10 —

Dr Sue Black left home and school at 16, married at 20 and had three children by the age of 23. At 25, as a single parent living on a council estate in Brixton, she decided to get an education. Sue studied maths at Southwark College, then gained a degree in computing and a PhD in software engineering at London South Bank University. She was head of a computer science department at the University of Westminster for several years before her current role: Senior Research Associate at University College London.

In 2001, Sue set up the UK's first online network for women in tech – BCSWomen. It was this that led her to Bletchley Park for the first time in 2003 and to starting a campaign to save it in 2008.

Passionate about the way that technology and education can change lives, Sue is now a social entrepreneur, writer and public speaker who has won numerous awards, including being one of the "50 most inspiring women in European tech". Sue writes regularly in the UK national press about technology. Her current startup #techmums works with disadvantaged families, teaching mums tech skills to empower them, build their confidence and get them excited about the opportunities that being tech-savvy brings.

Sue now has four children and has recently become a grandmother. Yay!

Saving Bletchley Park is Sue's first book. At the time of funding, it was the fastest ever crowdfunded book in the world. Sue would love to hear from you, so please tweet her @Dr_Black using the hashtag for the book #savingbletchley.

Stevyn Colgan is an author, artist, songwriter, public speaker and oddly-spelled Cornishman.

He is one of the "elves" that write the popular BBC TV series *QI* and its sister show, *The Museum of Curiosity*, for BBC Radio 4.

He has, among other things, been a police officer, a chef, a potato picker, a milkman and the official artist for the 2006 UK National Children's Book Fair. He's written briefing notes for two prime ministers, TV scripts for Gerry Anderson and *Doctor Who*, and helped build dinosaur skeletons for the Natural History Museum and movie monsters for Bruce Willis to shoot at. He's also been set on fire twice, been kissed by Princess Diana once, and Freddie Mercury once wore his helmet.

He is a creative consultant for Left/Field London and a visiting lecturer at a number of UK universities. He has given hundreds of talks across the UK and USA on a variety of subjects from problem solving to exobiology, and from Cornish mythology to why he believes that he wasn't intelligently designed. He was a judge for the 2014 Transmission Awards for the Communication of Ideas.

He is a contributor to various *QI* books and the author of *Joined-Up Thinking* (Pan Macmillan 2008), *Henhwedhlow* (Kowethas 2010), *Constable Colgan's Connectoscope*®(Unbound 2013) and *The Third Condiment* (deLune 2014).

He stops inordinately frequently for tea.

Saving Bletchley Park

Dr Sue Black
with Stevyn Colgan

unbound

This edition first published in 2016

Unbound
6th Floor, Mutual House, 70 Conduit Street, London WIS 2GF

www.unbound.co.uk

Typeset by Lindsay Nash

Art direction by Mecob

A CIP record for this book
is available from the British Library

ISBN 978-1-908717-92-4 (trade hbk)
ISBN 978-1-78352-167-8 (ebook)
ISBN 978-1-908717-93-1 (limited edition)

Printed in Great Britain

This book is dedicated to my little brother Stephen Richard Ambury who died during the campaign, to my best friend Hazel Jean Lapierre who died during the writing of this book, and to everyone who worked at Bletchley Park during WWII. Thank you all from the bottom of my heart.

Contents

Dear Reader,

The book you are holding came about in a rather different way to most others. It was funded directly by readers through a new website: Unbound.

Unbound is the creation of three writers. We started the company because we believed there had to be a better deal for both writers and readers. On the Unbound website, authors share the ideas for the books they want to write directly with readers. If enough of you support the book by pledging for it in advance, we produce a beautifully bound special subscribers' edition and distribute a regular edition and e-book wherever books are sold, in shops and online.

This new way of publishing is actually a very old idea (Samuel Johnson funded his dictionary this way). We're just using the internet to build each writer a network of patrons. Here, at the back of this book, you'll find the names of all the people who made it happen.

Publishing in this way means readers are no longer just passive consumers of the books they buy, and authors are free to write the books they really want. They get a much fairer return too – half the profits their books generate, rather than a tiny percentage of the cover price.

If you're not yet a subscriber, we hope that you'll want to join our publishing revolution and have your name listed in one of our books in the future. To get you started, here is a £5 discount on your first pledge. Just visit unbound.com, make your pledge and type savethepark in the promo code box when you check out.

Thank you for your support,

Dan, Justin and John
Founders, Unbound

Introduction

In April 2003 I made my first visit to Bletchley Park, the home of the codebreakers. Like many people, I knew very little about what had happened there. I certainly didn't know that more than 10,000 people had worked there during WWII, or that more than half of them were women, and young women at that; many of them were away from home for the first time. I also didn't know that the secret code breaking work carried out there had shortened the war by approximately two years, and at that time 11 million people per year were dying. This means there were potentially 22 million lives saved as a result of activities conducted at Bletchley Park.

22 million. Lives. Saved. Why did I, and so many others, know nothing about these amazing achievements?

Over the next ten years I learned much more about what had happened at Bletchley Park, and, amazingly, got to meet many of the people who made it happen. I went away after my first trip wanting to raise awareness of the achievements of the women who had worked at Bletchley Park – the "Women of Station X". (Bletchley was the tenth listening station, hence the X.)

Bletchley Park had got under my skin. But my interest in what had happened there, and the amazing contributions made by the thousands of people who worked there, contrasted starkly with the state of the site as it was at the time.

In 2008 I found out that Bletchley Park was, according to CEO Simon Greenish, "teetering on a financial knife edge". I thought, frankly, that this was a disgrace, and set out to do something about it. Campaigning to save Bletchley Park took over my life for the next three years. There was hardly a waking moment when I wasn't either taking action to raise awareness or thinking about how to get more people on board with the campaign. Looking back now, it seems like an obsession. At the time it just felt like an amazing whirlwind of energy and excitement; I was on a roller coaster ride. I'm very lucky that my family and friends supported me during that ride and even came along with me for parts of it.

I'm often asked what the major turning points were in the campaign. It's hard to pick just one, but if I had to I would say that for me the biggest turning point was working out how to use Twitter, and then using it to help build a massive community of love, support and goodwill towards Bletchley Park. Without it, I don't think we would have been nearly as successful as we were.

For years, whenever I mentioned Twitter and how it was a real catalyst for the campaign, I would get the same response: "I don't care what you had for breakfast!" For some reason, rather than embrace this new exciting medium, most people seemed to have decided that it was all about being vain and telling everyone the most mundane details of your life.

Not many people in the UK were using Twitter in 2008, but those who did were part of an exciting crowd of early adopters who I now feel very privileged to call friends. Many of these people became key influencers in the campaign. They are the ones that made all the difference with their enthusiasm, expertise, energy and, crucially, their response to a rallying call: *we must save Bletchley Park*.

Thankfully, Bletchley Park is now safe. I visited again in June 2014 to see the opening of the new visitor centre by the Duchess of Cambridge, whose grandmother and great aunt had worked there during the war. It was truly wonderful to see the newly restored huts and visitor centre, and to see the press there, jostling for position from behind cordons. At that time, Bletchley Park was on the front pages of national and international papers; just a few years earlier I had struggled to get any journalists interested enough to write a story about it at all.

This book is a personal story of how I started a campaign to save Bletchley Park, and of how hundreds, if not thousands, of people joined me to help save a site of fundamental international importance. This was a place where thousands of people worked around the clock for years on end, with no thanks at all, in the strictest secrecy. Many of the veterans of

Bletchley Park never told anyone at all what they had done and most of them received no reward. But what they did, and how they did it, ensured that we can enjoy the freedom we have today. We cannot thank them all now – most of them unfortunately are no longer with us. But we can preserve and cherish the place where they carried out their amazing work and ensure that our children, grandchildren and all future generations have the opportunity to get a glimpse of history, see what it was like, and hear the stories: of decoding messages straight from Hitler, of schoolgirls, away from home for the first time, arriving to work at Bletchley; of now famous codebreakers and inventors like Alan Turing, Bill Tutte and Tommy Flowers; of nicking the vicar's bicycle to go to a dance or sunbathing topless on the roof at Woburn Abbey. There are so many stories, so many of which were erased.

So let's treasure Bletchley Park and the people who worked there, and let's put those stories back into our history. Let's celebrate what we *do* have. Those stories are part of our heritage and should be taught to children in the UK and across the world.

We owe it to the people whose work saved 22 million lives.

Sue Black
London, September 2015

W hen the last members of staff left the Bletchley Park estate in 1945, they probably didn't give much thought as to what would happen to it. The war was over and the work that they had been doing was so secret that they undoubtedly believed that no one would ever know what had gone on behind those gates. Seven decades later, we now know a great deal about the extraordinary code breaking work that was done at Bletchley Park. However, what isn't so well known is what happened after those gates shut – both immediately after the war and in the 70 years since. This book tells the story of Bletchley Park's wartime activities plus, for the first time, the lesser known but equally fascinating story of how BP, as it was known to those who worked there, was saved for the nation. But before we begin, let's look briefly at what happened between 1945 and 1991, when one story ends and the other begins.

After the war ended, BP was effectively shut down. The specialist equipment that had been designed to assist the codebreakers was either destroyed or removed, staff were reassigned and, in order to protect secrecy, almost all paperwork and records of BP activity were destroyed. Once that was done, Bletchley Park settled into a long period of disuse and neglect of which very little has been written.

We do know that, for a short while after the fall of Berlin, BP was used by the Allied Military Government for Occupied Territories (AMGOT), which means that Germany was, at one time, "ruled" from Bletchley Park. Meanwhile, GCHQ, the government's intelligence service, continued to occupy part of the site until 1946 when they moved to Eastcote in Middlesex. During their short post-war tenure, the site was patrolled by security guards, but things had become very lax; local people frequently cut through the estate as a shortcut to Bletchley Park train station rather than walk the extra mile around the outside. When GCHQ left, they knocked down radar installations and all of the radio towers.

In the years that followed, several organisations moved onto the site and used some of the many buildings. In 1948, a teacher training college, run by a fearsome woman called Dora Cohen (who, if the tales told are true, ran the place with an iron fist) was set up in the Mansion House, and the General Post Office (what became British Telecom) set up a training school also in the Mansion and in G and H Blocks. The Civil Aviation Technical College was based on the site too until 1993, teaching future air traffic controllers, as were several radio clubs and amateur radio stations. But by 1996, all that remained on the estate was the Diplomatic Wireless Service Social Club which was based in Hut 4.

Between 1957 and 1958, some of the iconic huts were demolished and local people used the remains, stacked behind the Mansion, as firewood. Then, in 1965, vandals got onto the estate and smashed many windows which encouraged further degradation of the buildings, especially of the remaining wooden huts once the damp got inside. No one fought to save them because no one knew of their historical importance. BP trustee Sam Crooks first moved to the Milton Keynes area in 1970 and, in 1973, had occasion to speak to the College of Education based on the estate. He recalls that there was no reference to the history of the site then; in fact he wouldn't discover that anything interesting or unusual had happened there until the publication of Squadron Leader F W Winterbotham's book, *The Ultra Secret*, in 1974.

The Winterbotham book caused a sensation. Although some of the content subsequently turned out to be inaccurate, based, as it was, on a little knowledge supported by second-hand anecdotes, it nevertheless put the long-held secrets of Bletchley Park into the public domain for the first time. Local people began to talk about their wartime reminiscences of what went on in the Park, as did many of the people who had worked there. However, many veterans remained reluctant to break their vow of silence. Meanwhile, Dora Cohen's teacher training college moved off the estate in 1975 and a new college was installed, run by less formidable staff. Its open door policy soon led to it becoming the local centre of intellectual activity and it was here, among a group of amateur historians and archaeology enthusiasts, that many discussions took place regarding Winterbotham's revelations. It was from these humble beginnings that the campaign to save the Park would emerge.

At this time, the estate was roughly half-owned by PACE (Property Advisors to the Civil Estate) – the government's land agency – and by British Telecom. Neither agency did anything with it until there was a fire in 1983. Permission was then given for a property developer to demolish the damaged buildings, including the old Elmers School that had been subsumed into BP's wartime work (as a Japanese code breaking school), and to build a small housing estate – the first part of the BP estate to go. It was when the developers suggested plans for a large housing estate utilising the remainder of the site that people started to realise that Bletchley Park – and all of its history – was in genuine danger of being lost. It was one of several such development plans put forward during the coming years; on more than one occasion BP came very close to being reduced to nothing more than a commemorative plaque marking the spot where it had once stood.

In 1987, the aforementioned Sam Crooks became council leader for the Milton Keynes area, of which Bletchley is a part, and he began asking questions about how BP might be saved from the developers; since the publication of Winterbotham's book, a great deal more had been learned about the site's wartime role and he became convinced that Bletchley Park was simply too important to be bulldozed. What was needed was some kind of conservation order. However, obtaining anything like that was going to be an uphill struggle. In those days the Milton Keynes Development Corporation – now defunct – was very keen to capitalise on such a valuable piece of real estate. As Peter Wescombe, one of BP's foremost historians, explains: "You've got 55 acres of ground here, right by the railway station. People could get out of bed, brush their teeth and be straight on a train to London, without any need for parking. They would have their own supermarket and petrol station. It was a very valuable site indeed. With planning permission, it was worth an estimated £3m at the time." To make matters worse, Crooks had the site independently assayed by a heritage expert who expressed the view that it wasn't worth developing the site. By the late 1980s, the Park was being used less and less by its owners and, in 1987, it was finally decommissioned as a military establishment. With no one taking an active interest in preserving the estate, it was, quite literally, falling to pieces. Whoever did take on the task would face huge bills. Selling to a rich property developer was by far the easiest option for the owners.

In 1991, when BP was yet again under real threat of being demolished and turned over to housing, the Bletchley Archaeological and Historical Society – one of the intellectual groups that had been meeting on the site since the mid 1970s – formed a small committee with the aim of organising a farewell party to mark what appeared to be the inevitable demise of the site. The idea had come from Peter Wescombe who was friends with Peter Jarvis, a local GP and a member of the society. Wescombe recalls: "We invited ourselves to tea at the Jarvises. I said, 'Look Peter, what are we going to do about the Park? The council's decided it's a dead duck, how are we going to stop it happening?' I then suggested a big farewell party with all the WWII codebreakers at the Park. I could get their names. We requested a meeting with the Bletchley Archaeological and Historical Society because if we personally invited the wartime BP staff they'd say, 'Who on earth are Peter Wescombe and Peter Jarvis?' But if you say the chairman of the Archaeological Society invites you, that has some clout." The committee agreed to write the invitation letters on the Peters' behalf. However, getting permission to hold such a party on the estate proved to be more problematic. On his first attempt, Wescombe didn't bother to make an appointment and walked, unchallenged, straight through the front gate and into the estate administrator's office.* He was then told, in no uncertain terms, that he was on private property and was escorted off the grounds. Undaunted, however, he found a hole in the fence and snuck back to the administrator's office to carry on the conversation. It wasn't difficult; at this time the estate boasted a tiny skeleton staff of only nine people. His cheeky perseverance paid off and it was agreed that that the party could be held in Block E on the 21st of October – 50 years to the day from when Sir Winston Churchill had made a historic and very secret wartime visit to BP to congratulate the staff.

The Society put out feelers to locate and invite as many living veterans and their families to come along and say goodbye to BP. Over 250 people turned up on the day, most of whom had had no contact with each other since the end of hostilities. Chatting amongst themselves and with the party's organisers, many were finally able to talk about their top secret work for the first time in five decades. So powerful and extraordinary were those stories that the committee decided, there and then, that the story of Bletchley Park couldn't just end with demolition. They asked the veterans for a show of hands of all those who would support an attempt to save BP. The vote was pretty much unanimous.* At that moment, the party organisers decided that they would do all that they could to save BP for the nation. The Bletchley Park Trust was born.

One of the Trust's earliest prime movers was the late engineer Tony Sale who pushed, and pushed hard, for the site to become a national museum. He also began the seemingly impossible task of rebuilding some of the extraordinary machines that had been developed at the Park during the war. He had no plans, some boxes of parts – many more were missing – and no budget, but he soldiered on. Meanwhile Peter Jarvis and Peter Wescombe persuaded British telecom (BT) to allow the Trust to use part of the site. They even managed to persuade them to pay for some maintenance and utility bills. Two other big players at this time were local councillor and one-time mayor of Milton Keynes, Roger Bristow, and local MP Brian White. Remembering Sam Crooks' talk of preservation orders, they identified a number of important trees on the site – sequoias, maples and oaks among them – that dated from the 1880s and obtained a tree preservation order for them all. "At the time, the trees at Bletchley Park accounted for 2 per cent of all the mature trees in the city," explain Bristow. "We knew there would be some important specimens among them, and there were. For instance, we had a cherry tree that a Japanese expert got very excited about. He was even more excited when I told him we had two of them." The preservation orders made the site a very difficult prospect for developers; the roots of the

---

* Not all of the veterans were quite so enthusiastic. Peter Wescombe recalls hearing one veteran codebreaker telling a TV reporter that BP was finished and should be knocked down. This is an understandable reaction; many of the staff had quite unhappy lives during their time at Bletchley Park. "Broken marriages, unhappy love affairs, their husbands being killed in the war. One of the saddest things, they used to say, was young ladies sitting sniffing into their hankies down by the lake because their boyfriend or husband had been killed," explains Wescombe. "You can quite understand why some didn't want it back – it brought back some very unhappy memories."

various trees were all interlocking which made any attempt to install roads or other infrastructure – such as electricity, water and gas mains, etc. – almost impossible without killing some of them. It was a notable victory for the campaign.

Money was still a problem however. Or, more accurately, a complete lack of money. But the campaigners refused to give up. Roger Bristow even put his own money – including a substantial injury award he'd received – into saving Bletchley Park. He did so knowing that he'd never see a return on it, but, had he not done so, it's doubtful the site would have avoided development. By this time, BT owned the site in its entirety. When the Trust approached them about a sale price, Wescombe recalls that, "BT said we could have the site for about three million quid. Between us we had about £3.50."

The Bletchley Park site opened to visitors in 1993. To begin with, it was a very humble affair and it was open for just one weekend every fortnight. At this time, the Trust was operating from a single office with a single primitive computer and around ten people vying for space to work. There was no electricity across most of the estate and so old hand-cranked field telephones were used for communication. GCHQ kindly loaned the fledgling museum some exhibits, including Enigma machines, and the London Science Museum donated its old display cases when they installed new ones. One of the BP volunteers, a man called Clive Wallace, was part of a group that had amassed a collection of old military vehicles which they left on the BP site to help attract visitors, and it was one of these vehicles – a 1941 articulated lorry – that was used to collect the display cases. A few years later the Tower of London made a similar offer, and these too were collected in the vintage lorry. The Motor Vehicle Group was responsible for leading many expeditions to collect such things for the new museum. A small army of volunteers and passionate supporters of the estate gave freely of their time and energy in all weathers. Some even stood at the gate offering £2 raffle tickets to anyone they met; anything to raise much-needed cash.

1994 was a landmark year. Firstly, the museum was formally inaugurated by HRH The Duke of Kent, as Chief Patron. Then Chris Smith, the finance director for Milton Keynes council, was asked to bring his expertise to the Trust. Despite royal patronage and a now steady stream of visitors, the park was still not raising anywhere near the amount it needed. Things were still so bad that, at Smith's first trustees' meeting, the finance report was a printout from a cashpoint. Smith substantially improved financial management and developed several income generating streams, including the setting up of a shop and small café. Charity nights were organised and, in 1996, The Andrews Sisters showed their support by giving a fundraising concert (with their daughters as backing singers). Smith even organised a licence to have weddings conducted on site, and he and his wife Lindsey became the first couple to be married there. By 1998 the Trust had built a £25k operating surplus and a reserve of £59k. Consequently, the Trust was able to strike a deal with the landowners in 1999, obtaining a 250 year leasehold of the core historic areas of the Park with an option to purchase it for a nominal sum 25 years later.

For the next decade, the Trust worked hard to raise funds and develop the site. There were disagreements and some infighting between strong-minded individuals; some wanted to preserve the park as a living museum, in as original a form as possible, while others wanted to develop it into a more lucrative business venture, like a conference and conventions centre. But still the renovation work went on, mostly carried out by keen enthusiasts for no pay. Some, like Tony Sale who was working on rebuilding the Colossus computer, even used some of their own money. He was boundlessly enthusiastic about the rebuild and gave talks and lectures about the earliest days of programmable computing which kept public interest high in what they were trying to achieve at BP.

In 2002, the Trust's new leader, Christine Large began talks to nego-tiate a controversial but necessary sale of land to raise funds. It was not a popular decision; the Motor Vehicle Group left the Park when told that their area – the transport depot and H Block land – was being sold. And there was one moment of high drama around this time when one of the estate's Enigma machines went missing. To this day, no one knows if it was a genuine thief or someone disgruntled by the sale of the land. The good news, however, is that the machine was safely returned to Jeremy Paxman and the BBC *Newsnight* show.

The proposed sale also proved to be an issue for Tony Sale and his colleagues. By 2004, they had finished the rebuild of Colossus. The computer had recently been officially switched on by the Duke of Kent in the presence of Tommy Flowers, its original designer, and many wartime veterans. When told that the huge machine would have to be moved from H Block as the buildings were likely to be part of the land sale, the team began looking at various venues for relocation but none were appropriate. Therefore Tony and his colleagues set about forming a separate charity. In March 2005, The Codes and Ciphers Heritage Trust, which now trades as The National Museum of Computing (TNMOC), was formed. The land sale went ahead but H Block itself could remain on site if the TNMOC leased it from the Bletchley Park Trust. It meant that Colossus could stay in its rightful home in H Block, a building originally erected in 1944 to house six Colossus machines.

But despite any resentment, the sale of land generated much-needed cash. It meant that the estate shrunk to something like 21 acres, but this became a more manageable size; more than 70 buildings still needed renovation work. The iconic code breaking huts were damp and derelict, the Mansion had major leaks in its roof and issues with asbestos, and the annual heating bills alone were costing the estate half a million.

But even the land sale didn't guarantee the preservation of the site. When Christine Large left, Simon Greenish took over. He joined BP on a Monday and, at his first board meeting, the first question asked was, "Are we still open for the rest of the week?" Greenish began letting out buildings to companies and organising conferencing events. Gradually, the Trust built up the name of Bletchley Park and got visitor numbers increasing. Tim Reynolds became a leading light at this time, helping to create a successful Innovation Centre on site. The centre provided, and still provides, much needed revenue whilst ensuring that Bletchley Park's reputation as a centre of innovation is maintained. Greenish was forced to make some unpopular but necessary changes including cutting wages, losing some paid staff, encouraging more conferencing, organising professional catering and paying for good marketing, but it paid off and income improved. All of which meant that, now that finances were stable, if precarious, the real work of renovating the buildings could begin; Tim Reynolds had already renovated two, but many more needed attention. Plus there was a great deal more work to be done to ensure that Bletchley Park was saved.[*]

It was, more or less, at this point that Dr Sue Black entered the story. But I won't steal her thunder – the remainder of this book is the story of what happened next.

During WWII the staff of Bletchley Park managed to overcome difficulties that we today, with all of our computers and instant access to knowledge, would still find problematic. Much of what was achieved there is now public knowledge thanks to various documentaries and dramatisations (although, thanks to dramatic licence, the accuracy of some dramas has to be taken with a pinch of salt). We will tell that story in this book too. Throughout Sue's narrative you'll find accompanying text that will explain the historical significance of some of the people, projects and places she mentions. Every effort has been made to make the historical account as accurate as possible; unfortunately, what went on at BP was so shrouded in secrecy that almost no documentation exists and we are reliant on the memories of people who were there at the time. Much of the content is culled from interviews with surviving veterans.

An army of inspiring, wonderful people has spent the past 25 years working hard to save Bletchley Park for us and for the generations to come; the list of enthusiasts, experts, volunteers, funders, donors and visitors is simply too long to include them all here, and some of them, sadly, are no longer with us. In this 70th anniversary year of the end of World War II, all we can do is thank them and dedicate this introduction to them for performing such a selfless, noble service for the benefit of us all.

I now hand you over to Dr Sue Black who will take up the story of how Bletchley Park was saved.

Stevyn Colgan

---

[*]   I have skimmed through the post-war history of the park here for the sake of brevity. There is easily enough to fill another book. And there might well be such a book sometime in the near future.

Foreword: The Amazing Relay Race to Save Bletchley Park

Megan Smith, Former Vice President, Google

Several years ago, I was at an annual event called Silicon Valley Comes to the UK (SVC2UK.com). It brings together top British and American entrepreneurs for a few days each fall to engage with each other and to share insights and learnings with new start-up CEOs, university students and faculty, parliamentary leadership, high school students and others.

At one of the NESTA-hosted events, a woman with fabulous pink hair came up to me and said, "Alan Turing's papers are going up for auction at Christie's and we have to get them for Bletchley Park." This chance meeting with the incredible Dr Sue Black initiated our leg of an unlikely relay team, made more difficult by the fact that I did not know exactly what Bletchley Park was.

I do now and so should you.

The first time I was able to visit Bletchley with Dr Black, I was lucky to meet a woman who had lived at Bletchley as a child. Jean Cheshire was volunteering as a guide at the park and we met just inside the entrance to the Mansion.

It was there that she showed me a wonderful quilt hanging just behind the front door. It showed an aerial view of the Park, with her seven-year-old brother depicted in stitching, collecting duck eggs on the island in the middle of the small lake; her mother hanging laundry with her three-year-old brother on his tricycle; her father on his bicycle making a delivery; and Jean and her five-year-old twin sister making their way to the gate on their way to school. Their family lived in the stables area next to codebreaker

Dilly Knox's elite math team.

What she said next was striking: she said her mother used to try to keep all her children quiet, so they would not bother their hard-working technical neighbors, by saying, "Shh... the girls are working."

That still gives me chills, because I can see them, even though I had not imagined women as the elite math team, and it makes me think about the diversity of the Bletchley team.

More than half of the team working at Bletchley were women. It was a group of technical women and men who worked together at scale. And Alan Turing, who was gay but closeted because of the devastating oppression of the time, was part of all these different kinds of people who came together to make this possible – to crack the codes. Bletchley Park was a melting pot of brilliant minds set free by an atmosphere of tolerance. Social norms were swept away because of the extreme need and circumstances. What mattered was what a person could do – not their gender, sexual orientation, religion, national origin, or any other difference or supposed eccentricity. By removing these artificial constraints, Bletchley Park brought out the best in the fullest range of talent.

And that is really juxtaposed with the Nazis who decided that they needed to get rid of diversity – that groups of people literally needed to be killed. But here, in the middle of England at Bletchley Park, this group of diverse people beat them, hands down. What happened at Bletchley really happened because of diversity, not in *spite* of diversity.

The story comes together from many important and distinct strands: its roots with Polish cryptographers and their access to early Enigma designs gathered by French Intelligence; the creative sourcing of talent from across the UK by MI6 leadership and others; top mathematical faculty already visible to recruiters in Cambridge, Oxford and other campuses; discoveries like the incredible Jean Valentine, who had recently completed high school and applied for service, writing "cryptic crosswords" and "natural science" in the general interests section of her application form and cementing her path to the Park; and the clever, expedient designers of the Park operations – it is said that Churchill himself took the proposed list of those who would know the vital details of Bletchley's overall design and crossed off nearly all the names, much like removing most of the CCs on an email.

Heroic Engineering

What Bletchley stands for, for me, is heroic engineering. During World War II, so much innovation happened across the world because of the urgent need for mathematical computation.

Teams started to build and prototype and think through how to do these things. They built on top of earlier innovations, and their focused determination accelerated the beginning of the modern computer age. These wartime breakthroughs in computing and micro-electronics included Bletchley Park's Bombe and later the Colossus, the ENIAC, Mark I and more in the United States. Critical collaborations between the UK and US led to the creation of key technologies like radar, jet engines, and long-range navigation.

People think that technology is a dry thing – very scientific, very mathematical – but, really, it's not. In fact, it's a creative thing. I remember being at Bletchley with codebreaker Captain Jerry Roberts, who was sitting next to the Colossus, talking about having decoded a message from Hitler himself and saying, "We were so creative during the war."

"Scarcity breeds clarity" is what Google co-founder Sergey Brin always says, and I think these people were faced with incredible adversity and, therefore, had to take everyone's voice and work together. When the tech industry does that, we do our best work, and the more we can strive for those kinds of diverse, inclusive teams, the more successful we will be.

Bletchley is a big part of that story.

To quote Bletchley Park's founder Sir Winston Churchill, "the further backward you can look, the further forward you will see". This is what I think Sue knew instinctively from her earliest visits to Bletchley. Her own personal experience of coming to the technology industry later in her life than some and finding a striking lack of diversity echoed a serious problem all over the world today. Her work to expand inclusion by founding BCSWomen and #techmums aimed to grow access for all. Rooted in the Bletchley story of heroic engineering and breakthrough was a fundamental true story of humanity – one that was missing from history books and critically important to preserve on behalf of the future: that people can collaborate and rapidly innovate their way out of great challenges, and that women and men, working together, were a core part of that profound innovation. I was lucky to meet Sue that day in London, and to find a way to get involved and get others involved, like Lynette Webb, Simon Meacham and Alfred Spector from Google, where I was working at the time. Our initial teamwork on the Christie's auction donations helped secure Alan Turing's papers for the Park, and we later worked to co-host events and create short videos with Bletchley veterans to help preserve and promote these important stories. We are all so fortunate that Sue took up the leadership of this section of the relay race to save the Park – a relay to which so many have contributed over the decades – and now these critical stories are being preserved. There is no doubt they will change our future.

Technical women have always been part of the history of computing and innovation alongside men, even if their stories have until today been largely untold, excluded or, in some cases, written out of the story altogether. Ada Lovelace, Grace Hopper, Katherine Johnson, and so many more female innovators made elite technical contributions. The women and men working together at Bletchley are the same. It is critically important that we make visible all the stories in front of us, on behalf of the future – it's hard to be what you can't see. This is a challenge for technical women and minorities globally because of massive unconscious and institutional bias in society, the serious lack of visibility of their historic and current contributions, and media bias aimed at children and families which continues to skew the truth. How exciting to find out that Kate Middleton, Duchess of Cambridge's grandmother was a codebreaker at Bletchley! Perhaps she can inspire us to bring more children on field trips to visit the National Museum of Computing located at Bletchley Park – the ratio of boy to girl visitors has averaged 25:1 for some years. The UK needs both female and male histories told so that girls and boys might visit in equal numbers and learn of the stories of all their country's technical heroes.

I also hope our historians will see through the biases around them and pull all the stories from their hidden places... listening closely when those who were there reveal insights like "shhh... the girls are working". For example, in his wonderful book *The Secret Life of Bletchley Park*, Sinclair McKay reveals Dilly Knox's writing: "Miss M Rock is entirely the wrong grade. She is actually 4th or 5th best of the whole entire Enigma staff and quite as useful as some of the 'professors'. I recommend that she should be put on the highest possible salary for anyone of her seniority." This quote reveals that many of those without credentials in the teams had great talent and contributed well above their position but faced discrimination... we need to know of this talent so young women and men will include themselves and each other as equals in future innovation (as well as complete our global work on equal pay!).

I hope you will visit and feel the incredible pulse of "Station X", imagining 40 motorbikes per hour coming through the gate, all with different snippets of codes to be cracked, and people working busily in all of the different rooms, in all of their different sections. Be inspired by this group of heroic women and men who really came together and saved so many lives. Let their story captivate you like it did for Dr Black, for me and so many more. And let their innovation, success and diversity propel your confidence and imagination to consider how you might collaborate with other talent, anywhere and anyone in the world, to solve some of today's greatest challenges.

Many people want to work on the edge of innovation. If they were alive in those days, they would have been at Bletchley.

01
My first visit to Bletchley Park

My first visit to Bletchley Park was on 9th April 2003. I was attending the British Computer Society's Specialist Groups Assembly representing BCS-Women, the online network for women in computing that I set up in 2001. In 1998, I had set up a similar network called London BCSWomen, and it had been a massive success – so much so that we had appeared in a two-page spread about women and computing in the *Daily Mirror*. National publicity for London BCSWomen led to requests from women all over the country who wanted to join. I set up a national version and it quickly garnered a few hundred members. The idea behind BCSWomen was to support and encourage women in computing. I had found doing my PhD in software engineering on the whole enjoyable but sometimes lonely, with few women around, and I had often wished for a group of friendly women to talk to. I set up BCSWomen to bring together such a group and found many friends there.

April 2003

7th *MentorSET training day (Institute of Physics)*

8th *Reception to commemorate birthday of Isambard Kingdom Brunel (Institution of Civil Engineers, Westminster)*

8th *Presentation of Oxfam parliamentary briefing paper: "Hands up for girls' education" (Portcullis House, Westminster)*

9th *BCS Specialist Groups Assembly representing BCSWomen (Bletchley Park, Herts.)*

22nd *SQUFOL European project in software metrics (South Bank University)*

I'd heard of Bletchley Park but didn't have a very well-formed idea of what it was, and I had no idea what it looked like. I knew that it was something to do with code breaking and World War II. In my mind's eye was a picture of 50 or so middle-aged blokes sitting around in tweed jackets, smoking pipes and doing *The Times* crossword. I've since learnt that that view is not uncommon. In fact, I shared my image of the tweed-clad blokes with the wonderful Stephen Fry when he came to visit Bletchley Park in May 2009; he then used almost exactly the same words to describe his own preconception of Bletchley on *QI* – I wasn't alone in my thinking!

On the morning of 9th April, I got the train from Euston Station to Bletchley. I had no idea yet what a momentous visit it would prove to be.

I spent the day there, mainly in the mansion house ballroom, listening to BCS specialist group talks and chatting to colleagues in the break. At the end of the day, I decided to go and explore the grounds. Bletchley Park now occupies a 26-acre site, with many huts, blocks and various outbuildings, plus a lovely lake, so there was plenty to look at. I entered one of the blocks and started looking at the exhibits on display; moving from one room to the next, I saw a group of middle-aged men working on what looked like the most amazing contraption at the end of the building. It was probably seven feet high and six feet across, a wonderful vision of engineering, with wires and what looked like cogs of some sort. I walked over to take a closer look.

I started chatting to a man who told me that he and his team were rebuilding something called the Bombe machine. I first heard this as "Bomb" machine, which sounded almost *too* exciting, but I soon learned all about it.

That man was John Harper, who, with a team of enthusiasts, was rebuilding Alan Turing's Bombe machine, which was used during WWII to mechanise the breaking of Enigma codes. John told me that it was taking years to rebuild because they didn't have a complete set of instructions or information to help them reconstruct it. Most of the details of the construction of the Bombe had been destroyed at the end of the war, so they had the task of working with incomplete information to put together a plan and then rebuild the Bombe from scratch. They had a couple of photos and an incomplete plan that had been found on a window ledge in a toilet. But that wasn't the only difficulty. The parts for the Bombe were, of course, no longer manufactured, so they had to be scavenged, sometimes from old telephone switching equipment which had been thrown away, or sourced from various manufacturers, or especially designed and manufactured. It sounded like a very long, complicated and difficult task; I was completely in awe of this labour of love.

After John had told me all about the Bombe and what it was used for, he asked me why I was at Bletchley Park. I told him about the British Computer Society meeting and said that I was there representing the network for women in computing that I had started in 2001 and now chaired.

"Did you know that more than half of the people that worked at Bletchley Park during the war were women?" said John.

"No, I had no idea. How many people worked here during the war?" I replied.

"About 10,000."

I was astonished. For many years, I had been interested in women in computing, women in science and women's contribution to the world of work, but I'd never heard anything like this before. It was amazing to find out that more than 5,000 women had worked at Bletchley Park during the war, and more amazing still, considering their massive contribution to the war effort and my interest in women, that I had never read or heard about it before.

John then showed me a plaque on the wall listing all the names of the generous people who had donated their time and money to making sure that the Bombe was faithfully rebuilt. Some of them were women, and John said that they had worked with the Bombes during the war and that some of them were still around, working as volunteers at Bletchley Park. At the end of our chat, I thanked John and we said our goodbyes. As I exited the block, I bumped into a group of my colleagues, including Professor Jonathan Bowen and Conrad Taylor who had also been walking around having a look at the site and taking photographs.

We decided to head back to London together. On the way, I told them about the Bombe machine and repeated what John had said about the people that had worked at Bletchley Park and that how more than 5,000 of them were women. I wanted to find out more about the work that the women had done at Bletchley Park and asked everyone who I thought would be interested in funding a project which focused on researching and promoting this amazing story. By the time we arrived at Euston, I was resolved to find some funding to run an oral history project which would capture the memories of women who worked at Bletchley Park and bring them to a wider audience. The women that had worked at Bletchley Park deserved recognition, and I was determined to make sure that they got it.

Looking for funding

I started talking to everyone I knew about my trip to Bletchley, recounting my conversation with John Harper about the Bombe and the women who worked there. I was sure that if I talked to everyone who might be even the *slightest* bit interested, I would, at some point, come across someone who wanted to help – or at least someone who knew someone who would want to help.

Between 2003 and 2006, I talked to countless people about the women who worked at Bletchley Park, how many of them there were, how amazing their achievements had been and how we needed to record their experiences and raise the profile of their contribution. In those days, I had no idea who to talk to about funding and I also didn't know very many people who were actually in a position to help. Talking to lots of people, asking for help, and getting lots of (kind) rejections gave me some really good experience and taught me not to be put off by rejection. It was, looking back, very good training for what was to come.

Eventually, in late 2006, someone suggested that I apply for money from the special fund set up to support projects related to the British Computer Society's 50th anniversary. I applied for £5,000. At around the same time, I was encouraged to apply for matched funding from the UK Resource Centre for Women (UKRC) in Science, Engineering and Technology, so I did. I was delighted when both applications were approved, and I was granted £10,000 in total, £5,000 from each organisation. I quietly filed away what I'd learned: that it's usually easier to get matched funding than initial funding. No one wants to be the first one to jump in, but once one person or organisation has taken the leap, others will follow.

We get funding

After years of trying and failing to find funding, it was wonderful to finally get not only the financial backing for BCSWomen to run the Women of Station X project, but also the moral support and buy-in from established organisations and people. It gave me a great buzz when I found out that that others felt the same way I did about something important to me and wanted to help me make it happen.

Finally, I could get going with the project: we had £10,000 to work with. Unfortunately, the funding came through just as I was starting a new job. I had worked at London South Bank University full-time for about eight years, but in the summer of 2006 I got a job at the University of Westminster in Harrow as Head of the Department of Information and Software Systems. I was due to start at the beginning of 2007. It was my first management role and I was very excited about being able to make a real difference to students and to staff, but I was also worried about how I would manage the Women of Station X project at the same time. How could I run the project when I'd just started the most demanding role of my whole career?

Luckily Jan Peters, then working for the BCS, came to the rescue and offered to run the project. She found an interviewer, Ann Day, and put together a plan for the project. She got in touch with Bletchley Park to find out if they were happy to put us in contact with the female veterans. The plan was to interview a few female veterans in depth to find out about their experience of working at Bletchley Park.

Since first finding out about the thousands of women working there, I had wanted to make sure that their stories were captured for posterity. I was well aware that the veterans who were still around were aged 70 plus and weren't getting any younger. Everything that had happened at Bletchley Park was kept secret for such a long time – everyone who worked there had to sign the Official Secrets Act – and there had been almost nothing recorded about what happened there and what life was really like. There were a few stories floating around, but I knew there were more to be found. For one thing, I wasn't just interested in what the veterans had done at work, I was also interested in their lives outside of work. Many of them were only teenagers when they started working at Bletchley. Thousands of teenage girls carried out essential wartime work, so I knew there had to be some great stories there and I wanted to hear them and share them with the world.

Jan managed to persuade Bletchley Park to send around a letter to the female veterans asking them if they were happy to be interviewed by us. We then recorded several in-depth interviews, and Conrad Taylor made a short film about the women of Station X narrated by Sarah Winmill – a great friend and BCSWomen committee member.

Bombe rebuild switch on

On 17th July 2007, John Harper and his team's rebuild of the Bombe machine was complete and ready to be officially switched on. I was invited up to Bletchley Park along with others from BCSWomen and the BCS. My good friend Professor Wendy Hall had been invited to give a talk about the Women of Station X project, which she did with all of her usual intelligence and charm.

After Wendy's talk and the reception that followed, we went down to see the Bombe rebuild, which the Duke of Kent switched on. John Harper and his team had done a fabulous job of rebuilding the Bombe, and seeing

Presenting The Women of Station X oral history project to the veterans
in the Ballroom at Bletchley Park; my first talk at Bletchley Park

it work was incredible. It had taken many people several years to build and
was a remarkable feat of engineering. Hearing the sound of it working for
the first time was very evocative. The loud, rhythmic clicking of the drums
rotating on the Bombe machine made me wonder: "What must it have
been like for the women working there during the war?" It must have been
so noisy, day after day, month after month, working in a temporary hut
full of machines. The sound reminded me of the journey from Wickford
to Chelmsford when I started grammar school in the 1970s. I remembered
being 11 years old, sticking my head out of the window to drink in the sunshine and look at the fields, listening to the rhythmic sound of the train
going over the tracks as we flew past cows, crops and the odd tractor.

The women of Station X

Every September the Enigma Reunion is held at Bletchley Park, bringing
veterans from all over the UK and the world together to catch up, have
dinner and listen to a few lectures. In September 2007, while the Women
of Station X project was running, I was invited to Bletchley Park to speak

From L to R: Leah Black, me, Jo Komisarczuk, Daisy Bailey (veteran), Jill Dann and Lucy Hunt; all except Leah and Daisy Bailey are BCSWomen committee members

about the project.

I gave my talk in the lovely wood-panelled Mansion House Ballroom at Bletchley Park. I was so excited; it was the first time I had really had the chance to speak to any of the veterans. I spoke about my first trip to Bletchley Park, finding out how many women had worked there and wanting to do something to raise the profile of those women. How wonderful for me to now be standing in front of some of the very women that I had so looked forward to meeting. After I had finished speaking, several veterans came up to tell me how much they had enjoyed my talk and how grateful they were that I was seeking to highlight their contribution. I was so delighted to meet them, and we had the first of many discussions about what it was like working there during the war. It also drove home the point that many of these women had been teenagers when they had worked at Bletchley, and that going to work there had been the first time that they had left home. One woman told me how, wanting to do her bit for the war effort, she had gone along to the local office to sign up for whatever it was they thought she was suitable for. It was only upon leaving the office that she realised she was the only one there wearing Clarks sandals – she had been wearing schoolchildren's shoes.

Talking to the veterans reinforced my feeling that we really had to do more to help tell the full story of what happened at Bletchley Park. I left Bletchley that day feeling more resolved than ever to do my own bit to get the story out to the world.

Bletchley Park Veterans Day

bcs.org

23 September 2007

Several members of BCSWomen, the BCS group with 800+ women studying and working in IT, visited Bletchley Park on 23 September 2007 to attend the veterans day.

Dr Sue Black, founder and chair of BCSWomen, as part of the special talk to veterans, told the audience that she had first visited Bletchley Park some five years ago and been absolutely fascinated by its history.

But, when wandering around the Park she had been surprised to find that even though more than half of the people working there during WWII were women, there was almost no information at Bletchley about this. She went home determined to do something about it, to make sure that there was fair recognition for the contribution of the women that worked at Bletchley.

Funding was secured in 2006 from the BCS 50th Anniversary fund and the UKRC for Women in Science and Technology, and an oral history project is now underway recording the memories of women that worked at Bletchley.

Dr Ann Day and Dr Jan Peters have been working on the project this year and are currently working to produce a website and other resources in collaboration with Bletchley Park Trust to make sure that these stories are passed down to future generations and that the contribution is not forgotten.

02

"That is all you need to know"

"There was this song around at the time that went, 'We joined the Navy to see the sea, and what did we see? We saw the sea.' The Wrens sang a different version. We sang, 'And what did we see? We saw BP.'"

—JEAN VALENTINE WRNS

When 18-year-old Anne Pease[1] arrived at "BP" in July 1940, she had no real idea of where she was or why. All she knew was that a telegram had ordered her to report to a railway station to catch a particular train to somewhere called Bletchley in Buckinghamshire. The telegram had ended with the slightly ominous words "That is all you need to know". She later found that she was one of hundreds of young women who'd received similar mysterious requests. Some had been told even less than she had. One Wren[2] says that, "On arrival at Euston, we had no clues as to our journey so we enquired from the engine driver where he was going. He replied with a broad grin and told us that 'the Wrens get out at Bletchley.'"

"I travelled with three other newly fledged Wrens, all equally bewildered as to why we should have been sent about as far from the sea as it's possible to get in this country," says Anne. "When we arrived at Bletchley station we were met by a Leading Wren and marched up to a perimeter fence with sentries standing guard. We were then taken to an office in a grand Victorian mansion. We were told that the work we were going to be doing was of the utmost secrecy and vital to the war effort, and we were required to sign the Official Secrets Act. One was left with the distinct impression that contravening it would mean a spell in The Tower at the very least."[3]

The grand Victorian mansion in question was Bletchley Park, a country house and 58-acre estate in Buckinghamshire, some 50 miles north-west of London.

"We weren't told where we were going," says Lorna Fitch. "We just had a piece of paper saying catch this, do that, wait there and change trains here, and you just did. I was collected from the station and taken to Woburn Abbey where I was to be billeted. Then I was put on a coach to Bletchley Park. I had no idea what was going on." One Wren reports that, for her and some colleagues, things were even more mysterious than that: "Six of us were put in an enclosed van and driven away… "

Irene Humby was also quite alarmed by all of the secrecy, especially after being warned that if she ever mentioned anything about her work, there would be "someone on the train keeping a lookout". It made her feel nervous during every journey she took thereafter. Daisy Phillips was told that she would receive a minimum prison term of two years if she broke the Official Secrets Act.

We can only imagine how these young women – mostly aged between 17 and 21 – felt as they passed through the gates of Bletchley Park and walked up the drive towards the rather ugly and imposing Mansion House within. For many of them, it was their first experience of being away from home. In her memoir, Irene Young says that, "The establishment was ringed with barbed wire and guarded by men of the RAF Regiment whose NCOs kept discipline by threatening their men that misdemeanours would result in their being sent 'inside the park', as if it were some sort of madhouse."

The fact that BP was only ever referred to as "BP" or "Station X" by the staff on site must have added an additional flavour of melodrama to their situation.

Even the selection criteria that had brought them, and the thousands that were to follow, to BP was something of a mystery. Jean Valentine recalls, "After initial [Naval] training in Scotland, I was called in to find out what I'd be doing, expecting to be a driver or cook or steward or something. But they said, 'We won't be telling you what you're going to be doing because we haven't been told what to tell you.' We've just been asked to look out for people like you. They were looking for linguists, mathematicians, people who could think laterally. I'd put cryptic crosswords down in my list of hobbies." The very next day, Jean found herself heading to London for a further briefing. Shortly afterwards, and apparently solely because of her interest in puzzles, she received her instructions to travel to BP.

As the first young women started to arrive, they would have seen intense activity going on inside the grounds. Around the Manor House and its outbuildings, concrete roads were being laid, as were the foundations for a series of large wooden huts and a telephone exchange that would be built at the expense of a mature rose garden and a maze. A new water main was being installed along with miles of electricity and telegraph cables. Evidently, something very big and very important was going on. Security was watertight. Joan Eastman recalls that it was, "…a dreary, wet Monday morning and Bletchley was not the prettiest of places, not back then. I can remember very well going through the gates and all of the security guards." On her second day at BP, Margaret Broughton-Thompson was so tired that she forgot her pass and was held in a guardroom until someone could identify her. She didn't forget her pass again. No one was left in any doubt that, whatever it was that was happening at Station X, their position there was not to be taken lightly.

Some were not told what was happening, even when they got there. One Wren recalls that, "For six weeks I was kept in limbo at BP, quite free to move wherever I wanted, but no work – I was being vetted along with two other women with me. Then we were all admitted to the Park…" Some suspected that there were people spying on them and on their families, like Irene Humby's "someone on a train". In between selection and being sent to BP, one Wren says that, "There were questions asked around my mother-in-law's place – by an insurance man… "

Vetting complete, and after signing the Official Secrets Act, the young women were told that not only could they not tell friends and family about their work, but that they could never tell anyone. This wasn't going to be simply a change in their career paths; this was something that was going to affect the rest of their lives. Doreen Spencer, a BP wireless operator, says in her memoirs that, having learned Morse code with her father, her biggest sorrow was keeping him in the dark. "How I wish

I could have told him," she says. "He died in 1982 never knowing what I did or where I really was." Margaret Hamlin found herself having to lie to her parents: "My father was very interested in what I was doing and he used to make various guesses as to what he thought it was. But I couldn't tell him. He became convinced that it was something to do with the work in France, with spies and the secret service. I had to lie to him, in a way, by saying that what I was doing was secret and secretarial. He never did find out what I did."

Other veterans still refuse to talk about their experiences to this day. Sheila Deasy says, "We were told when we came here that if we talked about it, we would be shot. So we never ever talked about anything, even with each other, let alone anyone else. Even now it seems terribly wrong to talk about it. I suppose that it became so instinctive that you didn't ever mention it. I made a promise that I wouldn't say anything, and as far as I'm concerned, I will keep that promise."

"You have to remember that every single one of us had someone we loved who was fighting at the front," explains Jean Valentine. "The thought that letting something slip might harm them or get them killed kept us silent." And, if that were not enough, the authorities were there to ensure that you did. Joan Reed recalls how a young Wren who talked in her sleep suddenly disappeared one day, presumably because her bosses were worried about "careless words".

Men were arriving at Bletchley Park too; often middle-aged, tweedy men with the kinds of curious habits and eccentricities that marked them as academics and original thinkers. Some of them seemed unperturbed by the security or secrecy and gave the impression that this was a world that they were used to. Indeed, it transpired that some had been doing the kind of work they would now be expected to do for some time. A few of them had even done so during World War I. Others were slightly more nervous, having been recruited from universities, banks and the General Post Office (GPO) and being unused to military life.

The new arrivals at Bletchley Park were soon to discover that they had been selected because they had skills that might prove useful in code breaking. Germany and its allies – the Axis Powers as they came to be known – were using complex forms of encryption in order to pass secret messages among their senior staff, their armies, navies and air forces. A network of wireless listening stations along the south and east coasts – known as "Y Stations" – intercepted such messages and sent them to BP by way of motorcycle courier at a rate of 40 messages per hour.[4] It was Station X's job to try to break the encryptions and decipher the messages. In order to do so, it needed staff that had shorthand and typing skills, efficiency with the telegraph and Morse code, and the ability to think laterally and solve complex puzzles. Some recruits had even been identified by way of specially placed prize crosswords in the *Daily Telegraph* newspaper.

But not everyone could be a codebreaker and, in fact, the vast majority of the staff – particularly the women recruited to BP – were there in a vital support capacity to the codebreakers. And they would have to learn to be excellent multitaskers. "We learned to firefight and become first-aiders and a rescue squad," says one veteran. "We were warned that if we were bombed we would have to look after ourselves. Our job was so secret, no one would come to our rescue. So we had to be big brave girls from the start." Another recalls the training: "They used one of the huts with duckboards across it. We had to crawl over on our stomachs with a stirrup pump – the smoke created with burning oily rags – to find the fire. Funny thing is, in films you see people coughing and coughing, but really you're like a vacuum cleaner, gasping for air." Others received specialist training in everything from driving three-ton lorries to reading Morse code.

It turned out that the rather sinister sounding code name "Station X" was, in fact, simply a numerical designation. Bletchley Park was number ten in a network of communications stations receiving foreign radio and telegraph messages.[5] However, where Station X differed from other stations was that it rapidly expanded to become the hub of all such activity. The name "Station X" had originally applied to just the wireless station built into the Bletchley Park water tower, but it soon came to mean the entire complex. The use of the code name in all official communications became mandatory from the start.

There would be no more public mention of Bletchley Park.

03
The women of Station X

7th March 2008: the day of the Women of Station X launch had finally arrived. It was held at the British Computer Society's London offices on Southampton Street. There were about 20 veterans in attendance, along with many BCSWomen members including Jill Dann and Jo Komisarczuk, who had done a great job of listening to and transcribing the veterans' interviews. Jill had the good idea of bringing along *Colossus* by Professor Jack Copeland, about Bletchley's code breaking computers, and asking all the veterans present to sign it.

Jan Peters, the project manager, welcomed everyone and introduced the day. I gave a short talk about my first trip to Bletchley Park five

BCS President Rachel Burnett, Jan Peters, female veterans and me
at BCS HQ for the Women of Station X project launch

yearspreviously, when I had found out to my amazement that more than 5,000 women had worked there during WWII. I'd had no idea that any women had been involved in the code breaking effort and it left me wanting to document and showcase the contribution of the women who had worked there. I was so happy to have finally found some funding and for some veterans to have been interviewed.

Recognising Bletchley Park's unsung heroines
12 March 2008
Richard Thurston
ZDNet

Codebreakers like Alan Turing have been rightly celebrated for their wartime work but, until now, the women of Station X have been largely overlooked.

The project, launched on Friday, called the "Women of Station X" or the "Women of Bletchley Park", is the brainchild of Sue Black, chair of BCSWomen – a networking group within BCS that strives to support female IT professionals in the workplace – and the head of the department of information and software systems at the University of Westminster.

Next to speak was Simon Greenish, the Director of Bletchley Park at the time. Simon spoke about what had happened at Bletchley Park and its fundamental importance. He then made an impassioned plea, one that had a profound effect on me and would, in a sense, shape my life for the next few years.

Bletchley Park, he said, was "teetering on a financial knife edge".

They had no financial support from government or industry, Simon told us. Their main source of income was from gate receipts – the money paid by visitors for admission to the site. Simon was worried that if the visitor numbers dropped, the amount of money taken on the gate would fall

Me handing over the *Women of Station X* oral history project
to Simon Greenish at the project launch at BCS HQ

and Bletchley Park would have to close. If Bletchley Park closed, he continued, they probably would not reopen, as once operations shut down there it would be too hard to start back up again.

I was shocked. I knew that Bletchley Park had made a substantial contribution towards the war effort. It was also considered by many to be the birthplace of computing, since the world's first programmable, digital, electronic computer, Colossus, was invented and built at Bletchley Park and Dollis Hill during the war. It seemed so wrong that such a site might have to close down.

The Mansion House at Bletchley Park

Bletchley Park faces bleak future

13 May 2008

Richard Thurston

ZDNet

The secret home to Britain's World War II codebreaking efforts could face closure in two to three years unless it receives more funding.

Historians have postulated that, without Bletchley Park, the Allies may never have won the war.

But, despite an impressive contribution to the war effort, the Bletchley Park site, now a museum, faces a bleak future unless it can secure funding to keep its doors open and its numerous exhibits from rotting away.

Spending time in the company of the veterans that day was wonderful. I felt so in awe of them and the work that they had done all those years ago when they were in their teens and 20s and the world was teetering on the edge of disaster. I enjoyed the event immensely, but I was also disturbed by the news that Bletchley Park was struggling financially, and I left feeling worried about the situation and wondering what I could do to help.

My first email to CPHC

A few weeks later, in June 2008, Simon Greenish called my attention to a petition on the 10 Downing Street website which asked the Prime Minister and the UK government to save Bletchley Park. I signed the petition and then sent an email to all members of the Council for Professors and Heads of Computing (CPHC) asking them to sign the petition too. An email to CPHC goes to all heads of computer science departments and all professors of computer science in all universities in the UK. As a reasonably new member of CPHC I felt a bit shy about emailing all of the heads and profs in the country, but I was really keen to get support for the petition.

I remember sitting there thinking that I didn't know most of the people that would receive my email and hoping that they wouldn't be annoyed by my blanket message to them all.

Subject:	Saving Bletchley Park
From:	Dr Sue Black
To:	CPHC, Simon Greenish
Sent:	25 June 2008

Dear all,

There is a petition asking for action to secure the future of Bletchley Park. As many of you will know this historic site is run on a charitable basis and holds the national museum of computing along with many other amazing exhibits. I strongly urge you to sign the petition and to support the campaign to save Bletchley Park.

I first visited Bletchley several years ago for a BCS SG meeting and was amazed by the place, so much so that I went away determined to find some funding to record for posterity the efforts of the women who worked there. [...]

The text of the petition is:

As has been reported elsewhere, Bletchley Park "have two to three more years of survival."

The Bletchley Park Trust receives no external funding. It has been deemed ineligible for funding by the National Lottery, and turned down by the Bill & Melinda Gates Foundation.

Please do not allow this crucial piece of both British and World culture to disappear. If ever an example were needed of Britain leading the world, this surely would be it. To allow it to fall into the hands of developers would be simply unconscionable.

Please sign up here: http://petitions.pm.gov.uk/BletchleyPark/

Many thanks
Sue

After I sent the email, I read it again and thought about the more than 10,000 people who had worked at Bletchley Park during the war, many of them young women who had left school or university to help with the war effort. I now knew more about the conditions that these women had worked under – eight hour shifts, six or seven days per week, working in temporary huts that were hot in the summer and freezing cold in the winter. Most of them were doing quite boring, repetitive work, looking after the Bombe machines that were cranking through the various possible settings to decode messages sent by the German High Command to each other through Enigma machines, but it was absolutely crucial.

The petition stated that the Bletchley Park Trust received no external funding and had been deemed ineligible for funding by the National Lottery and the Bill and Melinda Gates Foundation. I really couldn't understand why funding was not being put forward by these organisations or any others. Why was no one taking any notice of Bletchley Park and its plight?

The petition mentioned the possibility of Bletchley Park disappearing, perhaps falling into the hands of developers. I was horrified by this thought. There was no way that would happen if I could possibly do anything to help stop it.

I checked my email a bit later and found to my delight that several recipients of my email had replied to me saying that they agreed and had signed the petition. I was relieved; although I was very passionate about saving Bletchley Park, I didn't know if my peers would share my enthusiasm. Imagine my astonishment, then, when I checked the Save Bletchley Park petition a few hours later and saw that many heads and professors of computing had signed the petition, including from Oxford and Cambridge and other major universities, the kind of people that made me feel a little awed. I was, to put it mildly, over the moon. Even though I was desperate to get the word out that Bletchley Park needed help, I was very conscious that I was, in my mind at least, at the bottom of the pecking order: I was a new head of department at a "new" university. I'd felt that there was a serious chance that I would get either no response at all to my email or that someone would kindly take me to one side and admonish me. I was therefore both very excited that *so* many heads and profs had signed the petition and also relieved that no one had asked me who I thought I was addressing all of these great (mainly) men as equals.

I needn't have worried. As well as seeing all the influential signatures on the petition, I also had many lovely and supportive emails from colleagues across the country, both well-known and new like me, male and female, young and old. My CPHC peer group agreed with me: *we must help save Bletchley Park*. I buzzed with new-found confidence. I was not alone in the opinion that Bletchley Park was an important place; others shared my desire to make sure its importance was recognised and that the site was saved for the country.

Jägerbombe

I carried on as usual for a few days, teaching my students and doing research. But I was keeping an eye on the petition as the number of signatories increased; all the time a thought was whirring in my head: *what else could I do to help Bletchley Park?*

After the Women of Station X launch I had received an invitation to a champagne reception at Bletchley Park in July. Not one to ever turn down champagne, and really keen to visit Bletchley Park again, I gladly accepted the invitation. I was allowed to take a guest along with me to the reception, and my thoughts immediately turned to John Turner, a colleague at the University of Westminster. John and I had had several chats about Bletchley Park at work, and he shared my interest in the place.

On the day of the reception, we travelled up to Bletchley together on the train from London. I was very excited, not least because for the first time I was to get a tour of Bletchley Park led by one of the veterans. We arrived at Bletchley station and walked the short distance to the entrance to Bletchley Park. It was a really nice summer's day, and as we walked past the gatehouse into the park, the fountain in the middle of the lake was sparkling in the sunshine. There was a large marquee on the lawn beside it, open along one side. The scene was idyllic.

John and I were greeted by Bletchley Park Director Simon Greenish, and after a quick chat we were put into a group and taken on a tour of the site. As I had not been on a proper tour of Bletchley Park before, I was very keen to see what else the site held.

First we went to The National Museum of Computing (TNMOC), which is based at Bletchley Park, and saw many old computers in various states of repair. As computer scientists, it was fabulous for John and me to see so many machines. They spanned the whole era of computing in the UK, from the 1943 Colossus rebuild through to Elliot Brothers machines, PDP11s, BBC Micros, and more. I challenge anyone interested in computing to go to TNMOC to see Colossus running and not get a tear in their eye. It is simply beautiful to look at, and hearing its sound when running is poetry in motion, very relaxing and hypnotic. At the same time, it is a reminder of the invention, ingenuity and innovation that occurred during WWII, at the dawn of the computing age.

After leaving TNMOC, our tour leader walked us over to Hut 6 and stopped us right in front of it, with our backs to the car park (which were tennis courts during WWII and are still referred to as "the tennis courts" by some!). We stood in the sunshine looking at the hut as our guide proceeded to tell us all about the amazing code breaking achievements that had happened just in that one hut.

He said that the work carried out at Bletchley Park had shortened the war by two years, and that at that time 11 million people per year were dying due to the war.

Hut 6 at Bletchley Park

11 MILLION PEOPLE.

Those words rang loudly in my head. So, the work carried out at Bletchley Park had potentially saved the lives of 22 million people. Unbelievable... but true. I stood there, looking at the hut, one corner of which was covered by a blue tarpaulin.

My brain was whirring fast. I thought, *This place saved 22 million lives and was the birthplace of the computer. What other place have I ever heard about in my whole lifetime that is as important as Bletchley Park?*

I couldn't think of a single one.

Professor Richard Holmes, a military historian, then gave a talk about Bletchley Park and its significance in World War II. I listened intently as he made a very compelling case for the survival of Bletchley Park. He mentioned that they needed funding and that he thought it was a place worth saving – "sacred ground" is how he described it. I found myself nodding in agreement.

> *"The work here at Bletchley Park... was utterly fundamental to the survival of Britain and to the triumph of the West. I'm not actually sure that I can think of very many other places where I could say something as unequivocal as that. This is sacred ground. If this isn't worth preserving, what is?"*
>
> —THE LATE PROFESSOR RICHARD HOLMES,
> MILITARY HISTORIAN

Professor Holmes told us what Sir Harry Hinsley, the official historian of British Intelligence in WWII, had said about what the effect of the code breaking work carried out at Bletchley Park, officially named "Ultra", had been.

> *"Ultra shortened the war 'by not less than two years and probably by four years'; moreover, in the absence of Ultra, it is uncertain how the war would have ended."*
>
> —SIR HARRY HINSLEY, OFFICIAL HISTORIAN OF
> BRITISH INTELLIGENCE IN WORLD WAR II.

Professor Holmes also mentioned the words of US President Eisenhower, who had said that the intelligence received from Bletchley Park had been "priceless" and a "decisive contribution to the Allied war effort".

> "The intelligence... from you [Bletchley Park]... has been of priceless value. It has saved thousands of British and American lives and, in no small way, contributed to the speed with which the enemy was routed and eventually forced to surrender... [It was a] very decisive contribution to the Allied war effort."
>
> —GENERAL DWIGHT D EISENHOWER

I stood there feeling more and more enthralled by the amazing contribution that the work carried out at Bletchley had made and the incredible achievements that had only happened because of those thousands of people working there. At the same time I found myself getting more and more upset that this fact was either unknown or unrecognised by so many, and that Bletchley Park was having such financial difficulties, and that it might have to close for good. It wasn't right; it wasn't right at all.

When Professor Holmes had finished speaking, John and I went over to see the rebuilt Bombe machine and the slate sculpture of Alan Turing by sculptor Stephen Kettle that was housed in B Block. Stephen gave a talk about how he had been inspired to create the one and a half ton, life-size sculpture of Turing from half a million small pieces of 500 million-year-old Welsh slate. He told us the statue had been commissioned by US billionaire Sidney E Frank, who made his money from Grey Goose vodka and Jägermeister – think about that next time you drink a Jägerbomb!

We stood looking at the life-size statue. It was incredible. We were all in awe at such a remarkable feat, half a million pieces of slate lovingly, painstakingly put together to create a fabulous sculpture of the great man. Stephen described how he had wanted to show Turing's personality through his sculpture and that one way he had done this was by including a slate recreation of Turing's tin tea mug, which he was said to have chained to a radiator in Hut 8 where he had been based.

I had noticed earlier that many of the people on the tour with John and me did not seem to be particularly interested in the computing aspect of

the tour. They weren't rude, but they were obviously not as engaged by it as John and I were. Now that we were all looking at a sculpture and speaking to the sculptor, however, they became much more animated and clearly felt much more at home. I thought about that and reasoned that they were probably more used to looking at and talking about art than old computers. Of course, as computer scientists, John and I were interested in *everything* there, and there was so much for us to look at. It felt like discovering an extraordinary Aladdin's cave of wonderful artefacts. But to this day, I still love the fact that Bletchley Park brings together the humanities and the sciences. It is the home of great historical and great scientific achievement. Can you think of another place in the world that does that?

At the end of the tour, we met up with Simon Greenish again. I had really enjoyed the evening and felt very passionate about helping Bletchley Park. I asked Simon how much money was needed to save Bletchley Park. He told me that, as a ballpark figure, around £10,000,000 would be necessary to carry out the renovation work, bring the buildings up to a reasonable standard, and keep the site going for a couple of years.

£10,000,000. You don't need me to tell you that that's a *lot* of money.

John and I got the train back to London together. We'd had a wonderful evening and seen many interesting and exciting things, but I couldn't help feeling restless and unhappy. Professor Richard Holmes' words were ringing in my ears, and so too was what Simon Greenish had said at the

Women of Station X launch:

"Bletchley Park is teetering on a financial knife-edge."

"Ultra shortened the war 'by not less than two years and probably by four years'."

"This is sacred ground. If this isn't worth preserving, what is?"

I spent the train ride home bending John's ear. How could we help raise awareness of the importance of the site and help it survive? What could we do? Not only to share the stories and legacy of Bletchley Park, but also to ensure that it didn't have to close its gates forever?

"We must do something about this," I said. "But what?"

I start a "Saving Bletchley Park" blog

I arrived in London that evening full of energy. John and I had had a great chat about how wonderful Bletchley Park was and how we wanted to do something to help raise awareness of its plight.

I decided that I was going to start a campaign, though looking back, I realise I had already started my campaign the week before, when I sent that first email to CPHC. I also decided that my campaign needed a blog. I wasn't quite sure how to go about setting one up, but luckily Chris Maigler, a great guy who's married to my friend Maria Margeti, offered to help. I had chatted to Maria and Chris a couple of times about Bletchley Park, and being computer scientists themselves they both felt the same way that I did and wanted to help. Chris has a digital design company, Brave Media and said that he would be very happy to set up and host a blog for me through his company. I jumped at the chance and I'm eternally grateful to Chris for giving me that encouragement and opportunity. The blog ended up being a very important part of the campaign.

I had taken a few photos whilst at Bletchley Park for the reception, so I wrote a bit of text about our trip to go along with the photos and hit "post", and, lo-and-behold, I was a blogger.

My first entry wasn't earth-shattering, but it described what we had seen and done at the reception. Reading it back now, my words seem ominous. I had no clue then what was going to happen over the next few years. I naively thought that if we started a campaign, it would take less than a year to make sure that Bletchley Park was financially secure. Little did I know it was going to take quite a bit longer than that...

That first ever post, along with all of my campaign blog posts, can be seen at savingbletchleypark.org.

Bletchley Park visit

Tuesday 1 July 2008

Went to a reception at Bletchley Park with my colleague from the University of Westminster John Turner who is also a passionate supporter. We had an interesting tour of the site. Although delighted to have a good look around the site I was quite shocked at the state of some of the huts which appeared to be almost falling down. One in particular was covered at one end by a blue tarpaulin to keep out the rain. I took a few photographs.

Hut 3

We saw the Colossus and Bombe machines which have been rebuilt over the last few years by two remarkable men: Tony Sale and John Harper, supported by teams of enthusiasts, their dedication is amazing and an example to us all. We also got to

John Turner, Alan Turing and me

see an Enigma machine and had a talk from the artist who has created a marvellous sculpture of Alan Turing.

We had a really interesting and educational visit to Bletchley Park, but on the way home I could not get the picture of the hut with the blue tarpaulin out of my head. I have to do something to ensure that it and the other huts along with the rest of the site are saved . . .

Me and the Enigma machine

A letter to *The Times*

Over the next few days I kept an eye on the Downing Street petition, started writing regular content for my blog, and wondered what we could do next. I met up with John after a few days and we had a chat over coffee in the University of Westminster refectory. I was really keen that we should do something else to highlight Bletchley Park and its situation. I had gained confidence from the reaction of the CPHC members. Many computer science heads and professors thought the same way that we did – that meant we had support from an important group of powerful people. Bletchley Park mattered and we needed to do something to make sure that everyone else realised both its significant achievements and its extreme financial need.

As we chatted, my mind was focused on one thing.

"What can we do next, John? We need to keep the impetus going!"

John had a great idea: "Why don't we write a letter to *The Times*?"

I thought it was a wonderful plan. A letter in *The Times* would hopefully mean that we'd draw some significant attention to Bletchley Park's situation. I'd never written a letter to a newspaper before, and wasn't quite sure what it should include, so I asked John to draft it and he said he'd be happy to. John emailed me a draft of the letter the very next day, and I sent it out to CPHC; I was sure that at least a few members would sign it and then I could send it in to the newspaper.

Subject:	Saving Bletchley Park
From:	Dr Sue Black
To:	CPHC
Sent:	14 July 2008 17:51

Dear all,

Many thanks to the very many of you who along with me signed the Bletchley Park petition recently. As Simon Greenish, the Director of Bletchley Park pointed out to me, the Bletchley Park petition now ranks higher on the popularity list than the petition asking for a knighthood for Bruce Forsyth. Excellent news, well done everyone ;-)

This email is a bid to take the campaign one step further. I went to Bletchley Park this month taking in a wonderful guided tour of the site. Whilst absolutely amazed by the history and the interesting and exciting stories of the fabulous work that went on there during WWII I was horrified to see the state of some of the huts where the codebreaking took place. One hut in particular is falling apart and has a blue tarpaulin nailed over one end (small photo attached), to be honest I found it quite distressing.

I came home determined to do more. So, I am appealing to you again to help me continue with the campaign to save Bletchley Park.

Pasted below this email is a letter drafted by John Turner, a colleague of mine at the University of Westminster, which I would like you to read and 'sign' if you agree by replying to this email with your name and affiliation. We will send the letter along with signatories to the Times newspaper in approximately ten days time. If you know of any computing pioneers or others whose signatures you think may add weight to the campaign please do feel free to forward this request.

Apologies for taking up your time with another email on this subject, but I believe that, not only is this a cause worth fighting for, but also that time is of the essence, a hut from the 1940s covered in a tarpaulin is not going to last for ever.

Best regards
Sue

Within five minutes of sending my email around, I had several "signatures" coming in. The first was Professor Bill Roscoe, Director of the Oxford University Computing Laboratory, who replied at 17:51, within seconds of reading my email. Professor Roscoe was followed swiftly by Professors Peter Jimack and Roger Boyle from Leeds University at 17:52 and 17:53 respectively, and then Professor Nigel Smart from Bristol University at 17:57. It was looking good – I was sure that we would get enough signatures for the letter after such an auspicious start, and indeed email "signatures" from professors across the country continued to come in all evening. By the time I went to bed that night I knew that we would have enough, and I fell asleep happy.

04
Establishing Station X

"Nothing I did at Bletchley had any connection with my degree course in mathematics. But important facets of one's mental make-up are deeply influenced by the nature ... of one's education. Characteristics which were in great demand at BP were a creative imagination, a well-developed critical faculty, and a habit of meticulousness."

—UNNAMED MATHEMATICIAN[6]

The establishment of Station X wasn't a response to war; it was a response to the threat of war. The house and grounds were bought in the spring of 1938 by Admiral Sir Hugh Sinclair for use as an evacuation site for the already well-established MI6 and the Government Code and Cipher School[7] should war break out and London be subjected to bombing raids. Astonishingly, he bought it with £7,500 of his own money – a huge sum back then – because he got fed up with waiting for the various Whitehall departmental bureaucrats to make a decision about who would fund the purchase. It's assumed that he never got paid back, as he died in November 1939.

Sinclair, known to his friends and colleagues as "Quex",[8] was, at the time of the purchase, a seasoned spymaster. He was the Director of British Naval Intelligence between 1919 and 1921 and then "C" – head of the Secret Intelligence Service (SIS), better known to us today as MI6. By 1938, he was running Section D, an MI6 unit dedicated to carrying out covert military operations and sabotage overseas. During the war, Section D would be amalgamated into the Special Operations Executive (SOE).

In September 1938, Sinclair organised a dry run of evacuation procedures by moving some of his codebreakers and other staff from London to Bletchley. Being something of a *bon viveur* he also took his favourite chef from the Savoy Grill, and the displaced workers ate very handsomely during the rehearsal. Known as "Captain Ridley's Shooting Party" – due to the move being organised by an SIS administrative officer called Captain W H W Ridley – the group of middle-aged men and young women selected by Sinclair and his staff must have made the villagers in nearby Bletchley wonder whether something scandalously naughty was going on at the big house. What Sinclair learned from the dry run was that more space would be needed for staff. Convinced that war was inevitable, he therefore engaged the previous owner of the Bletchley Park Estate, property developer Captain Hubert Faulkner, to build the iconic huts in which so much was later to be achieved.

Meanwhile, events in Europe were escalating. The German military had begun mobilising in August 1938 and, by May 1939, had invaded Czechoslovakia and signed pacts with Russia and Italy. The invasion of Poland in September would signal Great Britain's declaration of war. However, Sinclair had seen the signs and had made preparations.

Back in 1937, he had confided in Alastair Denniston, the head of the GC&CS, that he was convinced that war was inevitable. He then gave instructions for the school to locate and recruit the kinds of people who might be useful if war broke out. "The Emergency List" that was subsequently drawn up included many now well-known names such as Frank Adcock, Peter Twinn, Gordon Welchman, Hugh Alexander and Alan Turing. Then, in December 1938, Sinclair prepared a dossier for Prime Minister Neville Chamberlain in which he described Adolf Hitler as "possessing the characteristics of fanaticism, mysticism, ruthlessness, cunning, vanity, moods of exaltation and depression, fits of bitter and self-righteous resentment, and what can only be termed a streak of madness; but with it all there is a great tenacity of purpose, which has often been combined with extraordinary clarity of vision". Six months later, in August 1939, a month before the declaration of war, Sinclair began moving his staff into Bletchley Park.

The winter of 1939/1940 was very cold. In January, the snow lay thick on the ground and the lake was frozen. The ice was sufficiently strong to allow the staff to skate upon it. A photograph exists of the skaters but it is a rare treasure; even before the declaration of hostilities, secrecy was everything and no photography was allowed. Perhaps it was deemed safe to take this photo because it was outside of the buildings and revealed no more than people having innocent fun.

At this point Station X had around 250 staff, mostly working on analysing message traffic and early ciphers. This work was an invaluable build up to what was to come – the breaking of the complex Enigma cipher – as it provided the codebreakers with many of the common words and phrases that would provide "cribs", a best guess translation of part of a later Enigma-coded message.

The interception of enemy messages, or Signals Intelligence (SIGINT), had three distinct phases: Phase 1 was the signal interception itself. Radio operators trained in Morse code used log forms to record conversations and messages along with time, radio frequency, signal strength and direction. "We were there at that table, two or three girls. Everyone had a set. And we would listen for eight hours, every day," says Margaret Reardon. "We used to do running hand when the messages came in. I could barely speak French so I just tried to write it down as best as I could and hope people would understand it." Phase 2 was TA – traffic analysis. This used the information from SIGINT to plot up a map of where radio transmissions were originating from and of who was talking to whom. By doing so, they were able to focus resources on those sites that seemed to be most important. Some of this was done at Station X. The final Phase 3 was cryptoanalysis, the deciphering of any encoded traffic. As the arena of war expanded, so did the number of coded messages. At the height of its workload, BP was decoding and translating an average of around 4,000 messages per day.

The initial wave of codebreakers soon outgrew the space offered by the mansion. The huts weren't yet built and they couldn't move upstairs as that was occupied by MI6. So they spread out, first into the coach house/garage, then into the buildings around the stableyard, such as the fruit store. The tack and feed store had already been converted into three cottages, one of which housed the Budd family, who maintained the estate. Cottage 1 was used for meetings, but Cottage 3 was set aside for the top codebreakers. It was here that the first true breakthroughs occurred, led by the brilliant Dilwyn "Dilly" Knox, a veteran of WWI code breaking who was normally stationed at the Admiralty in London.

Knox, an expert in reading ancient papyrus, was a fellow at Cambridge when World War I broke out and he had received the call to join Room 40 at the Admiralty, a department involved in decrypting enemy communications. He was to stay there for the duration of the war and helped to decode many important messages, most notably the infamous Zimmermann Telegram. This was sent to the German ambassador in Mexico by Foreign Secretary Arthur Zimmermann who proposed that, if America entered the war, Germany would happily form an alliance with Mexico and support them in retaking Texas and some of the Southern states. The decryption of the telegram was a major factor in bringing the USA into the war. At the end of hostilities, Knox joined the GC&CS and eventually became chief cryptographer.

Something of an eccentric, Knox's office at the Admiralty was the tiny Room 53, which contained a bath. Many of his greatest breakthroughs came to him while soaking, a fact that inspired his colleague Frank Birch to pen the lines:

> "The sailor in Room 53
> Has never, it's true, been to sea;
> But, though not in a boat,
> He has yet served afloat,
> In a bath at the Admiralty."

Between the wars, Knox stayed on as a codebreaker while also continuing with his academic studies. A man known to get totally absorbed in his work, he was once so distracted that he forgot to invite two of his three brothers to his wedding, and he permanently damaged his eyesight while studying fragments of papyri in the British Museum.[9] Despite this, at the onset of war, he bought a motorbike and volunteered for night despatch work because, to his peculiar form of logic, his poor eyesight meant that he was as good a rider at night as by day.[10] Tall and angular – his uniform was said to have "hung on him like a sack" – and hesitant and shy, especially around women, he earned himself the nickname of "Erm" due to his tendency to become tongue-tied during conversation.

When the Enigma cipher machine became available in 1920, work at the Admiralty kicked up a gear. Enigma's inventor, a German engineer called Arthur Scherbius, had originally developed it for commercial use, such as in banking, but the German military soon saw its potential, adopting it for Naval use in 1926 and for the Army a few years later. Scherbius himself would never see the impact his invention would have on world events as he was killed in an accident involving a horse carriage in 1929.

By the time war was declared, Station X was already functioning as an efficient code breaking department. As the war progressed it would face huge, seemingly impossible challenges. But, as history can now show, it would not only face them but conquer them, helping to shorten the war by at least two years and saving an estimated 22 million lives.

05
Bletchley Park in the news

I woke up the next morning, thinking:

"A letter in *The Times* is great, but we need more publicity. If we are going to get support for Bletchley Park quickly, we need to make as big a splash as possible."

I went off to work ruminating on what else I could do to raise awareness and spent all day with that thought in the back of my mind. By the afternoon I had decided to ask for help.

A couple of years previously I had been awarded a National Endowment for Science Technology and the Arts (NESTA) Crucible Award. The award meant that I got to spend four long weekends over one year hanging out with 29 other people who had PhDs and were keen on public engagement, changing the world and making a difference. They were, and still are, a wonderful bunch of people.

Our weekends away were spent in a different location each time and involved listening to interesting and diverse lectures by experts on topics as different as economic forecasting, molecular gastronomy and modern art. We also had really uplifting, mind-changing sessions in areas like working out our Myers Briggs personality types. I learnt a lot and gained so much confidence from the Crucible programme.

One of the great people I met through the Crucible experience was Viv Parry. She led some of the sessions, including one on how the press and media work and how to work with them to best effect. I decided to ask Viv for help with my Bletchley Park campaign.

I sent her an email that afternoon telling her about the campaign and the letter, and asking for advice on how to get the issue more publicity.

Subject: Advice please

From: Dr Sue Black

To: Viv Parry

Sent: 15 July 2008

Hi Viv,

How are you? I hope that all is well with you. What exciting things have you been up to lately?

I'm emailing for some advice. As you probably know I have been involved for some time with Bletchley Park, especially highlighting the part the women who worked there played during the war. More recently, I have been involved with highlighting the dreadful state of repair that the place is in due to a ridiculous lack of funding.

I have copied below an email and related letter and photo that I sent to the Council of Professors and Heads of Computing yesterday asking them to sign a letter that we are going to send to *The Times*. In several hours, around 60 Professors and Heads of Computing have signed up and I have received emails of support from people, one who actually worked with Alan Turing!

Please can you help advise how to get this issue more publicity? It is a good story which links the efforts of many during the war, some of whom are still around and can tell a great tale, with the winning of the war and the history of computing without which we would not have the current and future revolution in society based around the internet. The photo of the hut (attached) portrays the desperate need for funds.

If you can help in any way I would be extremely grateful.

Best regards
Sue

Viv very kindly suggested I get in touch with Alok Jha at the *Guardian*, Mark Henderson at *The Times* and Roger Highfield at *New Scientist* and gave me their contact details. I emailed all three, as well as Chris Vallance from the BBC, who had interviewed me previously about women and tech, and Rory Cellan-Jones, the BBC technology correspondent, whose email address I had.

Luckily I had included my mobile phone number at the end of the email asking the journalists to get in touch. About 20 minutes after I sent the emails, my phone rang. I answered; it was Rory Cellan-Jones from the BBC. My excitement level went through the roof. I knew Rory from seeing him on TV but had never spoken to him before.

I chatted to Rory about Bletchley Park, their financial situation, why it was important that we help, and the letter that we were going to send to *The Times*. Rory listened patiently, and when I paused for breath, he said:

"Yes, of course we all love Bletchley Park. But I'm not sure that this is a *story*."

It was obvious that Rory cared about the fate of Bletchley Park, but I wasn't able to persuade him that the story was something that the BBC should cover. We said goodbye and I hung up the phone feeling crestfallen.

The BBC are quite intriguing

Later that evening, I received a nice email from Chris Vallance at the BBC. He was on holiday at the time, but had still taken the time to respond, saying that he was forwarding my email to his colleagues and adding, "It's a tale very much worth telling though! So we'll see what we can do."

I went to bed that Tuesday night cheered that Chris was interested, though slightly depressed that Rory wasn't and that I hadn't heard back from anyone else.

That Friday, out of the blue, I got another call from Rory. He introduced me to his colleague Mark Ward at the BBC, who was also on the line. We discussed the letter and Rory asked me when it was going to go into *The Times*. I'd not got around to contacting *The Times* about the letter yet, and told Rory this, hoping that he didn't think that made me seem unprofessional. Rory immediately asked me to carry on talking to Mark on the phone whilst he went offline for a moment. I thought it was a bit odd, but I carried on chatting with Mark about Bletchley Park, the women that worked there, the Park's current financial troubles and how it was one of the most important places in the world. I was getting more used to making a strong case.

A few minutes, later Rory came back online and asked me if I was OK with the story going into *The Times* alongside the letter the next Thursday. I said I was more than O.K. with that, I was *delighted* – though I was also curious.

"Why next Thursday?"

"If I told you, I'd have to shoot you!" he said.

I pleaded with him to tell me why, but he wouldn't. I let it go. We talked some more about the petition, the letter, CPHC and Bletchley Park's situation and then said our goodbyes. I wondered what sort of coverage the BBC would give the story and why on earth the letter needed to go into *The Times* the next Thursday.

Rory's royal shocker

The following Monday, I was sitting at home on my laptop, working on my departmental timetables, when my phone rang. It was Rory. I got excited.

"Hi Rory, how are you? Good weekend?"

"Hi Sue, great thanks. I'm going up to Bletchley Park now and I'd like to interview you up there. Can you come?"

I knew this was a great opportunity; it was exactly the sort of thing that I had been hoping would happen. I arranged to meet Rory at Bletchley that afternoon. On the train, I started wondering what to say. I was excited, but I was also suddenly aware that I had a big responsibility. How was I going to get the message across succinctly and in a way that would effectively convey exactly how important Bletchley Park was and how urgently we needed to save it – before any of the huts fell down, or worst of all, it was forced to close forever? I sat writing possible phrases and bullet points down in my notebook, over and over. I thought hard about what the site meant to me and why I was upset that it was in such a poor state. Would a site of similar importance, in the US for example, be left to fend for itself, as Bletchley Park had been? I was really hoping that I would do a good job. I'd had a bit of media training and Rob Watson from the press office at my workplace had given me a pep talk and a few tips. But I knew that this was a massive opportunity for the campaign, and I really didn't want to blow it.

It was a hot, sunny day. When I arrived I walked into the Park and up the main road towards the Mansion House. As I got to Hut 8 I saw Rory, Simon Greenish and a cameraman near Hut 6. Rory introduced me to the cameraman and said we were going to record something for radio and something for TV. *TV!* I thought. *Cool.*

We walked alongside Hut 6 and then stood in front of the hut looking straight into the bright sunlight while I said things like:

"Look at the state of this hut, the paint is peeling off…"

"I feel ashamed to be British in a way… why have we not looked after our heritage?"

"This site was fundamental in our winning the war and look at it now."

I hoped that what I was saying would get people interested and make them realise that action was needed. After about ten minutes of recording, Rory said:

"OK, that's great, thanks Sue."

"Was that all OK?" I wanted to know.

"Yes, great, thanks very much for coming up here."

"You're welcome!"

But there was one more question that I was dying to ask Rory. I took him to one side:

"Rory, why did you want the letter to go in *The Times* this Thursday, why was that so critical to you covering the story?"

"I can't tell you, if I did I'd have to shoot you," Rory said again, this time with a smile.

But then he whispered in my ear: "You mustn't tell anyone, OK?"

"Of course, I won't tell a soul," I said.

"OK, keep this to yourself: it's Prince Charles and Camilla. They're coming to Bletchley Park on Thursday."

"Aha!"

I understood now. The BBC were running the Bletchley Park story partly because it tied in with a visit from the Royal Family. It was another early lesson in campaigning for me: having celebrities and influential people linked to your cause can work wonders when you're trying to get media attention.

For now, it was time to go home. Just ten minutes or so after arriving at Bletchley Park I was saying goodbye to Rory, Simon and the cameraman and making my way back to the station. It was over already. After being so excited about the interview and putting so much thought and energy into what I was going to say, it felt anticlimactic. Had I done enough? Had I said the right things? Would people be interested? Actually, come to think of it… would the interviews even make it onto the radio and TV? What if that had all been for nothing? At least I wouldn't have to wait too long to find out.

The Times they are exciting

By the time I got back home my spirits were lifted again. Signatures for the letter to *The Times* were still coming in from all over the UK, as were some great suggestions for amendments to the letter for accuracy and impact. Professor Nigel Smart from Bristol University had put me in touch with Andy Clark from The National Museum of Computing (TNMOC), which was based at Bletchley Park. I had a chat with Andy about what I was trying to do and why. Andy was very supportive and offered his help if I needed it.

I was also in daily contact now with Bletchley Park CEO Simon Greenish, who was proving very helpful in getting the wording of *The Times* letter correct – the last thing we wanted was to say something inaccurate. And John Turner and I were still in very regular contact, writing and rewriting the letter, making amendments and corrections as appropriate when information came in from various sources. Just a few days after emailing CPHC with the original version of the letter we had signatures from 97 members. I was ecstatic to have such strong support from my community.

Finally, at 7pm on 22nd July, I sent our letter in to Angus Clarke at *The Times*. Rory had given me Angus' contact details and told me to send the letter through as soon as it was ready.

Subject:	Letter to the Times
From:	Dr Sue Black
To:	Angus Clarke
Sent:	22 July 2008

Dear Angus,

Rory Cellan-Jones spoke to you last week about the letter (attached) which has been 'signed' by 97 Professors and Heads of Computing in the UK. The community feel very strongly that Bletchley Park should be made a national museum and hence government funded. The current state of much of the Park is a complete disgrace. I attach a photograph of one of the codebreaking huts taken by me on a recent trip.

I believe that the situation at Bletchley is now critical, if serious funding is not secured soon some of the huts will fall down, time is of the essence.

As Rory mentioned we would be really grateful if our letter could be published this Thursday to coincide with his story about Bletchley Park for the BBC.

Also, as we have 97 signatures I would appreciate your guidance as to the best format in which to send you them, they are currently in spreadsheet form.

Many thanks for your help Angus,
Sue

I attached the letter and the photo of Hut 6, one end covered in a blue tarpaulin, that I had taken at the reception a few weeks previously. My email was quite strident in its tone – I was obviously very keen to get my message over!

After a few hours, I received a reply from Angus putting me in touch with Helen Chadney at *The Times*. We worked with Helen to get everything ready for publication, including working out which signatories should go on the actual letter in the printed edition. I'd not thought about this before, but it was obvious: *The Times* weren't going to be able to publish all of the 97 signatures in the actual newspaper. How would we decide which signatories to include and which to leave out?

I anguished about it for a bit; I really hate any kind of favouritism. But I realised that the best thing to do would be to put the most heavyweight signatures on the letter. I looked through the list. Professors from Oxford and Cambridge had signed; they should be included. Professor Keith van Rijsbergen had signed – he was currently one of the most high profile computer scientists in the country as he was chairing the Research Assessment Exercise panel, so he should be in too. I saw that Professor Robert Churchhouse had signed and that he had worked at GCHQ, so he should definitely be in. There was space for one more signatory. I looked through the 97 names. The one that stood out to me was Professor Ian Sommerville, whose book *Software Engineering* is like a bible to computer science students in the UK, especially to those like me who go on to do a PhD in software engineering. I decided to put him in to finish off the list and sent it through along with the letter to Helen at *The Times*:

We cannot let Bletchley go to rack and ruin

Sir, The work undertaken at Bletchley Park during the Second World War in breaking German wartime codes played a significant part in winning that war and securing our future. The work included the decryption of messages enciphered on the German Enigma machines and the breaking of the German "Fish" High Command teleprinter ciphers. Bletchley Park also played a significant role 65 years ago in the design and development of Colossus, one of the world's first programmable electronic computers. It is therefore fitting that the world's first purpose-built computer centre should be home to the National Museum of Computing.

Over the years, Bletchley Park has survived building redevelopment (1938), an air raid (1940), the destruction of sensitive material and information (post-1945) and more recently (1991), a second attempt at demolition and redevelopment. That Bletchley Park has survived to the present day is due to the foresight of Milton Keynes Borough Council, which declared the park a conservation area in February 1992, and the formation of the Bletchley Park Trust just three days later.

The trust currently runs this gem charitably, receiving no external funding. Although there has recently been some progress in generating income, without fundamental support Bletchley Park is still under threat, this time from the ravages of age and a lack of investment. Many of the huts where the codebreaking occurred are in a terrible state of disrepair.

As a nation, we cannot allow this crucial and unique piece of both British and world heritage to be neglected in this way. The future of the site, buildings, resources and equipment at Bletchley Park must be preserved for future generations by providing secure long-term financial backing. Is it too much to ask that Bletchley Park be provided with the same financial stability as some of our other great museums such as the Imperial War Museum, the Science Museum and the Natural History Museum?

Professor Keith van Rijsbergen
  Chair, 2008 Research Assessment Exercise, Computer Science &
  Informatics sub-panel

Professor Bill Roscoe
  Director of Oxford University Computing Laboratory

Professors Jean Bacon and Lawrence Paulson,
  University of Cambridge Computer Laboratory

Professor Ian Sommerville
  Professor of Software Engineering, University of St Andrews

Professor Robert Churchhouse CBE,
  Emeritus Professor, Cardiff University, formerly at GCHQ 1952-1963

Chris Smyth from *The Times* was also writing a piece to go in the paper to accompany the letter, so we corresponded about Bletchley Park facts and what to put in the article. It was all very exciting!

The next day I sent an email update around to several groups of people that I knew (well, at least hoped!) would be interested, including BCSWomen and CPHC. I let them know that I had been interviewed at Bletchley Park, that the interview would be on the BBC Radio Four *Today* program and possibly on the BBC News at 1 pm and 6 pm. I had also by now been approached by BBC News 24 and BBC *Radio Five Live*, who wanted me to speak to them at 6.50 am. I am not a morning person, so I was starting to feel quite stressed about having to think clearly at a time when I was usually still asleep.

I emailed CPHC explaining my rationale for choosing the six names that were going to be published in the paper version of the letter and thanked everyone for their support. I put out a plea asking everybody to talk to everyone that they knew about Bletchley Park and to spread the word about the campaign:

> "We need to preserve Bletchley Park so that our children and
> grandchildren know about and understand the massive effort put
> into cracking the codes and winning WWII and also the history of
> computing in this country."

I also included the sentence, "I'm really becoming quite confident that we do now have a good chance of getting some serious funding :-)." Looking back now, I think, *ah, I was so naïve!* It would be quite some time before some really serious funding appeared. But at the time, things were moving forward, and it felt like we had great momentum and support.

A publicity dream, so hard to beat

24th July 2008 was a big day for me.

I started very early, at 4.30am. I knew I was going to be interviewed by *Radio Five Live* about the letter in *The Times* soon, but I hadn't been able to sleep very well – I was too stressed and excited. I could see that the letter was already on *The Times* website, and there was an article on the BBC website too.

"Neglect" of Bletchley condemned
BBC News
24 July 2008

A call to save Bletchley Park has gone out from the UK's computer scientists. [...]

The academics were brought together by Dr Sue Black, head of the computer science department at the University of Westminster, who was moved to act after visiting Bletchley Park in early July.

"I went up there and felt quite upset by what I saw," she said.

Many of the buildings on the Bletchley estate were in a state of serious disrepair, she said. One building, where codebreakers worked during World War II, was falling apart, said Dr Black, and was protected by a blue tarpaulin that was nailed down over it.

Describing Bletchley as a "gem", Dr Black said it was a "national disgrace" that such a historic site was being allowed to fall into ruin.

"I do not know why they do not have funding as a national museum," she said.

The visit led her to contact other heads of computer science departments at universities up and down the country. Within hours, she had hundreds of responses – all of them backing her call.

Dr Black said she had been "overwhelmed" by the response which showed the depth of feeling about Bletchley and the position it occupies in the history of the computer age.

It must have gone up online at around midnight as I already had lots of emails from people around the world who had read it and wanted to show their support – including a lovely message from Professor Wendy Hall at the University of Southampton (sent at 2.08am!).

From:	Prof Wendy Hall
Sent:	24 July 2008 02:08
To:	Dr Sue Black
Subject:	RE: Bletchley Park update

Best of luck tomorrow – I hope it's a slow news day and you get all the slots.

Wendy

That morning, I had several phone calls from BBC *Radio Five Live*, who kept changing the time that I was going to be interviewed. Now that I'm a bit more used to dealing with the media, I know that this is reasonably common for a live news show as so much can change within the space of a few hours. I finally did my live interview sometime before 9 am; it finished just in time for me to listen to Rory's piece on the *Today* programme.

The announcer introduced the piece and then Rory's voice came on the radio. Rory described Bletchley Park, where it is, what happened there and its historic importance. He went on, saying that it is in a poor state of repair, and then he introduced me. It was very odd to hear myself on the radio! Then Simon Greenish was saying that it was a struggle keeping the site open and that they needed £200,000-£300,000 per year just to stay open. Rory then spoke to some of the visitors to the Park who said that it was a shame it was underfunded and that it looked shabby. The report then cut back to me saying, "Everybody in computing that knows about Bletchley Park wants it to be looked after properly... for us to understand what went on here and for our children... the state it is in now it's not going to be here when I retire."

Rory summed up:

"So secret was the work done at Bletchley Park that it was only decades later that its story began to be told. Now its supporters believe that it may not be here for future generations, many may not get the chance to hear about the place that helped shape their country's future."

It was a great report, and I was delighted. In just a few short days I had gone from gingerly sending an email to my peers asking for support, to being on the BBC *Today* programme. Rob Watson from the press office at work had told me that *Today* was the top media spot in terms of having influence in the UK with the people that mattered, so this was a very big deal.

I checked my email quickly. I had lots of messages from CPHC members congratulating me on raising awareness, messages from friends and family saying that they had heard me on the radio and Rob from Westminster saying that I was now a media star having also got onto page 9 of *The Times*. I checked the petition quickly and saw that there had been quite a few more signatures there too. Excellent.

Now that the *Five Live* and *Today* interviews were over, I started to worry about the BBC News 24 live interview I was going to be doing at around 11.30 am. Actually, to say that I was nervous was a complete understatement. I was beside myself with nerves.

Nevertheless, I got myself ready, put my best suit and make-up on and started my journey uptown to Millbank and the BBC studios. My phone had been buzzing all morning with calls from friends and radio stations. I agreed to do another interview for the BBC World Service in a radio studio at Millbank before the BBC TV News interview. Andy Clark from TNMOC had also been in touch, inviting me to meet him for lunch in the restaurant at Millbank after my news interview. I was looking forward to that, but not to the interview itself.

When I got up to Millbank I found the BBC studios and the contact that I had there. After waiting a few minutes, I was ushered into a small studio and told what to expect for the World Service radio interview. I was asked to sit down and put on headphones and told that someone would talk to me soon through them. I didn't have to wait long before a BBC interviewer spoke to me through the headphones, and we had a nice chat about

Bletchley Park and the letter to *The Times*. I wasn't too stressed during the interview, thankfully. It helped that it was being recorded for future broadcast and could therefore be edited if I said something incorrect or ended up at a loss for words, something which does frighten me.

After the interview I was taken into the TV studios. I sat in a chair with a couple of other people who were due to be interviewed on the same show. When I looked at the person sitting opposite me, I realised that he was Feargal Sharkey, lead singer of the Undertones. How cool: the Undertones song "Teenage Kicks" is one of my favourite songs. It comforted me a bit to note that even Feargal Sharkey looked just as scared as I felt about going on live TV. It wasn't just me, then. Phew!

Feargal was called in first, and I was told that I was straight after him, so I would be called in in about five minutes. My heart started pounding loudly in my ears and my palms got very sweaty. I actually started hoping that my body would give in and that I would have a heart attack and die. At that moment, the fear of being in a live TV interview was worse than my fear of death.

It was now my turn. I followed the BBC person over to a small booth which contained a camera, a chair and a TV monitor in it. I sat in the chair and thought, *O.K., what was the advice that Rob and my media training had given me for live TV?* All I could remember was that live TV was good because you could say what you wanted despite the questions you were being asked. So I didn't need to worry too much about answering the interviewers' questions per se, I just needed to say stuff that made some sort of sense and was vaguely on topic. I tried to calm myself down by doing some deep breathing as I thought about the main points that I wanted to get across.

It was still clear in my mind that one thing I really wanted to happen was an oral history project which collected interviews from all of the Bletchley Park veterans still alive. I wanted to capture as much information about what happened there as possible. As practically everything at Bletchley apart from the buildings was destroyed after the war, most of the knowledge about what went on there was in veterans' heads.

The BBC person appeared and said we were about to go live. The TV screen showed what was currently happening on the news programme and then they started talking about Bletchley Park and the letter that had appeared in *The Times*.

My pulse rocketed up to about two hundred beats per minute, but I also suddenly felt quite calm. Then I heard my name and a question addressed to me, and I started talking. The interview lasted about three minutes; I mentioned the veterans and oral history and talked about the letter and the overall importance of Bletchley Park. And then, as quickly as it had started, the interview finished. I hoped I had said the right things.

Still buzzing with adrenaline, I went to meet Andy Clark for lunch. Andy told me all about The National Museum Of Computing at Bletchley Park. He said they had a rebuild of Colossus, the world's first programmable digital computer, that had been built by a team of dedicated enthusiasts over many years. They also had several galleries full of computers of varying ages and were looking to build TNMOC into a world-class museum. In turn, I told him how I had got involved with Bletchley and how excited I was about all the media attention we had got from the letter in *The Times*. It was obvious that we both loved computing and Bletchley and wanted to raise awareness of Bletchley Park in the hope that it would increase in importance in the public psyche and hopefully bring in some funding.

After lunch, I had another interview with BBC Radio Wales. This time I was told that there would also be a Bletchley Park veteran in the interview. After the recording began, the interviewer introduced us, talked about Bletchley Park and the letter in *The Times* and spoke to the veteran, who was in Wales, about what she did at Bletchley Park. Again, I was totally in awe. The veterans are such remarkable people and every single one I've met has been very modest about his or her contribution. When it was my turn, I talked about the fundamental importance of Bletchley Park from both a wartime and a computer science perspective.

After the interview finished, I walked out of Millbank into the sunshine. I had been indoors all day and, despite feeling elated at the amount of coverage we had had with the story, I was feeling pretty knackered. I walked to Waterloo over Westminster Bridge, then got the train home. I was so looking forward to laying down on the sofa with my feet up and a nice cup of tea!

Prince Charles backs "crumbling" Bletchley Park

24 July 2008

MKweb

The fight to save Bletchley Park received a huge boost today when Prince Charles declared his support. [...]

Addressing Trust members, local dignitaries and park volunteers, Prince Charles said: "I woke up this morning, turned the wireless on and heard something about Bletchley Park.

I was so pleased to hear that attention is being paid to this amazing place.

You are the keepers of one of the greatest British success stories."

When I got home I made myself a cup of tea, sat on the sofa and attempted to catch up with everything that had been happening. I had loads of emails and texts from friends, family and others saying they had heard me on the radio or seen me on TV. I switched on the TV and put on BBC News 24. After a few minutes, they started talking about Bletchley Park and the letter in *The Times*. The narrator was Jon Brain; he started the piece:

"It survived German bombers, it's struggling to survive the ravages of time. It was here that the Nazis' Enigma code, once considered unbreakable, was cracked. The only cracks now are in the buildings themselves."

And then I saw and heard myself standing in front of Hut 6 speaking about the state that Bletchley Park was in: "I feel embarrassed that it is in this state. I feel ashamed to be British in a way, because, why have we not looked after our heritage? This site here was fundamental in our winning of the war, and look at it now."

Ok, maybe not the most eloquent speech, but at least it was reasonably clear and to the point!

Jon Brain went on to describe the park, saying, "Bletchley Park's very existence was kept hidden for years. Although it's now open to the public, it depends on charitable donations to keep it going, and it shows."

Some visitors then described what they saw – "bit dilapidated, buildings falling down"; "some of the huts in particular are dilapidated to the point of collapse almost, there's obviously a great deal of work that could be done, were they to have the resources" – before Jon continued his narration: "In addition to its wartime role the Park was also where Colossus, the world's first programmable computer was developed. Campaigners claim that it needs funding like any other major museum."

Simon Greenish, the Director of Bletchley Park, then came on, saying:

"We believe that £5 million is needed to put the infrastructure back into good order, and then we want to develop the museum as well, which could be anything from £5 million upwards. We've done the plans and we have got some fabulous ideas; I think this site could be a very important museum in the future."

Jon finished the piece: "The fear is that without an injection of cash, the site where they helped win the war will be lost."

I was so delighted that we had got Bletchley Park on the news. Hopefully offers of support would now come rolling in. I felt sure that once people saw the state it was in and found out that they needed funding, help would materialise.

People certainly seemed affected by what they were hearing, and we had got a lot of coverage. I had so many emails from people who had seen me on TV or heard me on the radio, saying that they supported what I was doing; one of them was from Mark Ward at the BBC saying that the piece had been running all day on BBC News 24 and was on the front page of the BBC website. Mark said that he thought the story had done really well and that he was going to follow it up with a call to the Heritage Lottery Fund people. He wanted to see if they would have anything substantive to say. I replied asking him to let me know what they said; I still thought that they were one of our biggest opportunities for funding.

Reading through my emails, I noticed one from a CPHC Professor who told me that she had recommended to one of the Bletchley Park Trust board members that they invite me to join the board. She also mentioned that she had heard that the Heritage Lottery Fund were "taking an interest at last", so hopefully the interest from the petition, *The Times* and BBC News would help to move things along. Christine Burns, a BCSWomen member, had kindly sent the links for the BBC coverage of the day around the BCS-Women online network, and great feedback was coming in about what members had seen in the media. Ann Appleton sent a link to a piece in *The Register*, "Scientists decry Bletchley Park's decline. Demand government action to save Station X."

SCIENTISTS DECRY BLETCHLEY PARK'S DECLINE, DEMAND GOVERNMENT ACTION TO SAVE STATION X

Lester Haines

The Register

24 July 2008

A group of the UK's leading computer scientists have demanded government action to save Bletchley Park from further decay, saying that 'the ravages of age and a lack of investment' threaten the future of Station X.

Some of the wooden codebreaking huts are in "a desperate state of decay" and, as we recently reported, the Bletchley Park Trust needs a cool £1m just to fix the central Victorian mansion's roof.

I also had emails from several people connecting me to others who they thought might be able to help with the campaign. One of these was Professor Derek Sleeman from the University of Aberdeen. He introduced me by email to Susan and Jonathan Michie whose father Donald Michie had actually been a codebreaker at Bletchley Park during the war. I got in touch with them and arranged to meet up with Jonathan later that week for a chat.

I read Donald Michie's obituary in *The Telegraph*. He had been a friend of Alan Turing during the war and had worked out the solution to *Tunny*, the German Lorenz cipher machine, before going on to a distinguished academic computer science career.

Professor Donald Michie

The Telegraph

9 July 2007

Professor Donald Michie, who died in a motor accident on Saturday aged 83, was a pioneer in the creation of artificial intelligence; during the war he worked on breaking German codes at Bletchley Park and later, as Professor of Machine Intelligence at Edinburgh University, helped to bring about the world of robots, computer games and search engines.

Known to his colleagues as 'Duckmouse', Donald Michie was one of the great multi-disciplinarians of his generation. A classical scholar at the start, he worked with mathematicians – and especially Alan Turing – at Bletchley, then went into genetics until computers caught up with his ambitions to 'build a brain' before putting together his team at Edinburgh.

The story had also reached the international press and media. Vladimiro Sassone from the University of Southampton sent me a link to an article in Italian newspaper, *La Repubblica*, which had covered the story; I even heard from friends in the US and Canada who had been surprised to see me pop up on their TVs on BBC America. Incredible; so wonderful that the story had reached so far. I'd had no idea what would happen when I'd had that first chat with Rory; this was way beyond what I had hoped for.

A pezzi l'edificio dove gliinglesi decifrarono il Codice Enigma"

La Repubblica

24 luglio 2008

LONDRA – La chiamavano la 'Stazione X', perché fu il decimo centro segreto di questo tipo ad essere costruito in Gran Bretagna. Tra la mura di Bletchley Park gli inglesi decifrarono il Codice Enigma, creato dai tedeschi per comunicare tra loro.

Bletchley Park in the news

Several journalists contacted me over the next few days to talk about the petition, the letter to *The Times*, the state of Bletchley Park and to ask what was needed to save it. I was starting to get to know more about Bletchley Park, its history and its current position. There were many questions that I couldn't answer, but thankfully Simon Greenish was happy to help. I also had Andy Clark and Stephen Fleming from TNMOC to talk to; they had been really helpful in sending me information about Colossus, TNMOC and its many delights.

I received many emails and phone calls around this time from various people who wanted to help or who wanted to put me in touch with people who they thought might be able to help, particularly with funding. I remember one particular conversation with a key figure – I'll call him Sir X. I had been told that Sir X cared about Bletchley Park, was influential in government, and would be able to advise me "off the record" about possibilities for serious funding. We had a really good chat about potential scenarios and what might and might not be possible.

As I got to know more and more about Bletchley Park and its financial situation, I started thinking that surely the best idea for its future would be for it to somehow become a joint venture, with shared ownership between the Imperial War Museum and the Science Museum. In my mind Bletchley Park was unique; it was the only place that I knew that was so fundamentally important in both a historical and scientific way. Its contribution towards the shortening and the winning of World War II made it a site of great historical significance, while the industrial code breaking effort that led to the world's first programmable digital computer, Colossus, had solidified its scientific significance. Surely, I thought, these remarkable achievements and the site and artefacts at Bletchley would be valuable assets to the Science and Imperial War museums.

I put forward this case to Sir X and he agreed that, in principle, it sounded like a reasonable idea. He then went on to explain why it would not happen: partly because of institutional and governmental politics and partly because the financial instability of the Park meant that neither museum would consider it worth investing in. Still, we had a really interesting discussion. I greatly valued his interest and his candour in speaking to me, as I was an unknown quantity to him.

I also had another email from Viv Parry, who had been so helpful earlier in sending me names and contact details for several journalists. This time, after congratulating me on getting great media coverage for the story, she suggested that I get in touch with Simon Singh, the well-known mathematician and author, who might be interested in what I was doing. I found Simon's contact email on his website and sent him a message.

Simon very kindly got back to me the next day, congratulating me on the media coverage and offering to help. He included his home phone number and suggested that I give him a ring the next day to discuss things further. We had a great chat about how important Bletchley Park was. We were both in agreement that it needed to be preserved for the nation, and we spoke about the best way to make this happen. I told him about my ideas around the joint venture between the Science Museum and the Imperial War Museum and my conversation with Sir X. Simon gave me some campaigning advice and lots of encouragement and told me to get back in touch if he could help in the future.

Subject:	Saving Bletchley Park
From:	Dr Sue Black
To:	Simon Singh
Sent:	29 July 2008

Dear Simon,

You may have seen our letter to the Times last week and some of the resulting publicity in the press and on TV and radio.

As you are a supporter of Bletchley Park and, I have heard, as passionate as I am about the place :-) I am writing to ask for your help in our (currently at an early stage) campaign to save Bletchley Park. Anything that you can do towards the cause would be extremely welcome.

Best regards
Sue

Meanwhile, I had been approached by Maggie Holland from *IT Pro* as she wanted to write an article about Bletchley. Maggie had written several articles about women in computing so we had talked previously, particularly as she had covered our BCSWomen Bletchley Park oral history project. This time Maggie wrote the great piece entitled "SOS Bletchley Park" – a rallying call for support, which asked people to sign the petition and help raise awareness of its financial state and also highlighted the contribution of the women that had worked there. I had previously sent Maggie some of the audio files from the BCSWomen oral history project and she had obviously listened to them. There was a nice mention of my colleague John Turner as well; after all, if he hadn't had the idea to write a letter to *The Times*... would any of this have happened?

Maggie's article was accompanied by the photo of Hut 6 that I had taken at the reception on July 1st. Reading the article I couldn't believe that it had been only four weeks previously that I had stood there in front of Hut 6 with a tear in my eye, listening to an account of all the amazing achievements that happened there during World War II. So much had happened since then.

SOS Bletchley Park

Maggie Holland

ITPRO

29 July 2008

Is the hospital/house you were born in still standing? How would you feel if it was there but not there – a decrepit shadow of its former self? Not good, one would imagine. Yet that's exactly what is happening to the birthplace of computing and the place that played home to the code breakers during World War II.

Bletchley Park is an absolute goldmine of historical significance. It is incredibly exciting – even nail biting – to think of what went on within its walls during the war, and it is attracting visitors from around the world. The gems on offer to those visiting are akin to those found in many of Britain's great museums. Indeed, the site now serves as home to the National Museum of Computing.

But, unlike the majority of museums, Bletchley Park receives no government funding. As a result, there is a real danger that this piece of history could be consigned to just that: history.

06
Enigma

"Hut 6 would never have gotten off the ground if we had not learned from the Poles, in the nick of time, the details both of the German military version of the commercial Enigma machine, and of the operating procedures that were in use."

—GORDON WELCHMAN

The Enigma machine was a fiendishly clever device. It encrypted messages by substituting one letter for another, as most ciphers do. However, the machine used a series of rotors to run a series of substitutions for every letter it coded. Therefore, unless you knew the starting positions for each rotor, the possible combination of substituted letters ran into the hundreds of thousands. But that was just the start; Enigma was far more complicated than even that.

Depressing a letter on the keyboard – let's say the letter "P" – sent an electrical signal to Rotor I. The signal then passed from one side of the rotor to the other, but the two sides wired each input letter to a different output letter. So the input letter "P" may have been wired to the output letter "G", for example. The output letter "G" then passed to Rotor II where it was output as, let's say, an "S". The "S" passed to Rotor III which output it as a "Q". After leaving Rotor III, the signal would hit a component called the Reflector which changed the letter again – a letter "H" for these purposes – and then the character would travel back through the three rotors. However, the return journey would be different to the outward journey because the rotors, as their name suggests, rotated. Rotor I was called the fast rotor and would advance by one position after each key depression. Consequently, if you pressed a single key – our "P" for example – several times, each keystroke would generate a different output letter. Rotor II (the middle rotor) also rotated one position after the fast rotor had completed a full circuit of 26 positions. In addition, a sliding ring bearing the letters of the alphabet could be set at any of the 26 positions on each rotor. If the letter "A" on Rotor I was turned into an "R" by Rotor II, then re-setting the ring by one position on Rotor I would mean that "B" would code to an "R". You could also decide which letter position would trip Rotor II and set the position on Rotor II that would trip Rotor III after Rotor II had completed a circuit. Finally, the finished cipher signal would light up one of 26 letters on the face of the machine, displaying the letter that your initial letter "P" had now been coded into.

Input/Output	Rotor I	Rotor II	Rotor III	Reflector
P	P to G	G to S	S to Q	Q
R	Y to R	B to Y	H to B	H

But that's still not the full process. Each machine came with three rotors, all wired differently. Plus, each rotor could be placed in any of the three slots in the machine. So apart from needing to know the starting position of the three rotors, you also had to know what slots the three rotors were in, as there were 60 possible combinations (the Naval Enigma added two more rotors to the mix so that you then had to work out which three of five were in use and their positions). In 1930, a plugboard was also added to the military machines whereby any two letters of the alphabet could be randomly wired together in pairs causing them to be reversed. This added another layer of complication to encryption.[11]

This was why Enigma was so efficient as a coding device; every letter in a message was coded using a different cipher to every other letter. To decode a message, you needed to know which three rotors were being used and what positions they occupied (*Walzenlage*). You also needed to know the initial starting position for each rotor (*Grundstellung*), the ring settings that dictated which letter was being coded into which

(*Ringstellung*), the trip position that would trigger rotation of the next rotor, and the chosen paired letters on the plugboard (*Steckerverbindungen*). The total number of possible ways in which a standard Enigma machine with plugboard could be set up was 60 *Walzenlage* x 17,576 *Grundstellung* x 676 *Ringstellung* x 150,738,274,937,250 *Steckerverbindungen*. That's around 158 million million million possible ways to set up a machine. Therefore it was believed, with good reason, that no one would ever be able to crack the Enigma code system. As Tony Sale, the late curator of Bletchley Park, once said: "Unless you had the exact key, you couldn't get anywhere with it all. This was the major difference from any of the code systems that had existed prior to that. There was no sense of nearness; you were never nearly at a solution. You'd either got the solution or you hadn't got the solution." Codebreaker Howard Smith recalls that a colleague described breaking Enigma as "the frenetic equivalent of blindfold three-dimensional chess".[12]

But someone *did* break Enigma.

In 1939, shortly before the invasion of Poland, a group of Polish cryptographers revealed to the GC&CS that they had been working on military Enigma machines since 1932 and, after receiving documents from a disgruntled German clerk and from French Military Intelligence, they had worked out the scrambler wiring on the machine's rotors. This was very useful information indeed. Dilly Knox was already familiar with the commercial Enigma machine but this didn't have the plugboard, nor were the rotors wired in the same way. But Polish mathematician Marian Rejewski had figured out the differences and, what's more, had built a replica machine that he called an *Enigma Double* to test encryptions. He had also built an electromechanical machine called the *Bomba Kryptologiczna* (Cryptological Bomb) that used a series of six connected Enigma rotors to speed up the working out of possible combinations.

Poland, sandwiched between Russia and Germany, was ripe for invasion and so the Poles agreed to hand over everything they had to the Allies, including all of their research, an Enigma Double and a Bomba. Sadly, changes in the German operator instructions, and the addition of two extra rotor choices, made much of this work obsolete very quickly. But as Peter Calvocoressi, head of the Luftwaffe section in Hut 3, has remarked, "According to the best qualified judges it accelerated the breaking of Enigma by perhaps a year. The British did not adopt Polish techniques but they were enlightened by them."

Initially, attempts to break into Enigma were made using *Zygalski Sheets*, named after Henryk Zygalski, a Polish mathematician who worked as a cryptographer with Marian Rejewski and Jerzy Różycki. Zygalski had noticed that Enigma had a curious quirk; occasionally – about one in eight depressions of the same key – it coded a letter into the same letter twice. So rather than a key depression being a random 1/26 chance, there were often repetitions. He called these repetitions *samiczki* (females), and there were only a relatively small number of Enigma machine configurations that would generate females. This was good news for the codebreakers. Tony Sale again: "Repetitions give codebreakers a toehold. Repetitions are always bad news in cryptography." Anything non-random meant that patterns could be detected, and if enough females occurred during a day's message traffic, it might be possible to find the unique configuration from which all of these doubles could be generated.

Zygalski Sheets[13] were sets of 26 large cards, each with a vertical and horizontal axis bearing the letters of the alphabet, rather like a map's grid reference system. The 26 × 26 matrix represented the 676 possible starting positions of the middle and left (slow) rotors. Each sheet was different, with holes meticulously cut out with razor blades, to represent every rotor configuration that could possibly produce females. By laying these sheets on top of each other, working through each of the six possible rotor orders (1-2-3, 1-3-2, 2-3-1, 2-1-3, 3-1-2, 3-2-1) and then through the 26 possible left (slow) ring letters, you had 156 chances of finding the Enigma configuration that generated the females you'd spotted in a message.

"When the sheets were superimposed and moved in the proper sequence and the proper manner with respect to each other, the number of visible apertures gradually decreased," wrote Zygalski. "And, if a sufficient quantity of data was available, there finally remained a single aperture, probably corresponding to the solution. From the position of the aperture one could calculate the order of the rotors, the setting of their rings, and, by comparing the letters of the cipher keys with the letters in the machine, likewise the entire cipher key."[14] "It was like solving a very difficult crossword puzzle", says Pam Hemsted who worked with codebreaker John Jeffries on the sheets. "But you could actually see it happening. And the triumph when you found it worked! That was fascinating, marvellous. There's really nothing like seeing a code breaking. That is really absolutely the tops." And Leslie Yoxall, a cryptographer from the Naval and Japanese sections, recalls: "People were very reluctant to go home at the end of the shift. They wanted to hang in there."[15]

The Zygalski method worked wonderfully until the Germans changed their operating procedures. For a while, the Allies were back to square one and it seemed that the only way they were likely to get back into Enigma was by capturing enemy code books. At the Admiralty, all kinds of audacious plots were hatched to achieve this goal. Personal Assistant to the Director of Naval Intelligence, Commander Ian Fleming – later to achieve huge success as the author of *Chitty Chitty Bang Bang* and the James Bond books – came up with the idea of crash-landing a captured German plane into the sea and then overpowering the crew of the ship or U-boat that answered its distress call. The appropriately named Operation Ruthless was never implemented, however.

But then, on a cold evening in February 1940, a young codebreaker and colleague of Dilly Knox called John Herivel had a sudden, brilliant flash of inspiration. In Sinclair McKay's *The Secret life of Bletchley Park*, Herivel describes that moment to the author: "Something very strange happened; I may have dozed off before the fire – a dangerous thing to do as I often smoked a pipe and might have burnt a hole in my landlady's carpet, or worse – and perhaps I woke up with a start and the faint trace of a vanishing dream in my head. Whatever it was, I was left with a distinct picture – imagined of course – in my mind's eye, of a German Enigma operator. I seem to have taken Aristotle's advice, that you cannot really understand anything thoroughly unless you see it growing from the beginning."

By putting himself into the mind of one of the German operators, Herivel imagined the long hours, the fear, the working conditions – maybe not so different from the pressure of work and conditions at BP

– and realised that maybe the operators might not be as on the ball as they could be. What if tiredness, or distractedness or even laziness made them do something silly, like not resetting the ring settings on the Enigma at the start of a new day? Acting on his hunch, Herivel worked out exactly how such a mistake could be spotted. What became known as "The Herivel Tip" or "herivelismus" proved to be the next great breakthrough.

Meanwhile, other mistakes had been noticed by Dilly Knox and Gordon Welchman. They christened them "Dilly's Sillies" or "Cillis" after finding what seemed to be a shortened version of a woman's name – CIL – as an indicator for the day's codes. Similar slipshod or lazy operator practice included snippets of poems, proper names, common and non-random typed letter sequences like ABC or QWE, and even swear words.

It's a chilling thing to consider, but had John Herivel not had his moment of brilliant intuition, and had the German operators displayed a little more of the efficiency that dogs their national stereotype, Enigma would not have been broken for many more months and the course of the war may have gone a very different way.

07
Bletchley Park heroes

In the days after the letter to *The Times* was published, things started to get back to normal, though there were still a few emails per day coming in from people all over the world who were interested in Bletchley Park. I did a few more interviews with radio stations overseas, including one with an Australian station, ABC Radio Canberra, on the Ross Solly show. I was finding that the non-UK audiences seemed to find it incomprehensible that Bletchley Park wasn't government-funded. I agreed with them. I had used the phrase "ashamed to be British" whilst talking about Bletchley Park and its situation, and though this had now become a phrase my family used regularly to take the piss out of me, I still felt that on some level it was true: I was ashamed that the government hadn't stepped up to save this important historical site from ruin.

When I went back into the office that week and checked my voicemail, I found that I had a message from someone called Captain Jerry Roberts, asking me to get in touch with him. I immediately looked him up online. He was a Bletchley Park veteran and sounded very distinguished. How exciting! I gave him a ring and we chatted for some time about how the Park needed funding. We were like minds. Jerry had been a linguist and senior codebreaker during the war, and he had served as a shift leader in the Testery, one of the vital components of the code breaking operation at Bletchley. Jerry concluded the conversation by very kindly inviting me over for lunch the next week at his flat in Pimlico.

Lunch with Jerry and his wife Mei was wonderful. They were both such lovely people and obviously keen to tell the world about what had happened at Bletchley and how important it was. Jerry told me a bit about

Captain Jerry Roberts

his work at Bletchley, about decoding messages from Hitler himself and about working for months in a room with Bill Tutte, the codebreaker and mathematician who made a crucial advance in cracking the Lorenz cipher, *Tunny*; Jerry said he'd thought Tutte was not "earning his corn" until his major breakthrough with Tunny, when of course it became apparent that he'd been hard at work.

Jerry had so many great stories. I asked him if he had written down all of his experiences and said how great it would be if he published an autobiography. Jerry said that he wanted to, but that due to his age he was finding it difficult. He was nearly 90 years old, and although he was extremely sharp mentally, his body was starting to let him down. His stamina was not what it had been, and he had to have a nap each afternoon.

Over lunch, Jerry told me that he was dedicating the rest of his life to highlighting the importance of Bletchley Park and the "three Ts": Bill Tutte, Tommy Flowers and the Testery. Jerry had worked with Bill Tutte and told me that it was shocking that Tutte had received almost no recognition at all from the government for his fundamental work at Bletchley. He had gone to Canada after the war and carved out a career as a distinguished mathematician there, but no one knew that his work had been pivotal in winning the war. Tommy Flowers had also received little recognition. He had, at his own expense, built Colossus, the world's first programmable, digital computer, to industrialise the breaking of the Lorenz code at Bletchley. Flowers was a Post Office engineer working at Dollis Hill during the war; he invented and built Colossus there and then took it up to Bletchley. Like everyone else who worked at Bletchley, Tommy Flowers signed the Official Secrets Act, and he, like Bill Tutte, received little credit after the war had ended.

The Testery was an operational unit at Bletchley Park. It was named after its leader, Ralph Tester – a protocol at Bletchley Park was that the operational units were named after those who led them (so, for example, Max Newman ran the Newmanry). Jerry had worked in the Testery with Bill Tutte, serving as shift leader, so it was the site of many of his memories and experiences. As Jerry spoke to me about his time at Bletchley Park, it became clear that we shared a common bond: the desire to make sure that the profile of Bletchley Park was raised and its future safeguarded. At one point his wife Mei mentioned his hobby, the stock market:

"How much was it that you got last week from your buying and selling shares, was it £6,000?" she asked him.

"£65,000," came the matter-of-fact reply. I really do love it when people belie their appearance, especially when someone as unassuming and humble as Jerry reveals through his intellect and humour a fascinating inner life that is barely discernable to the outsider.

We talked for a few hours that day and parted fast friends with a shared purpose. It was clear that Jerry knew an incredible amount about what had happened at Bletchley and why it was important. I was so happy to have met and spent time with him and Mei. I also really wanted to find someone to help Jerry write his autobiography. I felt, and still feel, a real sense of urgency about finding people who worked at Bletchley and capturing their memories. Even at the time very few people had a complete picture of what was going on at Bletchley Park during the war. We now need as many memories from as many people as possible to build up our understanding. I left resolved to find someone to help Jerry write his autobiography; his was an important story that needed to be heard.

Funding and an important visitor

Pretty good progress began with an exciting announcement: IBM and PGP Corporation were giving $100,000 to The National Museum of Computing at Bletchley Park.

I was invited up to a celebratory lunch at Bletchley Park. The President of PGP, Phil Dunkelberger, gave a very entertaining talk, followed by Andy Clark from TNMOC. It was wonderful to see all the press interest. It was also good to meet some of the professors who had signed our CPHC letter to *The Times* in person; previously I had only interacted with them online. I had a chat with a couple of them about the success of the letter. We had a lovely lunch in the library at Bletchley Park followed by a tour of the site. I have to say that even now, several years on, having probably been on thirty or more tours, I still enjoy every single one. I also find out something new every time, which to me once again underlines the importance of the site: there is so much just waiting to be discovered.

I also got a call from my friend Professor Caroline Wardle at the beginning of September. Caroline is an academic, a computer scientist and someone who enjoys supporting and encouraging other women in computer science. She held a senior role at the US National Science Foundation for a number of years, and we became friends after she moved back to the UK. Caroline was calling to ask if we could arrange a visit to Bletchley Park for a friend of hers who was visiting from the US. The friend, who had taught Caroline computing at university in the US, turned out to be the first female winner of the Turing Award (the computer science equivalent of the Nobel prize), Fran Allen.

 Sue Black
@Dr_Black

Off to Bletchley Park again tomorrow. This time with Fran Allen (Turing award winner!) + Mavis Batey, last surviving female codebreaker :-)

10:54PM – 18 Sep 08

Fran was coming over to the UK to speak at a British Computer Society conference and really wanted to visit Bletchley Park while she was here. I was happy to facilitate this; I got in touch with Bletchley Park, and they organised a wonderful visit for us. I hadn't known at the time, but Fran was coming to the UK to talk about a code breaking system that IBM built for the National Security Agency (NSA) in the late 1950s. Fran had spent a year at the NSA delivering a programming language, Alpha, that she and her colleagues had developed with the NSA. Fran was also really interested in the women at Bletchley Park, and I was excited to meet her.

Subject:	Bletchley Park on Friday?
From:	Fran Allen
To:	Caroline Wardle
Sent:	10 July 2008

Let's plan to go to Bletchley Park on Friday since they sometimes rent out space for events and that's probably more likely to happen on weekends. I may not have mentioned why I am so interested. My talk at the conference will be about a code breaking system IBM built for NSA in the late 50's. I spent a year at NSA delivering a programming language, Alpha, we had developed with NSA. Also I couldn't possibly miss whatever they have on the women who worked there.

Fran, Caroline and I drove up to Bletchley Park together. When we arrived we were met by Simon Greenish and taken into the Mansion for tea. Simon introduced us to Frank Carter and Brian Oakley, Bletchley Park experts who would be our guides for the day. We were also introduced to the local MP, Phyllis Starkey, who was to join us on our tour. We sat down and introduced ourselves. Brian Oakley and I were sat next to each other, and he told me how wonderful it had been for him to see all of the coverage of Bletchley Park in the media. He had tears in his eyes; it was obvious that he cared very deeply about Bletchley Park. One of the greatest things at this stage of the campaign was meeting other people who felt as passionately as I did about Bletchley Park – it gave me so much confidence that I was doing the right thing.

On our tour, Frank and Brian talked about various aspects of Bletchley Park. Frank gave a demonstration and explanation of the Enigma machine, while Brian told us about some key breakthroughs in World War II that had been enabled by intelligence from Bletchley Park. This included the Battle of Cape Matapan, which Churchill regarded to be the greatest Royal Navy victory since Trafalgar. The victory effectively removed the Italian Navy from the Mediterranean and therefore the war. The code breaking breakthrough had come from a 19-year-old codebreaker working as one of Dilly [Knox]'s Girls at Bletchley Park. Her name was Mavis Batey, and we actually got to meet her that day. Michael Smith, author of *Station X*, interviewed Mavis for his book. He pays tribute to Mavis, her fellow female codebreakers, and the thousands of other women who worked at Bletchley Park, writing on the Bletchley Park website:

> "It is often forgotten, amid the inevitable concentration on brilliant codebreakers like Alan Turing and Dilly Knox, that the vast bulk of the people who worked at Bletchley Park during the war were women, and while many of these worked in what might be regarded as menial positions each was important to winning the war. More than that, there were women among them who were themselves quite brilliant codebreakers and Mavis Batey was certainly one of these women. The Battle of Matapan was described by Churchill as the most important British naval victory since Trafalgar, and despite her long-standing modesty on the subject, considerable credit for that victory must go to Mavis."

When we met Mavis, she was accompanied by her husband, Keith Batey, who had also worked at Bletchley Park. They were lovely, and although both in their 80s, they were very sprightly. At some point during the day, some-one asked Mavis how she and Keith had met. She told us that they had both been working in the cottages at Bletchley Park during the war. Mavis liked the look of Keith, so had devised a test to see if Keith felt the same way about her. One day, while walking past his desk, she "accidentally" dropped a pencil on the floor next to him, reasoning that if he picked it up, he was interested. Ah, those were the days... I wonder if that would work now! (In fact when I asked Mavis if he had picked up the pencil, she said that he hadn't – but they got together anyhow and were happily married for over 60 years.)

In addition to visiting the Colossus rebuild at The National Museum of Computing, we also got to see a new exhibit at Bletchley Park, which Mavis

Mavis Batey (L) tells Fran Allen (R) and the group all about her experience working at Bletchley Park.

The Enigma machine

had curated: "From Bletchley, with love". The exhibit highlighted James Bond author Ian Fleming's work as a liaison officer between Bletchley Park and the Director of Naval Intelligence throughout the war.

As always, it was a wonderful visit. Meeting Mavis and Keith and hearing about Mavis' incredible code breaking achievements at the age of just 19 was very special. I found myself wishing we had heard more of these kinds of stories growing up. I remember reading about Edith Cavell and other war heroines when I was at school; I would so love to have known about Mavis Batey too. Role models are important for young girls.

That afternoon Fran, Caroline and I said our goodbyes. As we drove home, Fran remarked that the American Computer History Museum in Mountain View, California couldn't even hope to get across the same kind of understanding of code breaking and computing history that Bletchley Park and TNMOC did. Having now been there several times myself, I know what she means. They are both fabulous museums and I heartily recommend visiting them both if you have the chance, but the edge that Bletchley Park has over the Computer History Museum is that so much history actually happened *right there*, on that very site. More than ten thousand people worked round the clock to shorten the war and save millions of lives. Visiting Bletchley Park, walking on site there, is like stepping back in time. I've been there so many times now, and still, every time I walk through the gate and up towards the Mansion House I get a frisson of excitement... *this is where it all happened.* It's a magical place.

Now we're funding for the ceiling

Time rumbled along. I was spending several hours per day thinking about the campaign, contacting people, and talking to everyone I met about Bletchley, telling them what a wonderful place it is and asking them to sign the online petition.

Some great news came via a call from Jerry Roberts. He had received a call from the BBC to say that they wanted to interview him, along with Professor Jack Copeland, author of *Colossus*, a collection of reminiscences about Colossus from a range of people who had some involvement with it. I was thrilled to hear this; it meant that the BBC were taking Jerry's story seriously. Perhaps it could even lead to a documentary about him and his time at Bletchley. Jerry told me that the BBC were going to put together a programme about Tommy Flowers: more great exposure for Bletchley! (This became the BBC documentary *Codebreakers: Bletchley Park's Lost Heroes*, which aired on British television in 2011. It tells the story of Bill Tutte and Tommy Flowers and their massive contribution towards shortening the war.)

Just the next day I got some more great news, this time directly from Bletchley Park, but I was sworn to secrecy...

The exciting news was that Bletchley Park was to receive a grant of £330,000 from English Heritage, which could be used to carry out urgent repairs on the roof of the Mansion House. Water had been leaking through for some time and if not sorted out promptly could cause all sorts of damage to the building. The money had come just in the nick of time.

Simon Greenish rang to tell me the news.

"I think this has come out of the publicity this year with your contribution being a major factor," he said. It was moving to hear that he thought the campaign was really working!

The story was linked from the BBC homepage; it was also front of the BBC Technology page. The story was picked up by more press than we were expecting. This was important, indicating not only that the media were now happy to run stories about Bletchley Park, but also that they wanted to run positive stories. It also showed that national funding institutions were willing and able to grant money to Bletchley Park. This was a major turning point. Perhaps it was no longer seen as such a huge financial risk to

Simon Greenish, Director of Bletchley Park, with Sir Francis Richards and
Dr Simon Thurley, Chief Executive of English Heritage at Bletchley Park

grant funding to Bletchley. Perhaps people were really starting to envision
the wonderful future that Bletchley could have. Simon Singh and Angela
Shepherd shared my excitement about the grant in their comments on the
online BBC News story:

New lifeline for Bletchley Park

BBC News

6 November 2008

Britain's code-cracking and computing heritage has won a
lifeline in the form of a donation from English Heritage.

The grant of £330,000 will be used to undertake urgent
roof works at Bletchley Park – where Allied codebreakers
worked in World War II.

> It is terrific that English Heritage have recognised the value of Bletchley Park. I hope that this investment will trigger a plan to bring Bletchley Park back to life so that future generations can learn about the extraordinary events that took place in and around the mansion.
>
> *Simon Singh, 25 November 2008, 16:49*

> So pleased to hear of the English Heritage grant – at least the roof of the main building will be sound. Shameful, though, that Bletchley Park still not deemed worthy of direct Government aid. Well done, Sue Black, for achieving so much media attention.
>
> *Angela Shepherd, 15 November 2008, 17:18*

Station X does not mark the spot

I'd been blogging all of the key things that had happened as a part of my campaign at savingbletchleypark.org for about six months at this stage. It was the first time I'd written a blog. I was never much good at keeping a diary, so it wasn't always easy to remember to do it or to know what to write, but I'd managed to write a few posts, and I was really glad that I had. The blog was valuable if only as a record to remind me of what I'd done as part of the campaign, but it was also heartening to start receiving comments from people that I didn't know at all – it meant the campaign was having wider-reaching effects.

> My father, Professor Donald Michie, worked at Bletchley Park with Alan Turing and others cracking codes and developing the first computer. He would have been delighted by the progress made in saving this historic site, as am I. I hope this is only the beginning of the support that its role deserves.
>
> *Professor Susan Michie, 13 November 2008, 10:03*

Congratulations! Dr Black's efforts have not been in vain. Bletchley Park can be the inspiration for the coming generations as the seat of technology creation that is British... Where all good things begin.
Patricia Miller, 6 November 2008, 13:41

I think its wonderful that people are finally starting to recognise the value of this place... Its a national treasure and and should be preserved along with all the other important parts of our history. I have over 150 students visiting Bletchley Park this week and they would all like to add their support as well. :)
Gavin Peake, 6 November 2008, 00:57

I cannot think that there is another country on this planet which would take the view that somewhere as important as BP does not merit public funds! WHAT DOES IT TAKE to get Governments to grasp reality?
James E. Siddeley, 5 November 2008, 15:03

They included a lovely one from Professor Susan Michie, daughter of Bletchley Park codebreaker Donald Michie. Donald Michie had been a close friend of Alan Turing and was one of the few people who could hold his own playing chess with him. I like this story about Turing and Michie from Michie's obituary in the *Telegraph* in 2007:

"Fearing a German invasion might devalue his bank account, Turing turned his savings into bullion and buried the bars at several sites in the surrounding countryside.

For 'security reasons' he did not make a map, and after the war he asked Michie to help him retrieve the silver using a home-made metal detector; the only stash they located was under a stream and impossible to recover. Offered a third of the proceeds or £5 per visit, Michie had shrewdly chosen the latter."

Michie went to work at Bletchley Park in the Testery, working on Tunny when he was just 18 years old. Wanting to help with the war effort, he had taken a course in cryptography and then been recruited to Bletchley Park from Balliol College, Oxford University where he had been studying classics.

It was lovely to get some feedback on my blog and to hear that people I had never met – some of them with direct connections to Bletchley! – thought that Bletchley Park was worth saving, too. The people around me, my partner Paul, my children, my friends and many of my colleagues at work, were of course supportive of what I was doing. But having positive feedback from people who were completely outside of my circle gave me confidence that I was doing the right thing and that at some point the change we wanted would happen. Surely it wouldn't be too much longer before Bletchley Park received the recognition and, just as importantly, the funding it needed to sustain itself. I was confident that soon a major technology company and/or the UK government would pick up on the idea that supporting Bletchley Park would earn them valuable kudos. So, I thought.

And so we had a cup of tea...

The next Sunday, I was invited to lunch again with Jerry Roberts and his lovely wife Mei. The lunch had been arranged so that Jack Copeland and I could meet and discuss the campaign. I took along my copy of *Colossus*, thinking to myself how cool it would be if they would both sign it for me. After arriving and making introductions we all sat down with a cup of tea and started discussing Bletchley Park. Jack has an amazing knowledge of its history, along with a deep knowledge and understanding of code breaking from both a theoretical and historical point of view.

I felt like I was in heaven during that conversation. I had to pinch myself. I was sitting in the house of an amazing Bletchley Park codebreaker, having lunch with him, his wife and a Bletchley Park expert who knew all kinds of interesting things about what happened there and what effect it had on WWII.

After a long chat about Bletchley Park and code breaking we turned to the subject of the campaign:

Captain Jerry Roberts, me and Professor Jack
Copeland (author of the book *Colossus*)

What can we do to help Bletchley Park?

We talked all through lunch; after lunch Jack left, Jerry went to have a lie down, and I wrote down a list of the ideas that we had discussed. When Jerry awoke from his nap we had another cup of tea and continued our chat. I talked to Jerry about writing his autobiography. I was desperate to ensure that all of his memories about Bletchley Park and his time there were captured; Jerry said that he found writing hard as it took a lot of energy. (Now, having written this book, I know what he meant!) When I got home, I emailed the list of ideas to Jerry and Jack; a day or two later I had a reply from Jerry:

Subject:	Saving Bletchley Park
From:	Jerry Roberts
To:	Dr Sue Black
Sent:	19 November 2008

Dear Sue,

Thank you for your imaginative and practical list!

This reply a bit delayed because we were down at German Dept. UCL yesterday. We had a really wonderful day. Prof. Kord arranged this visit and she looking after us so well, we also had lunch and the Champagne. It was fun, a great day out, and we both really enjoyed, it was certainly one of the best birthday at my 88!!

With Jack together, we visited DIVERSE already (prod.co) and now await the reactions to our "pitch" of last Thursday. It seems a very interesting subject to them. We will follow up approach to other companies.

I need time to digest your excellent list, will try to follow up on it. Meantime, well done!

Best wishes,

Jerry

Even at the age of 88 Jerry was out there pitching to a production company a television programme about Bletchley Park. His enthusiasm amazed me and continues to inspire me now. When I began writing this book, Jerry was still alive; sadly, he died in April 2014.

And now it's only falling apart

About a month later, I got some great news from Simon Greenish: "It's been a record year for visitors this year, with 70,000 regular visitors plus 5,000 schoolchildren. With all the publicity that Bletchley Park is getting I'm sure that numbers will keep increasing."

It certainly did feel like Bletchley Park was becoming more visible. Around the same time, I was delighted to see that Mavis Batey, the Bletchley Park codebreaker that we had met during our July visit, had been interviewed by CBS News. (I wonder if Fran Allen had talked to CBS when she got back to the US…)

The CBS report, "World War II Code Breaking Compound Crumbles", focused on the importance of Bletchley Park, the achievements there and its current state of disrepair. Mavis told the reporter about the message that she had decrypted, Simon Greenish showed the reporter the inside

of one of the huts, and Tony Sale gave a demonstration of the Colossus rebuild.

The report also showed Mavis and her husband Keith as they were during the war, as well as today. It was lovely to see them, especially as Keith and Mavis – like Jerry Roberts – are sadly now no longer with us.

One of the most wonderful things that has happened during my involvement with Bletchley Park has been getting to know some of the people who worked there, like Jerry Roberts and Mavis Batey, most of whom are in their 80s and 90s. It's obvious to anyone who meets them that they are interesting and important people. They have a certain spirit, an intelligence, and a matter-of-fact way of looking at life. Everyone that I have met has been an absolute pleasure to speak with, and listening to them talk to each other, sharing stories about what they did at Bletchley Park and what they have done since, is an even more joyful experience. Knowing that these wonderful people would not be around much longer helped me to redouble my efforts throughout the campaign. I wanted everyone to realise and experience the same feeling that I had: *these stories must be heard.*

In November 2008, I sent 5 tweets

08
The Ultra effect

"Those people who worked at Bletchley Park could be thought of as a living jigsaw. Each piece dependent on those around it."
—CHRIS HICKEN, BLETCHLEY PARK PADRE

In February 1941, Dilly Knox's team broke the *Abwehr16* cipher, which helped the Allies to find and sink the German battleship *Bismarck*. By this time, Knox was very ill; he'd been treated for cancer for several years and would not live to see the end of the war. But it was his team's work on Enigma that would have the biggest impact. The fact that they had broken the code in 1940 immediately became one of the Allied Forces' most well-kept secrets. If the Germans got even a hint that their ciphers were compromised, a few simple changes in operating procedure could easily render all of the code breaking work useless. This was, in part, why activity at Bletchley Park was so very secretive. Careless talk really could have cost lives.

Quite apart from the complication of the ciphers, the biggest problem faced by Station X was the sheer weight of message traffic from not only the Germans, but also the Italian, Russian and Japanese military forces. It meant that between 2,000 and 6,000 messages needed decoding and translating *every day*. "Chaos is a mild term to describe our condition at the outset," says Edmund Green, who worked in the Naval Section. "I am told that I once swapped a small and incompetent typist for a large and priceless card index." And cryptanalyst Harry Hinsley adds: "At one time the Germans were operating concurrently about 50 Enigmas, some in the Army, some in the Air Force, some in the Navy, some in the railways, some in the secret service. And so you were faced not merely with understanding the machine and with breaking a key regularly, but with breaking 50, sometimes regularly at once, or as many of them as you could without delay."[17]

In October 1941 some of the senior codebreakers broke all military protocol and wrote directly to the Prime Minister bemoaning the lack of resources to deal with such huge numbers of messages. They emphasised that their needs were small when compared to other areas of the military but that investment would produce results of staggering importance. "Our reason for writing to you direct is that for months we have done everything that we possibly can through the normal channels, and that we despair of any early improvement without your intervention," they wrote. "No doubt in the long run these particular requirements will be met, but meanwhile still more precious months will have been wasted, and as our needs are continually expanding we see little hope of ever being adequately staffed. We have felt that we should be failing in our duty if we did not draw your attention to the facts and to the effects they are having and must continue to have on our work, unless immediate action is taken."

Churchill understood, agreed and immediately directed: "Make sure they have all they want extreme priority and report to me that this has been done." The message was famously marked "Action this day". This was when the building programme at Bletchley Park really took off.

"As soon as the government knew how much could be done at Bletchley Park they pumped more money in. It turned from a cottage industry into a production line," says Mavis (Lever) Batey. Station X grew into a network with outstations in Middlesex and at Adstock, Gayhurst and Wavendon in Buckinghamshire. "There simply wasn't room at Bletchley Park to allow for more huts to be built," explains Bombe operator Anne Pease. "So outstations were formed, usually in large country houses in the area, with special huts built for the Bombes, and there were also two big purpose-built outstations at Eastcote and Stanmore, near London. The first outstation I went to wasn't far from Bletchley, in a village called Wavendon. After a few months, we were transferred to Wavendon House so we were able to live and work in the same place."

Sorting the important messages from the admin was vital but, even after distributing them around the now fully operational huts, each of which had a particular area of focus, there were simply too many to handle with pencil and paper alone. The process of passing messages quickly between huts had been solved mechanically with a "Lamson" vacuum tube system between departments, and the wooden box tunnel between Huts 3 and 6 contained a permanently rolling conveyor belt. But the business of decoding needed to be mechanised too. Therefore, Alan Turing proposed the construction of a machine based on, but quite different and significantly more powerful than, the Polish *Bomba*. With help from Gordon Welchman, he designed a new electromechanical device that they christened the *Bombe* and called upon the services of Harold Keen – chief research scientist at the British Tabulating Machine Company in Letchworth, Hertfordshire – to construct it.[18]

"At my interview in London they told me to stand up and sit down again," says Jean Valentine, a wartime Bombe operator. "At the time I didn't understand why. And I don't think they knew why either. I only found out why when I saw my first Bombe." The Bombe consisted of a bronze-coloured cabinet within which were set a series of rotating drums – each performing the same role as an Enigma rotor. The drums were stacked in twelve banks of three with every bank of three emulating the slow, middle and fast rotors. As a result, each Bombe acted like 36 Enigma machines working simultaneously and at a higher speed than a human. In addition, another cabinet behind emulated the Enigma plugboard settings. The reason that Jean Valentine and many other female Bombe operators were asked to stand up and sit down at their interviews was to gauge their height. The Bombe stood at over seven feet tall, and taller operators were needed for the higher drums and plugs.

At midnight every night, the enemy Enigma operators would all change the settings on their machines. This meant a new selection of plugs on the plugboard, new selection of rotors, new ring settings and trip settings, and new rotor start positions. The details of what settings to use each day were contained in codebooks and key sheets; a typical entry might have looked like this:

Datum [Date]	Walzenlage [Rotors]	Ringstellung [Ring settings]	Steckerverbind-ungen [Plug board settings]	Grundstellung [Initial rotor settings]
3	I III II	S M C	EA DH LO NS CW JM	H P W
4	III II I	G K R	SL OH FA BK JF MW	D M A
5	II I III	T B Q	XT DA RB PQ LE KS	M D C

So, every day, Station X had to figure out what the new settings were from the 158 million million million possibilities. However, they did have several clues to help them.

Firstly, one supposed strength of the Enigma machine was that no letter could ever be coded as itself, no matter how many times you pressed a key. You could jab at a letter M for all eternity but it would never generate an M. However, this supposed strength was actually a weakness. Removing one variable significantly reduced the number of possibilities and therefore helped the codebreakers.

Secondly, as John Herivel had surmised, the enemy operators were so confident that the messages were undecipherable that they sometimes got a bit lazy. At midnight, after setting the machine, they would then send their first coded message accompanied by something called an Indicator – three letters chosen at random and typed twice.[19] This Indicator allowed the receiver to check if their machine was set up correctly to decode messages; Enigma machines decoded as well as coded. For example, the sender would type three letters twice, let's say HIT HIT, and the machine would encode it into YGD UPL. They would then send this message to the receiver. If they have set their machine up correctly using that day's settings, typing YGD UPL into their machine would then generate a repeat of three letters, in this example HIT HIT.

If this happened, they could be confident that they'd set it up correctly. The Enigma operators were supposed to use three letters at random but they often took the lazy route and used, as predicted by the Herivel Tip, three adjacent letters on the keyboard or even the same key three times.

Thirdly, the codebreakers noticed that certain words and phrases appeared fairly frequently in communications. For example, many German messages ended with HEIL HITLER and many weather reports began with WEATHER REPORT. These became known as "cribs" – best guesses as to what small portions of a message were. Dilly Knox had a particular knack for recognising patterns of language. If he felt that a cipher took on a kind of rhythm, he looked at popular German poems and nursery rhymes and would sometimes find that an operator had typed them in an idle moment. These too became cribs.

The combination of cribs, Cillis, lazy operator practice, and the fact that no letter would code as itself helped the codebreakers to reduce the number of possible settings for the Enigma machines by discounting those that couldn't work. But there were still many more variables to consider, which was why the Bombes were so necessary. By October 1944, the Bombes were averaging 35,000 hours of operation per week, and by the end of the war there were over 200 Bombes in operation.

Using what they knew, the codebreakers would give the Bombe operators a "menu" of how to set up the rotors and plugboard. The operator would set up the first bank of three rotors, then set up the next bank with the rotors moved by one position, then the next, then the next, etc. The Bombe would then run, looking for the Indicator by disproving every incorrect combination. Once they had the Indicator they could decode messages sent using Enigma. "The menus came from Huts 6 and 8 – I think Hut 8 was naval signals and Hut 6 others," says Anne Pease. "We never knew what the messages were about. Although we did get snippets of information, and some codes like weather forecasts were much easier to break."

"We were thrilled when we got a 'stop'. It meant that we'd been successful," says Daisy Phillips. "When the Bombe had found a possible setting for the Indicator, the machine would stop and a bell would ring. We would pass on the settings and then wait. If we got back the message 'job up', it meant that we'd been successful and we'd have to strip the machine and put in a new menu. We usually had no idea what message we'd helped to translate but occasionally they'd put up a notice to tell us. We were delighted when we got it right." Another Wren remembers that, after each run, one row of drums would be removed and another placed in situ. Then the removed set had to be "inspected and trimmed – the circles of copper wire brushes were set at an angle and if a single rogue wire bent and caused a short-circuit, that run was invalid and had to be repeated".

The Bombe operators, nearly all women, worked in teams of two with one operator setting the rotors and one setting the leads on the plug-board. A third operator would use a Letchworth Enigma machine to check the Indicator before passing the details on to the code breaking team for that unit. If it turned out that the crib and the menu were wrong and the Indicator didn't work, they would be sent back to the codebreakers for a rethink.

Initially, Post Office engineers would do running repair on the Bombes but, over time, many of the female operators became maintenance staff. "I got a rudimentary idea of how the Bombes worked, so would maintain them, do soldering where it was needed," says Anne Pease. "Coaching others in the technical details to pass the promotion tests was more interesting than just operating a Bombe." It was not a job free of danger, however, and electric shocks were common. One technician describes an incident in which a Wren got more than she bargained for: "She was prettying herself using a metal mirror which slid across two large electrical terminals. There was a bright flash, the mirror evaporated and her lipstick shot across her throat. I was working nearby. The scream made me look up. I thought she had cut her throat."

In recent years, much attention has focused upon the codebreakers – particularly Alan Turing – while the army of people who supported them has remained largely unnoticed. But the facts speak for themselves: at the height of wartime activity Station X had 10,471 personnel, an eclectic mix of "Boffins and Debs" of which 80 per cent were women.[20] They came from a wide variety of backgrounds, Wrens, WAAFs and debutantes, all working side by side to support the code breaking effort, or indeed, working as codebreakers themselves. There were also 152 house staff – cleaners, handymen, etc. – five barbers, and four people who ran the NAAFI.[21] There were 151 maintenance workers, 139 catering staff, 14 medical staff and 29 people sorting out the billeting. Add to that the registry and despatch staff, the people looking after the staff records, the finance department, the five Air Raid Wardens and the three people who ran the recreation group, and the numbers start to swell. One of the largest departments was Transport, which boasted 169 drivers, 50 of whom were women. Security on the estate was covered by a 44-strong corps of Military Police and a Home Guard platoon.

Not everyone could be a codebreaker, but every person had an important job to do.

09
Tweeting Bletchley Park

I signed up for Twitter in June 2007 on the recommendation of my friend Eileen Brown, a BCSWomen committee member. I didn't know it yet, but that was a momentous occasion: Twitter would prove to be an absolutely invaluable tool for the Save Bletchley Park campaign. At the time I was mildly curious; I filled out the registration form and played around with Twitter for a bit, but I couldn't really see the point of it. After half an hour, I thought to myself: *It's rubbish. I don't see what use it could possibly be.*

I closed the browser window and forgot all about it for a few months.

Fast forward to December 2008. I was at a conference at the Institution of Civil Engineers (ICE – what a great acronym!) in Westminster. I was sat at the front of an audience listening to a guy called James Whatley talk about social media. Quite early on in his talk he asked,

"Who here is on Twitter?"

I put my hand up. So did both of the guys sitting either side of me, so I leaned over and whispered,

"Its rubbish, isn't it?"

About ten per cent of the eighty or so people in the audience had put their hands up – not very many. James carried on talking about Twitter, telling us that his Twitter ID was @Whatleydude. I remember thinking, *what a cool name.*

The guy sitting on my right has since become a great friend. His name is Professor Jonathan Raper, but he's known on Twitter as @madprof – another great name. He replied to my comment about Twitter being rubbish by asking me if I was using it through the app on my mobile or just through a web browser. I told him that I'd only used it on my laptop at home – I didn't have it on my phone.

"Aha!" he said. "Download it now. It's so much better on your mobile. You'll love it."

I wasn't convinced, but I downloaded it all the same. Once I had the app on my phone, Jonathan tweeted me, I tweeted him and we tweeted James on stage, and my other neighbor, Roland Harwood (@rolandharwood), who I'd met through the NESTA Crucible programme and known for a couple of years, joined in too.

We tweeted at each other throughout the session. It was surprisingly enjoyable.

During the day we carried on tweeting each other; it was especially useful when we were not in the same room together. We could have conversations about various topics of interest but also address logistical issues, such as, "Where are you now?", "Is the talk you are in any good?" and so on.

By the end of that day, I was in love with Twitter. It gave me another completely new way in which I could connect with people, and it was fun. It was cool to be able to interact with a speaker whilst he was on stage giving a presentation, for instance; it was also nice finding out how things were going with people in different parts of a conference – a bit like having your own private spies reporting back to you.

Looking back now, knowing that it was about to become such an important part of the Save Bletchley Park campaign and my life more generally, it's amazing to remember my first tentative foray into the world of Twitter. One of the many things I love about Twitter is that you can look up and find conversations that you have had in the past. In a way it's like writing a diary together with your friends: as everything is recorded you can just look it up, even years later, remember, and reminisce. While working on this very book in 2013, I tweeted James, Jonathan and Roland to tell them that I was writing about them:

 **Sue Black**
@Dr_Black

@whatleydude @madprof @rolandharwood Hey Dudes! I'm writing about you guys + that day when I started tweeting at ICE unbound.co.uk/books/saving-bletchley-park

2:37PM – 3 May 13

Initially James didn't remember the day, but then I got a tweet from him containing a link to our actual tweets from the 3rd December 2008 – the day I discovered how useful Twitter could be:

Sue Black
@Dr_Black

Good to meet you @whatleydude

3 Dec 08

James Whatley
@Whatleydude

@rolandharwood @MadProf @Dr_Black Well met! Surprising (in a good way) to find fellow Twitterers in the room today :)

3:10 PM – 3 Dec 08

Roland also tweeted. He remembered the day.

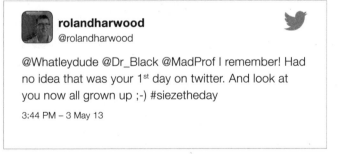

rolandharwood
@rolandharwood

@Whatleydude @Dr_Black @MadProf I remember! Had no idea that was your 1st day on twitter. And look at you now all grown up ;-) #siezetheday

3:44 PM – 3 May 13

Jonathan, saying that there had been days when Twitter had changed the course of his life.

Jonathan Raper
@MadProf

@Dr_Black @whatleydude @rolandharwood We were young then eh? There have been days since then when Twitter has changed the course of my life.

3 May 13

I completely agree with that. It has changed the course of my life many times since that day in 2008.

Sue Black
@Dr_Black

Good to catch up with @rolandharwood today and to meet @madprof and @whatleydude. Hope to see u again soon

4:54 PM – 3 Dec 08

I may not have had a sense yet of the role Twitter could play in the Save Bletchley Park campaign, but my interest had been aroused.

And a growing obsession

Towards the end of December 2008, I went away on holiday to Cornwall with my partner Paul and young daughter Leah. It was a good time to start really playing around with Twitter – there were lots of great photo opportunities and memorable moments.

I was starting to use Twitter more and more as the days went by. I loved posting photos and using the "Nearby" function on the Tweetie app, which allowed me to strike up conversations with tweeters nearby, most of whom I didn't know. I also enjoyed interacting with people I *did* know – when Rory Cellan-Jones tweeted that his wife, the economist Diane Coyle, had received an OBE, I was able to congratulate them right away.

 **Sue Black**
@Dr_Black

@ruskin147 Big congrats to Mrs CJ :-) my friend
Wendy Hall become a Dame :-D a great start for
2009.

11:17 AM – 31 Dec 08

I was starting to find some really interesting people on Twitter. The process I followed went something like: follow people I know; have a look at who they're chatting to on Twitter; follow the interesting ones; have a look at who they are chatting to on Twitter; follow the interesting ones; and so on. In pseudo computer code that would be something like:

```
10 Find friends on Twitter
20 See who they are talking to
30 Identify interesting people
40 Follow interesting people
50 GOTO 20
```

There is a problem with this program. Have you spotted it? Yes: it never ends. This was manifesting in real life, too. I was finding myself so interested in finding and talking to interesting people on Twitter that I was spending hours at a time doing it. The downside was that my partner Paul was becoming a Twitter widower. He was spending evenings on holiday sitting on the sofa watching TV, and I was sitting next to him completely absorbed by my iPhone. Poor guy.

I was starting to realise why my first dabble with Twitter several months previously hadn't got me very far: I hadn't really known what to do with it or, more importantly, what I was looking for. But once I had met and spoken to friends who were not only using it but actually finding it helpful, it was like being launched into another dimension: there were so many possibilities. Poking around and following the little Twitter start-up algorithm above had led me to find some very interesting people. This was how I came across David Bott, for instance, who worked at the Technology Strategy Board (TSB). As I had written several successful funding proposals to the TSB in the past, I knew who they were and I was interested in what they were doing. David had tweeted on New Year's Eve, asking whether we thought the internet was a success or not. I love computing, the internet, and everything techy, so you won't be surprised at my response:

Sue Black
@Dr_Black

@david_bott the Internet has revolutionized our lives and will continue to do in ways that we can't yet imagine. A massive success.

7:25 PM – 31 Dec 08

Those tweets marked the beginning of one of my many great Twitter friendships. I was starting to learn something really important about Twitter: it wasn't just a passive, mindless time-suck; the connections you could form through it could be real and lasting.

A social media campaign

We'd had a lovely holiday in Cornwall.

I'd also had an intriguing direct message from a guy called Mike Sizemore (@sizemore) during our time away. He said that he had seen my Saving Bletchley Park blog, which was linked in my Twitter profile, and was very interested in helping with the campaign. Although I had put the blog URL in my profile and had mentioned it a few times in tweets, I hadn't actively done much to call people's attention to it, so it was exciting that someone was taking an interest already.

Mike suggested that we chat on the phone once we were back at work. He said that both he and a friend of his, a guy called Christian Payne (@Documentally), were really keen to help out.

 **Documentally**
@Documentally

Getting excited at the possibility in helping to Save Bletchley Park . . . http://www.SavingBletchleyPark.org

3:32 PM – 6 Jan 09

 Sue Black
@Dr_Black

@Documentally thx very much for the link to my Bletchley Park blog savingbletchleypark.org and for getting excited about saving BP

4:57 PM – 6 Jan 09

On the 6th of January, Christian tweeted a link to my blog, saying that he was getting excited about helping to Save Bletchley Park. I was also getting excited – it was wonderful to think that such cool people were interested in becoming part of the campaign. I had a great chat with Mike on the phone. He reiterated that both he and Christian wanted to help with the campaign: what could they do? I told Mike about everything that had happened so far: about my first visit to Bletchley Park, shattering my image of it as a small place with a bunch of old blokes in tweed jackets smoking pipes and doing *The Times* crossword, learning about the women of Bletchley, meeting the amazing Jerry Roberts, and so on. I told him that Jerry was going to be giving a talk about Bletchley Park at UCL the following week; why didn't he and Christian come along? Mike thought that was a great idea.

We arranged to meet before the talk, and we also arranged to go to Bletchley Park the day after. I really wanted them to have the full Bletchley Park experience. I also wanted Simon Greenish and Kelsey Griffin (Director of Operations at Bletchley Park), with whom I was working fairly closely, to understand why I thought Twitter could be so useful for Bletchley Park. My time tweeting over the last month or so had already helped me to realise that Twitter and social media, if used wisely, had massive potential for raising awareness of our campaign and for finding, bringing together and building a community of people that were interested in and cared about Bletchley Park. It was going to be an interesting couple of days.

40s Four Ts

The day of Jerry's talk arrived. I made my way into London, arrived at Goodge Street tube, and walked out of the station and into the café next door. I tweeted Mike and received a reply saying that he was in the Starbucks, which is just a few metres away from the station. I went over to Starbucks and saw Mike straight away, recognising him from his Twitter profile pic. We said "Hi", and he introduced me to his friend Jamillah Knowles (@Jemimah_Knight), who worked at the BBC. We had a quick chat about Bletchley Park and Jerry Roberts and how excited we all were to be going to listen to his talk.

At UCL, I introduced everyone to each other, Jerry and Mei introduced us to Professor Suzanne Kord, who was organising the talk, and then we all walked over to the lecture room together.

There was an audience of around 30 in a small room. Our group went straight to the seats at the front and sat down. The anticipation was immense.

 **sizemore**
@sizemore

Interview with the good Captain today and then tomorrow off to Bletchley Park where they have an Enigma machine set up for us! #bpark

12:41 PM – 13 Jan 09

We were not disappointed. Jerry is a great speaker, quiet and measured, and he had us hanging on his every word. He told us many stories about his time at Bletchley Park, including the time when he deciphered and translated a message that ended with: "Adolf Hitler, Führer".

How incredible must that have been? Jerry told us all about what he called the "four Ts" (an updated version of the "three Ts" he'd told me about when we first met): Tommy Flowers, Bill Tutte, Tunny and Alan Turing. Tommy Flowers had invented Colossus. Bill Tutte had shared an office with Jerry at Bletchley Park during the war and cracked Tunny ; and Alan Turing, of course, is one of the best-known codebreakers from the Park.

Jerry told us some great stories, including how in 1941 we had almost lost the war during the Battle of the Atlantic because we were losing almost all of our supply ships. If it hadn't been for the intelligence received at Bletchley Park, which enabled us to locate and destroy some of the U-Boats that were taking out our ships, Britain, as we know it, probably wouldn't be here today. The room was silent in awe and contemplation.

 Jamillah Knowles
@jemimah_knight

At UCL W @Sizemore. Captain Jerry Roberts has the grace and charisma of an old movie star #bpark

4:04PM – 13 Jan 09

 Sue Black
@Dr_Black

 @jemimah_knight that's so true!

7:04 PM – 13 Jan 09

At the end of Jerry's talk, we made our way over to a local café; Mike and Jamillah had arranged to interview Jerry there. However, it was clear that Jerry had run out of energy. He apologised and said that he needed to sit quietly for a bit as he was worn out from his lecture. Because Jerry was so engaging and interesting, we had lost sight of the fact that he was nearly 90 and didn't have quite as much energy as he might have had a few years before.

We apologised and after making sure that Jerry and Mei were alright to get home, we all parted ways. It had been a great afternoon. Jerry losing his energy after giving his talk brought back the feeling of urgency that I'd first felt with the Women of Station X project. We really needed to capture as many veterans' memories as possible, as quickly as possible. Time waits for no man... or woman.

 Sue Black
@Dr_Black

thx so much @sizemore + @jemimah_knight 4 today. Have blogged here: http://www.savingbletchleypark. org/ see you tomorrow! #bpark

12:38 AM – 14 Jan 09

That evening, I wrote a quick blog post about the day and tweeted Mike and Jamillah the link. It had been a great day, but the next day might be even better. I was taking them and Christian Payne to meet Simon Greenish and Kelsey Griffin at Bletchley Park. I really hoped that they would feel the same way that I did about the place. After our successful trip to Jerry Robert's talk, I was optimistic that they would.

 Sue Black
@Dr_Black

Really looking forward to introducing @sizemore and @documentally to the wonder that is Bletchley Park tomorrow :-) #bpark

2:22 AM – 13 Jan 09

Living on video

The next morning, I had a quick breakfast with my daughter before she went to school and then got the train into London, meeting up with Mike and Jamillah at Euston. We left the train at Bletchley and walked over to the entrance to Bletchley Park itself. As always, I had a sudden rush of excitement as we walked on site. This time there was a great sense of anticipation too, as I was here with people that I was hoping were going to make a big difference to my campaign. Mike, Christian and Jamillah are all remarkable people, and they all had expert knowledge of a world that I knew little of: the media, both traditional and social.

 Direct To Consumer
@dtcdeals

Many thanks to @Dr_Black for following – Sue has recently been campaigning to save Bletchley Park

8:51 AM – 14 Jan 09

 Sue Black
@Dr_Black

@dtcdeals thx very much. I'm on my way to Bletchley Park now with @sizemore @documentally + @jemimah_knight who will b reporting live #bpark

9:17 AM – 14 Jan 09

We headed up to the Mansion House where we were greeted by Simon, Kelsey and Christian. We all went into the morning room for some coffee and biscuits. As soon as we got there, Christian did a quick video of us and posted it online straight away.

This was a great start. I'd not met Christian before and didn't know much about him, but he is one of those people who, once met, is never forgotten. Friendly, smart and extremely talented in so many ways, he is an absolute phenomenon – he's been a shepherd in Italy, a social media advisor to leaders of UK political parties, a photographer of Kurdish freedom fighters, and so much more. As he started videoing us all, it became clear that these three people I'd brought up to Bletchley Park were going to make a massive difference. They were all game changers, people who had expertise and influence in a sphere that neither Bletchley Park nor I did.

After we had chatted for a bit, Christian set up a Twitter account for Bletchley Park: @bletchleypark. He showed Kelsey how to use Twitter to its full advantage, and he set up a Flickr account and group so that everyone who was interested in Bletchley could add their own photos and find other Bletchley Park-related images. Christian also came up with the hashtag #bpark, which has been used ever since to share news and thoughts about Bletchley Park.

Once we were done with social media setup, we had a grand tour led by Kelsey. We even went to the Bletchley Park Post Office and Toy Museum (unfortunately no longer on site). In the Toy Museum, I was amazed to see a book that I had read when I was about six years old; it brought me back to my childhood, and even in this old place, with all its history, I felt momentarily rather old myself! As always the tour was fabulous, very evocative and with something for everyone. We moved on to the cottages where some of the top codebreakers worked, then to The National Museum of

Computing – which is of course Mecca to a geek like me; I could spend all day in there. In fact Mike said exactly that as we were leaving the museum:

"This place is the geek Mecca." We all agreed.

We then walked down to have a look at one of my favourite places at Bletchley Park – the furnace. It is where all of the paper used for writing down the codes/decrypts were burnt. As Christian said, it's "like the forerunner of the modern day shredder". It feels like a very symbolic place to me. I can just imagine people walking down there every night during the war with the paper used that day, burning it in the furnace (which was located on land that's unfortunately no longer owned by Bletchley Park). Even as the day's paper burned, there would probably already be messages coming through which needed to be deciphered for the next day. The position of the wheels on the Enigma or Lorenz machines was changed every day, which meant the code had to be cracked afresh every 24 hours; many of the workings, notes and messages from the previous day were therefore no longer useful and so were taken to the furnace and burnt.

Next for us was the Bombe rebuild, where I'd had the very conversation that had sparked my interest in the Women of Station X almost six years previously. John Turner gave us a demonstration of the Bombe rebuild which was, as always, awe-inspiring, then we had a look at the other exhibits in the same block and finished up in the gift shop. Jamillah suggested that she interview each of us for her BBC *Pods and Blogs* show. As she interviewed Mike and Christian, I walked over to the lake and spent a few minutes thinking about all of the people who had worked there, most

L to R Christian, Mike, Kelsey, and me

sadly no longer with us. That reflection inspired a fantasy that Bletchley Park should become a living museum. Just imagine if visitors could really get a sense of what it was like there during WWII: you arrive at the entrance and are questioned by a sentry and not allowed in until you show the correct ID; once you've gained entry, there are people sitting by the lake who will talk to you about their jobs running the Bombe and Colossus machines; and there's someone playing the role of Alan Turing, walking or riding around on his bicycle, happy to answer questions about his life there...

 Jamillah Knowles
@jemimah_knight

RT @Documentally: Ditto . . . Thanks to @bletchleypark & @Dr_Black for inviting us. @sizemore & @documentally Wowed. #bpark

8:49 PM – 14 Jan 09

 Sue Black
@Dr_Black

@sizemore @documentally @jemimah_knight thank u all so, so much 4 today it was absolutely wonderful. I really can't thank u enough #bpark

10:49 PM – 14 Jan 09

The thing about Bletchley Park, of course, is that history does seem to come alive there; it's a very special site, and it had been absolutely fabulous to spend the day there with people who were equally convinced that it needed to be saved. It was very exciting to hear about the digital tools that Mike, Christian and Jamillah knew that Bletchley Park could use to help get a whole new audience involved. As I had hoped, it really seemed that Bletchley Park wasn't properly funded not because people didn't care, but because not enough of the people that cared knew the reality of the situation.

I left with a real sense of hope that we had taken a massive step forward with the campaign. Mike, Christian and Jamillah are wonderful people who really care about the important things in life. I felt very honoured to have met and spent a day with them. None of them *had* to be there at Bletchley Park that day; they had all volunteered to come along. I thought that their involvement could really help make a dramatic difference to Bletchley Park over the next few months, and I left looking forward to seeing how their influence and input would play out.

Can Twitter save Bletchley Park?

A few days later, Jamillah let us know that she had produced a podcast about our two-day Bletchley Park fest, starting with Jerry Roberts and then moving on to our visit to Bletchley Park and TNMOC. One of the students who had been at Jerry's talk had written a blog post about the talk, in which she'd written:

> "It was a true honour for me to listen to him talk and describe how
> they broke the code and what understanding the code meant for the
> war effort... It was an inspiring talk about what our studies can bring
> to us, and to see him so humble and carefully describing to us his
> experiences and answering our questions was very enlightening.
>
> Thank you Captain Roberts. Not just for today, but for your work
> at Bletchley Park to you and the others in the team, who are often
> not thought about. If it weren't for you, life as we know it may not
> be there!"

I completely agree.

That evening I wrote a quick blog post of my own, pointing people to Jamillah's podcast on the BBC *Pods and Blog* page, linking to the blog post about Jerry Roberts' talk, and including another plug for the online 10 Downing Street petition.

I was starting to think that Twitter could actually play a key role in the campaign and that it could be the one thing that made all the difference.

Sue Black
@Dr_Black

Hey wouldn't it be cool if Twitter saved Bletchley Park! Ideas anyone? #bpark

12:35 PM – 24 Jan 09

An extreme programme of blogging

Back in 2006, while working as a reader at London South Bank University, I received a very nice email out of the blue. It was from a guy called Jason Gorman who was working as a consultant at Symbian, a mobile operating system producer. He had been reading my PhD thesis, was interested in my research, and suggested meeting up for a chat. After I got over the shock of finding out that someone had, of their own volition, read my PhD thesis, I felt very happy that I would have someone to talk to about my research. We met up a few days later and had a good chat about code, software systems and ripple effects. We were both interested in finding solutions to help programmers visualise the ramifications of any changes they might make to the software they were working on. We chatted about this for some time over a couple of beers and became fast friends.

 Sue Black
@Dr_Black

Right! Time to get ready and go uptown for Extreme Tuesday 'Blogging for Bletchley' talk. Hope I do a good job…it's so important #bpark

5:16 PM – 27 Jan 09

Over the next couple of years we had lots of discussions about software and coding; we both felt that a practical, problem-based approach to coding was the right way forward.

jasongorman
@jasongorman

And don't forget Blogging for Bletchley at the Extreme
Tuesday Club tonight – 7:30pm

9:56 AM – 27 Jan 09

Sue Black
@Dr_Black

And don't forget Blogging for Bletchley at the Extreme
Tuesday Club tonight – 7:30pm (via @jasongorman)
#bpark

10:10 AM – 27 Jan 09

Jason was also involved with a group called Extreme Tuesday, which
held regular meetings for people interested in Extreme Programming. I
had spoken to Jason many times about Bletchley and how important it
was, and in January 2009, he invited me to talk to the Extreme Tuesday
club about Bletchley Park. On the 27th January, I met up with Jason and the
other Extremers in a pub in the City and told them all about how Bletchley Park needed saving. They were a small but lovely group of interested
people. For me it was particularly memorable; it was one of the first times
I spoke to a *group* of people about Bletchley Park; up to this point I had
mostly been talking to people on an individual basis.

It was over the course of that evening, too, that Jason coined the phrase
"Blogging for Bletchley". After I had given my talk, he put a great amount
of effort into mobilising people to write blog posts about Bletchley Park to
raise both awareness and funds. In Jason's words:

Blogging For Bletchley –
Meeting in London, Tues Jan 27th

From Jason Gorman's Software People Inspiring

20 January 2009

Do you use a computer? Do you have a blog?

If the answer to both of these questions is "yes" then Bletchley Park needs you!

Bletchley Park is a country estate in the South East of England where two very important things happened:

1. Some very clever people cracked the German Enigma code, which allowed the allies to intercept vital information and even spread vital disinformation that led directly to victory in World War II.
2. The same very clever people did this by inventing the world's first electronic computer

To my mind, this makes Bletchley Park the centre of the post-war universe. It's a very important part of our modern heritage.

Bletchley is now a museum and tourist attraction. But years of neglect and a crippling lack of funds have left the place in a shocking state. I struggle to think of any nation worth their salt who would have let such an important part of their history end up as run down.

Bletchley needs love and attention. It also needs about 10 million quid to make necessary repairs and to restore it to its former glory.

You can help by spreading the word on your blog, and by asking other bloggers to spread the word, too. Every single one of us owes Bletchley a massive debt of gratitude for creating the very industry that feeds and clothes us (and runs our XBox 360's). The least we could do is say a few words and alert our readers to Bletchley's plight.

Dr Sue Black, Head of Information & Software Systems at University of Westminster, has been campaigning tirelessly to save Bletchley Park. Sue has kindly agreed to come along to the Extreme Tuesday Club at The Counting House, 50 Cornhill, London to tell us all about the campaign and to educate us on what we can do to help.

If you're in town and are interested in blogging for Bletchley Park, please drop in. Sue's talk will start at 7:30pm (it won't take long, leaving plenty of time for socialising afterwards).

If you're too far away to make it, I'll be videotaping Sue's talk so you'll get to see it, too.

Coincidentally, Sue's PhD was on the ripple effect in code (y'know, you change one bit of the code and it ripples out to dependent parts of the software). Let's see if we can't start our own ripple through our network of blogs and get the word about Bletchley out to as many people as possible.

I couldn't have put it better myself.

There are lots of opportunities

Looking back through my tweets from this time, I can see that I was always searching for opportunities to connect with people who might be interested in the campaign. On the way to the pub to meet up with Jason and Extreme Tuesday, for instance, I'd had a chat on Twitter with Lewis Shepherd, who was a manager for Microsoft in the US, and had asked him if he knew about Bletchley Park and its amazing history and achievements. That evening Lewis kindly tweeted a link to my savingbletchleypark.org blog and said that he would spread the word. Excellent news!

 Lewis Shepherd
@lewisshepherd

@Dr_Black Looked at your great website, will solicit help/support from friends! www.savingbletchleypark.org #bpark

5:49 PM – 27 Jan 09

Sue Black
@Dr_Black

@lewisshepherd Fabulous! Thank you so much :-) Do let me know if I can help #bpark

6:00 PM – 27 Jan 09

It's also clear from my tweets that campaigning can be exhausting. When asked if I had seen a screening of *Enigma* on television, a film based on the book by Robert Harris and something that I had really been looking forward to watching, my reply was:

jonwinterbourn
@jonwinterbourn

Curious to know what @Dr_Black made of Enigma. Shame it wasn't filmed @bletchleypark, else the cast might be asked to join the campaign.

8:40 AM – 26 Jan 09

Sue Black
@Dr_Black

@jonwinterbourn I fell asleep! :(gonna try again soon. 4 kids, working full time and campaigning on the side = tired at weekends ;)

11:18 PM – 27 Jan 09

It was tiring, constantly thinking about how to make the change that I wanted to see happen and move the campaign forward. But it was also extremely exciting, especially when some of the people that I spoke to agreed with me, and, like Jason, went off and did something themselves to make the change happen. Jason also went on to organise a comedy fund-raiser for Bletchley called "Boffoonery" starring Robert Llewellyn, Maggie

Philbin and Stephen Fry among others, which raised thousands of pounds. That was a great feeling; it gave me real hope. Just like when I'd found that the Heads and Professors of Computer Science across the country felt the same way that I did about Bletchley Park and signed the petition to save it, having the active support of Jason and others gave me strength and confidence. I wasn't alone – there was an army of people out there that felt the same way as me, I was sure of it. The challenge was to find and mobilise them.

So I was always looking for opportunities to talk to new audiences about Bletchley Park, to find new groups of people that I could tell about the campaign. I had approached the organisers of the International Conference on Software Engineering (ICSE) 2009, which was to be held in Vancouver. I asked them if I could give a five minute talk to the conference delegates, the top software engineering academics in the world, and they very kindly agreed. I had wanted to go to ICSE since I started my PhD in 1994 but had never had the funds to attend, so I was very excited to be going. Finally, I would get to meet some of the people whose papers I had been reading and citing over the years.

 Sue Black
@Dr_Black

have been accepted to give a 5 minute talk about Bletchley Park at ICSE2009 in May to raise awareness, am very excited :-) #bpark

12:59 AM – 29 Jan 09

By the end of January 2009, my brain was going into overdrive. I was tweeting so many people, sharing my and others' ideas for how to get recognition and funds: codebreaking iPhone apps, a short film with Stephen Fry introducing celebrities and Bletchley Park veterans saying why it should be saved, a "World Geek Forum" with a team programming competition at the Park, a "Song for Bletchley". It actually makes me feel a bit sad now to read through my tweets from that time, knowing that we still haven't managed to do some of these things.

Sue Black
@Dr_Black

How about an iPhone app that's codebreaking related, game possibly, where money raised goes to BP? Anyone wanna write it? #bpark

9:38 AM – 31 Jan 09

 Sue Black
@Dr_Black

@sizemore how about short film w sfry intro asking celebs+BPvets etc why BP should b saved. Show it b4 films and @ CS confs. Like ur #amp08

9:35 AM – 31 Jan 09

 Sue Black
@Dr_Black

@bletchleypark how about holding a team programming competition at BP? World geek forum or something?

9:05 AM – 31 Jan 09

 Sue Black
@Dr_Black

Hey! Does anyone know any musicians that could put together a "Song for Bletchley"? I'm happy to play the triangle ;) #bpark

8:59 AM– 31 Jan 09

One thing that did happen, however, was that Kelsey Griffin mentioned to me that Adam Ficek from the band Babyshambles was from Bletchley and that he was interested in visiting. I started tweeting with Adam, and he visited Bletchley Park and then wrote a song called "Bletchley Park"!

One of the most amazing people I met during the campaign was a man called Brian Oakley. I had met Brian a few months previously when I'd gone to Bletchley Park with Professor Caroline Wardle and her friend Fran Allen – the first female winner of the ACM Turing award. Brian had been one of our tour guides, and he was obviously moved by the fact that Bletchley Park was getting more notice and publicity. It had been clear to me then that he cared very deeply for the place. We kept in touch after that meeting, and, after finding out that we lived only five miles from each other, Brian invited us round one afternoon for tea with him and his wife Marian. My partner Paul and my youngest daughter Leah came along and we had a lovely afternoon. I somehow hadn't realised until then that Brian had been director of the Alvey Programme, a government-sponsored research programme, which had given some focus to software engineering and formal methods, two of the areas that I had carried out research into during my PhD.

> Bletchley Park was a key in the defeat of Nazis efforts to invade this country and dominate the world, it is the least that this country can do to preserve what little remains of that invaluable establishment for future generations to see just what happened in this country during WWII
> Johnmcleod, 28 January 2009, 21:35

The Alvey programme had in fact funded much of the research that I had read about and built upon during my PhD, including the research of my PhD supervisor Professor Robin Whitty and his supervisor in the area of software measurement and that of several of my friends. What a coincidence! Brian had also been president of the BCS the year before I started my degree and maintained a keen interest in computer history. My partner Paul has a PhD in formal methods and similar interests, so it made for very interesting discussions.

© Paul Boca

Brian Oakley and me, Epsom Downs, Surrey

Brian had also spent many years producing documents relating to Bletchley Park. Towards the end of the afternoon, he took me up to his study to show me all of the work that he had done, including a month-by-month account of what had happened at Bletchley Park and a database of people who had worked there; this database formed the basis for the current "Roll of Honour" on the Bletchley Park website – an incomplete list of everyone that worked at Bletchley Park and its outstations during WWII: http://bit.ly/1KHq4DR

Brian's month-by-month account of what happened during the war was called "Sixty years ago at Bletchley Park" and was available for free as a monthly newsletter in the Mansion House (http://bit.ly/1lgcndJ). It appeared every month from July 1999 to August 2005. The account was also accessible via the Bletchley Park website and available in the Bletchley Park shop as *The Bletchley Park War Diaries*.

What a great man, and what wonderful work to have done. We left at the end of the afternoon absolutely honoured to have spent a fabulous few hours with two really special people.

In January 2009 I sent 468 tweets

10

A famous tweeter joins the campaign

On the 3rd February 2009, I was sitting in the living room at my PC when I noticed that Stephen Fry was tweeting about being stuck in a lift at Centre Point in London. He had posted a photo of himself and the other people that he was stuck with in the hope that Twitter would help rescue them.

I was always looking for influential people who could help raise awareness of the fact that Bletchley Park was operating on a financial knife-edge with no government funding. So, when I saw the photo I thought to myself, *Hmmm... does Stephen Fry like Bletchley Park?*

I Googled "stephen fry bletchley park" and several hits appeared, including a quote from a few months earlier in which Stephen Fry, responding to a journalist's request for comment about the state Bletchley Park was in, had eloquently condemned the lack of funding:

"To me it is equivalent to letting Nelson's Column fall down or Wellington's victory arch crumble to dust. An outrage to think we have not the will nor the historical understanding to save it."

Fabulous! Stephen Fry knew and cared about Bletchley Park. I was on to a winner, I was sure. This seemed like it might be an ideal opportunity to draw some much-needed attention to Bletchley Park. I searched for @StephenFry on Twitter, and luckily he was following me, which meant I was able to send him a few direct messages (DMs). He was more likely to respond to a DM than a tweet, but he was also following thousands of people, so there was a good chance that he wouldn't even see them. What the hell, I thought. What did I have to lose? Fingers crossed he would see my DMs and then maybe, *maybe*, tweet about Bletchley Park.

I sent him three messages in total:

Hi Stephen, I'm campaigning to save Bletchley Park. It would be really wonderful if you could tweet about them to raise awareness of their plight.

The work done there by 10k people shortened WWII by 2 years, possibly saving 22mill lives. They have no govt funding and need money.

Please help by drawing attention to them, I'm sure that if you tweeted it would make a real difference. Thank you *so* much.

At the time Stephen Fry was being followed by 116,000 people. So if he was interested and tweeted about Bletchley Park, that meant that there were 116,000 potential recipients of the tweet. Not bad for a few seconds of work!

It was getting late. I went to bed wondering if Stephen Fry would see my DMs and if he did what he would think. I knew that he must get many such requests every day, that there was a very slim chance that he would even see mine, and an even slimmer chance that he would actually respond. Still, it was worth a chance. I knew that he was interested in and cared about Bletchley Park – after all, he had spoken to the press fairly recently about the situation it was in.

At about 11 the next morning, I got an email from Twitter:

@StephenFry has DMed you

and then another:

@StephenFry has mentioned you in a tweet

My first thought was, *What! OMG! Let me have a look at this, what has he said?*

Stephen had tweeted about my savingbletchleypark.org blog and pointed people to the petition to save Bletchley Park on the No. 10 e-petition website.

 **Stephen Fry**
@stephenfry

#bpark You might want to sign the Save Bletchley Park petition. Read @Dr_Black's reasons why on http://is.gd/ikEh – BP won us the war!

10:11 AM – 4 Feb 09

I immediately replied to Stephen:

 "Thank you! Thank you SO much Your tweet will really make a difference to Bletchley Park"

Moments later I got a phone call from Kelsey Griffin at Bletchley Park. Everyone was thrilled that Stephen Fry had tweeted about the campaign – our conversation went something like this:

Kelsey: "Stephen Fry has tweeted Save Bletchley Park!!!!"

Me: "Yes!! Isn't it amazing?! I wonder how many people will sign the petition now..."

Kelsey: "Maybe he would like to come for lunch at Bletchley Park – can you invite him?"

Me: "Sure! What a great idea."

I DMed Stephen Fry again:

Bletchley Park just phoned me. They would love to invite you for lunch at Bletchley Park, would you like to visit?

Five minutes later I had a reply:

I would absolutely love to, please thank them for inviting me

Hundreds of people had already retweeted Stephen's message, my Twitter ID, @Dr_Black, had trended on Twitter, and, as I found out the next day, I had 8,000 hits on my blog instead of the usual 50 or so. Wow!

I continued my DM discussion with Stephen, he put Kelsey Griffin and me in touch with his PA, and a date for lunch was arranged. It was quite hard to calm down after all that excitement. I sat back at my computer and carried on with my emails for a bit, but it was too hard to concentrate. My mind was buzzing like crazy. I couldn't believe that I had just had a private conversation with Stephen Fry (albeit over Twitter) and that he had tweeted a link to my Saving Bletchley Park blog.

After I had finally calmed down I checked my email again. I had messages from people all over the world asking me about my campaign, offering support, and requesting more information. There was also a flurry of comments on my blog from supporters of Bletchley Park.

My mother worked in a related military-support role, just down the road and "knew something was there" (at Bletchley) – so cool. I feel BP's place in our world today is terribly underrated and the UK Gov should recognise BP as much as it does other key wartime monuments. I dropped into BP in 2002 to visit someone who rented an office there and was awestruck by it's modest presence. Good luck to all involved. – AB
Alan Bristow, 4 February 2009, 12:45

Has Britain no respect for its history? This single most significant undertaking of any armed conflict. This IS history. For heavens sake Gordon, forget slipping the sly fiver to the investment bankers and invest in Britains (and the free worlds) heritage. This is something all Britons and allied countries should be immensely proud of!
David Goll, 4 February 2009, 12:06

Flabbergasted this is happening – all the millions being handed out to greedy/inept bankers, and something that epitomises what is actually great about this country left to rot.
Vince, 4 February 2009, 10:43

Bletchley Park is so important for so many reasons. What a travesty it would be if it were allowed to rot away.
Chris Dick, 4 February 2009, 10:17

On that day my Twitter ID, @Dr_Black, was the most retweeted ID on Twitter, @StephenFry was second, and @Mashable third. This meant the message was really getting out there.

You can see my excitement in the blog post I wrote later that month about the day:

Stephen Fry Tweets "Save Bletchley Park"
Sunday 22 February 2009

On the evening of 3rd February I decided to send a tweet or two to Stephen Fry asking him if he would tweet about saving Bletchley Park, I went to bed afterwards and forgot all about it.

At 10am the next morning I got an email saying that I had received a direct message from Stephen Fry. He said that he had sent out a tweet to all his followers! I checked Twitter to find this:

Stephen Fry
@stephenfry

#bpark You might want to sign the Save Bletchley Park petition. Read @Dr_Black 's reasons why on http://is.gd/ikEh – BP won us the war! 2:11 AM Feb 4th from web

This may not seem like a big thing for the campaign, but believe me, it's massive! Stephen then had about 116 000 followers on Twitter, he now has 222 690. Twitter has been incredibly powerful in terms of spreading the word.

Well, guess what happened? Everything went crazy! I had people emailing me from all over the world, and many people retweeted Stephen's original tweet which meant that even more people got to hear about the situation that Bletchley Park finds itself in. I had 8000 hits on my blog and the petition to save Bletchley Park on the No. 10 Downing Street site went up by over 1000 signatures. A very unusual day :)

I went to most retweeted person of the day, with Stephen Fry in second place. Thank you so much Stephen Fry and thank you so much Twitterers, you are really helping to save Bletchley Park.

I was absolutely amazed. Through one very influential person on Twitter, the Saving Bletchley Park campaign had reached a whole new audience. It was a real turning point in the campaign and a great lesson for me about the value of seeking out influential people who were interested in the message I was trying to get across to everyone. I was learning how to conduct a social media campaign.

I'm ashamed to be British

A couple of weeks later, an opportunity came through that was too good to miss. I was asked to write a piece for the *Daily Telegraph* about Bletchley

Park and my campaign. I had not written a piece for a national newspaper before so I was excited about the opportunity, but also apprehensive about my writing skills. I called upon my friend Judy Corbalis to help me and we met up for a quick coffee to discuss what I should include and how to structure the piece.

I really wanted to get across how important Bletchley Park is and explain my theory that if Bletchley had been in another country, there was no way that it would be in this precarious situation. I found some information online about the Australian War Memorial and how it is treated with such respect by Australians, and I found out more about the Computer History Museum in Mountain View, California. Why were Bletchley Park and The National Museum of Computing in the UK having such a difficult time getting the financial support they needed? It was wrong.

Judy and I spent our lunch hour on the piece; I finished it off after lunch and sent it through. About an hour later, it was up online and already attracting comments.

Save Bletchley Park: Why I'm ashamed to be British

16 February 2009
The Telegraph

Bletchley Park is an example of British brains at its best and we must act to preserve it, writes Sue Black.

Have you heard of Bletchley Park? It's just north of London, where more than ten thousand men and women worked during WW2 to decode messages sent between the German forces, most notably by Hitler, and the German high command. The cracking of the codes, the use of the intelligence gained and the subsequent related actions of the Allies is said to have shortened WW2 by two years possibly saving an estimated 22 million lives.

Bletchley Park is also the birthplace of the computer. The

world's first programmable, digital, electronic computer, Colossus, was invented and built by Tommy Flowers and his team at Bletchley Park and Dollis Hill during World War Two. It automated a critical part of the process of deciphering encrypted German messages.

If all that work, carried out by thousands of dedicated people for years on end, had not happened many of us would not be here now. Thousands of us today had relatives working at Bletchley Park: many of us may not know it due to the Official Secrets Act, fortunately some of us do.

Bletchley Park needs sustained government funding to preserve it. But then of course we're in an economic downturn – so how could the government afford it?

Well, here's a comparison. In the short term Bletchley Park needs £10 million, which is a pittance compared to how many millions, or is it billions now, that have recently been given to the banks? And how much more than the original estimate is being spent by us on the Olympics?

In Canberra, Australia, there stands the Australian War Memorial which is a place that every Australian citizen visits at least once in their lifetime to get an appreciation of the contribution made by Australians to the war effort.

In California stands the Computer History Museum a national museum of great importance that is treasured by US citizens.

The UK equivalent of these museums is Bletchley Park and the National Museum of Computing which is housed there.

Bletchley Park is an example of British brains and British thinking at its best. Have we no national pride? Is the UK government ashamed of British achievements? Where is our debt of gratitude for the efforts of so many to achieve so much? In Britain we can't even manage to preserve what we have.

This is why I'm ashamed to be British. I hope you are too.

The comments were interesting – some people were in support of the campaign, some were against, and some were just strange. But it was interesting to find out what the general public thought when reading my opinion piece. Of course it was great to read the supportive comments, like these ones:

> SAVE BLETCHLEY PARK...As an ex-GPO/BT engineer I remember spending many weeks at Bletchley Park training for my apprenticeship. At that time, in the 70's, the Park had an air of mystery about it...we knew it was something to do with the war but none of my colleagues and myself knew what. To find out what an important and pivotal role it played adds to my fondness of it. It was the first time I stayed away without my parents, my first steps into manhood and the first time I drank to much...therefore you could say it played a pivitol role in my life as well as WW2. Don't let this be lost.
>
> *Paul, 17 February 2009, 02:43 AM*

> Come on the British Government and the people. If you're going to put a stop on the bonuses the banks were going to pay their employees then have the money redistributed to Bletchley. If it isn't it should be a listed building for its heritage factor alone. I am appalled at the British lack of enthusiasm for OLD TECHNOLOGY.
>
> *Amanda Reed, 17 February 2009, 02:51 AM*

But there were also comments such as this one:

> Yawn. Yet again The Telegraph is giving space to people who want to tell us that we stink because of some grievance or another.
>
> If you're ashamed to be British, why bother preserving anything? Just more to be ashamed of really. Maybe you shouldn't ask "Have we no national pride?" in the same article as one asking us not to have any pride.
>
> Pride goes beyond some gap in funding. The only person who should be ashamed is you.
>
> *David, 17 February 2009, 02:59 AM*

I felt a bit embarrassed that someone was saying that to me. There were several comments even worse than this one, and since then I've had quite a lot of negative comments as well as a lot of overwhelmingly positive and supportive ones. It is something that I, and everyone else who puts their head above the parapet, has to get used to. If you stand out from the masses, some people will feel the need to shoot you down, whoever you are and whatever you are doing. I've talked to quite a few people about this phenomenon. Being perhaps a bit naïve, it was one of the things that really surprised me, particularly as the campaign began to get more exposure. Why would someone who doesn't know you at all behave as if they absolutely hate you? I was very bothered by this kind of behaviour to start with; it contrasted so starkly with the wonderful sense of connectivity and community that I'd found through Twitter and other social media channels. But, although I still don't understand it, I've got used to dealing with it over the years. If you are in the public eye and have any sort of opinion about anything at all, someone will hate you and make sure that they let you know.

One way that I have learnt to deal with this is whenever I feel confused and upset by someone's opinion towards me, I look at all of the positive feedback I've had and comfort myself that the positive outweighs the negative. In this case, many more people were expressing support for Bletchley Park than were attacking me and my views, and that was what was important. *Nil desperandum.*

Spent time at BP training at the CAA 20 years ago. Wasn't until over 10 years later that I got to realise the importance of all those derelict wooden huts! I hope the powers that be and the public have the sense to save what is a very important part of our heritage.

  Nick B., 6 February 2009, 14:01

My mother was a Bletchley Park girl during the War. Good luck with all you are doing. Keep that history alive!

  Charles Nove, 4 February 2009, 23:56

Given that last year, we are trying to raise public awareness of WW1 & WW2 and through different displays and exhibitions with the 'speak to and learn from the veterans' I think that it is an important part of our history that has got to be kept. Also, it may make the gov't re-think where our money goes and actually put it into something useful for a change.

  BabsnRay, 4 February 2009, 17:15

Flabbergasted is right, I can't believe a site like BP isn't already protected. Thank you for bringing it to our attention. I've signed of course and will be passing the details on.

  Sheryl La Bouchardiere, 4 February 2009, 15:07

Just saw the piece in the online Telegraph, and immediately signed up. Here in Boston MA, the Museum of Science has a small display dedicated to BP... it's of such international importance. Good luck!

  Richard, 16 February 2009, 22:12

Is there any way for those of us in America to help? I could send money, but is there a more tangible way to help? I noticed the petition is only available to British Citizens...
As a former student of World War II, and as a current employee of a technology company – I've long known of Bletchley Park. In fact, in my last working visit to London, I specifically took an afternoon to visit Bletchley – even bought a souviner mug with "enigma" on it!
Let us know...
Yours,
A.J. Murray, FSA Scot

A.J. Murray, 16 February 2009, 19:57

I absolutely and entirely agree with you Sue, but you are dealing with a government who lack integrity and have only a superficial interest in anything 'British'. We are witnessing the destruction of our national heritage and culture, we're on a downhill spin and I doubt that nay amount of protests and petitions by genuine, caring British people will make nay difference.

David Mills, 16 February 2009, 19:08

The Fry effect

As time went on, I was getting more comfortable with Twitter and experimenting with various ideas about how to get people excited about Bletchley Park. I developed a routine: I would find influential people through Twitter, chat to them about Bletchley Park and how fab it was, encourage them to visit, and then put them in touch with Kelsey Griffin at Bletchley, who would organise the visit.

Sue Black
@Dr_Black

@Dave_Gorman are you watching Enigma on BBC1?
Are you interested in helping to save Bletchley Park?
Be great to have you on board.

10:49 PM – 8 Feb 09

 Sue Black
@Dr_Black

@Schofe ru watching Enigma on BBC1? Bletchley Park
needs ur help. Www.savingbletchleypark.org 4 details.
Not a joke but may take ur mind off

11:47 PM – 8 Feb 09

I can see from my tweets at the time that I was tweeting lots of people, trying to get them interested in the campaign. As more and more people were starting to use Twitter, I was trying to catch them before they had too many people following and tweeting at them and my voice got lost in the "crowd".

 Sue Black
@Dr_Black

@mrskutcher Hi! Did you know that the world's 1st
programmable computer was built at Bletchley Park:
www.savingbletchleypark.org

12:48 AM – 6 Feb 09

Meanwhile, the "Fry effect" had meant that traffic to my Saving Bletchley Park blog had increased dramatically.

Sue Black
@Dr_Black

Wednesday was a fab day 4 saving #bpark >1k sigs on petition, 8k hits on my blog, lots of offers help + no.1 RT on Twitter! Thx all!

9:55 AM – 6 Feb 09

Stephen Fry's tweets and support meant that the number of signatures for the "Save Bletchley Park" 10 Downing Street petition had gone up by over 1,400; it was now in 5th place. I was really hoping that it would come 1st and get enough signatures to warrant a response from the government.

Sue Black
@Dr_Black

1.4k sigs on #bpark petition since last Tuesday, now in 5th place, well done everyone :) Can we get 2 4th place? 2k more needed!

11:52 PM – 7 Feb 09

Encouraged by our social media trip to Bletchley in January and now the amazing response to Stephen Fry's tweets, people at Bletchley Park were starting to understand that social media really was a way of bringing in and engaging with a whole new audience. Simon, Kelsey and I worked well together, and social media was proving useful for all of us. We were in touch several times a day to discuss where we were with various issues. Whenever I was given a tip off from either of them about some particular aspect of the campaign needing attention, I would rally the troops online.

Sue Black
@Dr_Black

267/367 voted in support of MK council contribution to @bletchleypark http://tinyurl.com/dyz3hx (via @kirtle) #bpark

4:55 PM – 12 Feb 09

Kelsey and I also set up a Facebook group and encouraged people to start populating it.

Sue Black
@Dr_Black

#bpark facebook group now up and running: http://bit.ly/2V57 do join and tell ur friends, thx :)

12:32 AM – 8 Feb 09

Kelsey Griffin
8 February 2009 at 01:28

Dr Sue Black, founder of BCSWomen, is truly one of the most incredibly ardent supporters the Trust has ever had. I cannot thank her enough for her ongoing support and the attention she has generated. K x

The Flickr group that Christian Payne had set up was proving popular, too. It was great that everyone taking photos of Bletchley Park could hashtag them and make them available to others wanting to see what Bletchley Park was like, and also to showcase all the amazing exhibits on display there.

Sue Black
@Dr_Black

Remember to upload ur #bpark pics to the Flickr group http://bit.ly/Cipi and if uv never been, have a look and c what ur missing!

1:28 AM – 8 Feb 09

I set up a LinkedIn group called Saving Bletchley Park. It seemed like another good avenue for finding people and giving them the opportunity to interact with the campaign online. With LinkedIn being a more professional networking site, I thought we might be able to get through to people in the tech industry and maybe even find some tech companies who would be able to support Bletchley Park either by direct financial sponsorship or by holding conferences or events there.

Meanwhile, I was excited to be attending my first "Twestival" – Twitter Festival. In just a couple of months, Twitter had changed my life. I had met lots of really interesting people online, and I was excited to be going to Twestival; it was an opportunity to finally meet some of them "In Real Life" (IRL) for the first time. The first Twestival of 2009 was held in Shoreditch. It was freezing cold and snowing, but I was so excited about attending that I hardly felt it. I joined the end of a long queue waiting in the snow.

After I had been standing there for a few minutes, I spotted Rory Cellan-Jones walking past me and the rest of the queue to the front. He got a few good-natured boos and jeers from the crowd.

Sue Black
@Dr_Black

FURY as Rory Cellan-Jones JUMPS the queue at LDNtwestival. For shame! (via @DailyWail)

7:41 PM – 12 Feb 09

Sue Black
@Dr_Black

@lindiop thx. Yes I can only just use my thumb to send tweets! Only about 50 people ahead of me now.

7:42 PM – 12 Feb 09

While I was in the queue I was, of course, constantly checking Twitter – luckily I got to the front of the queue before my fingers became frostbitten! I was given a label and a black felt tip pen and asked to write my Twitter ID on it and stick it on myself. I did so, and then walked into a large room full of people chatting to each other. I got myself a (free) beer and looked around. How on earth was I going to find the people that I knew online?

Sue Black
@Dr_Black

@GianninaRossini hey! Great to meet u! :)

8:37 PM – 12 Feb 09

I needn't have worried. Giannina Rossini (@GianninaRossini) saw me almost immediately and came over to say hello – we were following each other on Twitter and she recognised my Twitter ID. We had a great chat about tech education and then joined in another discussion with @digitalmaverick and @eyebeams, two other tech educationalists. What a great start. I'd arrived having met hardly anyone there in person, and within five minutes I'd already had an interesting discussion with three people who were as passionate as I was about tech education in the UK. After a while, I bumped into Jemima Gibbons (@Jemimag), who I'd actually met at a women in tech talk at Google's Victoria offices a couple of years previously. Jemima introduced me to her friends @anniemole and @utku and another interesting discussion ensued. I had another (free) beer and thought to myself: *This is wonderful.* All of these people, brought together by Twitter, chatting and sharing ideas... I was having a great time. Twitter, I realised, was becoming my lifeblood – my main source of information, humour and friendship, as well as my primary campaign weapon.

Sue Black
@Dr_Black

@DavidLammyMP Hi David, any chance that u cud pop in @bletchleypark on the way? I'm sure they'd luv 2cu :) savingbletchleypark.org #bpark

2:09 PM – 26 Feb 09

Just the two of me

I think it was Mike Sizemore who first introduced me to Tuttle, a social media meetup that took place in London every Friday morning on The Mall, at the Institute of Contemporary Arts (ICA). It was a wonderful place to go to meet up with the Twitterati of London. I started going every week, if possible, so that I could meet new people involved in tech, startups and social media. It gave me lots of ideas for courses and events in my department at the University of Westminster – I always wanted to be ahead of the curve. It was also a source of inspiration for the Save Bletchley Park campaign.

Sue Black
@Dr_Black

@tom_watson hey Tom, ru going to b @bletchleypark tomorrow for the first @StationX? Coolest place on the planet to b tomorrow #bpark

10:45 AM – 15 Feb 09

Christian Payne had the great idea of setting up a similar regular meetup at Bletchley Park to give people from the local community who were interested in social media somewhere to meet and chat. Not only would they benefit from meeting, but Bletchley, being the host, would benefit from the attention it would get from people who were tech and social media-savvy – the local influencers. It was a genius idea.

The first "Station X" was held on 16th February 2009. About 30 people turned up, all of whom were interested in social media and Bletchley Park and wanted to see the place for themselves. Kelsey Griffin, Clare Unwin (@bparkevents) and Lin Jones (@Linjones) from the Bletchley Park and The National Museum of Computing came along to chat to people. There were also several members of staff from The Open University, which is just down the road, as well as people like Lee Martin (@HighKeyLee) and Benjamin Read (@Bookpirate) – people from very diverse backgrounds, but all with an interest in social media, geekery and Bletchley Park.

Everyone chatted for a while in Hut 4, the Bletchley Park canteen/café, and then we all had a tour of the Park which included the Colossus rebuild and The National Museum of Computing. It was great to see everyone so animated and excited about its history, artefacts and ambience. It really reinforced my feeling that to get people to truly understand what a wonderful place Bletchley Park is, you need to get them there to see it for themselves.

Station X itself was actually a small room at the top of the Mansion House which was being used by the local Milton Keynes Amateur Radio Society. It's a really tiny room with just a couple of chairs and radio equipment and was set up by MI6 in 1939 as a secret UK Foreign Office covert radio station run by Charles Emery. Christian made a short video about it, called "Inside Station X", and posted it on Vimeo.

The first Station X social media café was a really positive experience. Christian had taken the great idea of Tuttle, which brought together early social media adopters, and set it up in a location that everyone would feel a strong connection to because of its important place in geek history. It was, as Mike had said earlier, "the geek Mecca". Everyone left buzzing with excitement about what they had seen and heard.

 Sue Black
@Dr_Black

Wow! I went over 1000 followers today . . . thanku all :) If ur interested in savingbletchleypark.org do follow @bletchleypark 2 #bpark

8:10 PM – 16 Feb 09

I carried on promoting Bletchley Park on Twitter and pointing people towards my blog and the Bletchley Park website so that they could read all about the history, the museum and the campaign. Through Tuttle, I was starting to meet lots of interesting people, such as Bill Thompson from the BBC Archives. I'd hoped he would be interested in Bletchley Park and Station X, and I was delighted to find that in fact he was; he has been a massive supporter. I also tweeted Bryan Glick, who was editor of *Computer Weekly*, asking him if he would run a feature on Bletchley Park.

 Sue Black
@Dr_Black

@bryanglick fancy having a feature on Bletchley Park #bpark? See savingbletchleypark.org for details of campaign

4:36PM – 19 Feb 09

Sue Black
@Dr_Black

@billt in case u haven't seen it @StationX has just
started at #bpark social media cafe

3:31 PM – 19 Feb 09

Other influential people that I tried to recruit to the campaign at that
time included Alastair Campbell, former Labour government spin doctor;
Gyles Brandreth, comedian; Maggie Philbin, TV technology reporter and
geek icon; and Padmasree Warrior, CTO of Cisco.

Sue Black
@Dr_Black

@campbellclaret Hi Alastair, can u help save Bletchley
Park? Www.savingbletchleypark.org any ideas or
advice gratefully received #bpark

11:46 PM – 20 Feb 09

Sue Black
@Dr_Black

@gylesONESHOW hi Gyles. Do u have any ideas for
www.savingbletchleypark.org ? Have u visited there?
#bpark

11:58 PM – 20 Feb 09

Sue Black
@Dr_Black

@maggiephilbin great 2 hear that ur interested in www.
savingbletchleypark.org was thinking about getting in
touch with u about it :) #bpark

1:48 PM – 21 Feb 09

Sue Black
@Dr_Black

@Padmasree Hi there. Would Cisco be interested in helping to Save Bletchley Park? See www.savingbletchleypark.org and #bpark

7:41 PM – 21 Feb 09

Not all of my attempts to contact key influencers this way met with success, but Maggie Philbin responded to my tweet saying that she was interested, and we arranged to meet at Tuttle the following week. By the time we met in person, we had chatted quite a bit on Twitter, so I think we both felt that we knew each other a bit. The following Friday, I spotted Maggie soon after I walked into the ICA. I went over and started talking to her about Bletchley Park. She seemed a bit less friendly in person than she did online, which was unexpected. We discussed the possibility of her being part of a group of people I wanted to get up to Bletchley for a visit on the Enigma Reunion Day, with the aim of recording interviews with some of the veterans that had worked there. Maggie seemed very distracted, and when our conversation ended I went to get a drink, feeling surprised and a little disappointed. After about five minutes, though, Maggie came over and told me why she'd been behaving so oddly. It turns out that ten minutes before our conversation, she had spoken to someone else who had looked like me; when Maggie had asked if she was me, she had said yes. So before I had arrived, Maggie had already had a conversation with someone pretending to be @Dr_Black. We still talk about it now when we meet up – it was very strange! (And a good reminder that as positive a force as Twitter is, misunderstandings can happen.)

Things were improving at Bletchley. Visitor numbers were rising and Kelsey was sure that was due at least partly to Twitter.

Sue Black
@Dr_Black

RT @bletchleypark: Fab day today! Around 500 visitors! I am certain that this is down to Twitter! Please keep spreading the word! #BPark

21 Feb 09

I was continuing to find great uses for Twitter in my life as well as for the campaign. One revelatory day was a grey Sunday in February 2009. Paul, Leah and I had gone to Brighton and were on the beach, feeling a bit peckish. We decided that we wanted fish and chips for dinner, but there were so many fish and chip shops in Brighton. It was hard to know which to choose, but after a few indecisive minutes I thought, *Hang on! I can ask people on Twitter, I'm sure someone will have a recommendation...*

I tweeted, asking if anyone knew where the best fish and chip shop was in Brighton, and waited to see if I would get a response...

> **Sue Black**
> @Dr_Black
>
> Anyone know where best sit down fish and chip place is near Brighton pier? We r getting hungry :)
>
> 5:37 PM – 22 Feb 09

Within just a few minutes I had several responses, a couple of them mentioning the same chip shop which, as it turned out was just a couple of hundred metres away. Result! We had a fabulous meal there. I tweeted a photo of my meal and ended up having a hilarious conversation with fellow Twitterers, featuring lots of silly fish puns.

> **Sue Black**
> @Dr_Black
>
> My 5 year old daughter says we r all naughty old people (on Twitter) :)
>
> 7:12 PM – 22 Feb 09

Pretty much every day I would tweet asking people to sign the "Save Bletchley Park" petition. As we left the chip shop I checked it again to see how many people had signed, and I was happy to discover that numbers had gone up quite a bit.

Sue Black
@Dr_Black

Hey just checked the #bpark petition: 19 014! U guys rock! X

7:35 PM – 22 Feb 09

Even on a day out with my family I was honing my Twitter skills and knowledge. Our day trip to Brighton had been a great lesson: I now knew that Twitter was an incredible tool for very quickly getting recommendations and ideas from experts, and then being able to interact with those experts – even if it was just to make puns.

In February 2009 I sent 468 tweets

11
Dilly's Girls

"Dilly Knox had so many ideas; bright idea after bright idea, going off like a Catherine Wheel."

—MAVIS BATEY

As the war became larger and ever more complex, Station X expanded to cope with the needs of the military. In addition to the mansion and garage, several brick-built structures popped up and were named Blocks A-H. Between them they handled such things as intelligence, code breaking, transmitting and receiving radio and telegraph messages, and traffic analysis. Block D was involved with Enigma decoding along with huts 3, 6, and 8. Block F housed the Newmanry and Testery (of which more later). And Block H was home to Tunny[22] code breaking and Colossus – the forerunner of all modern computers.

Then there were the huts. At the peak of activity there were 18 large operational huts and scores of smaller huts containing baths, changing rooms, a barber shop and other amenities. They were around 40ft by 16ft in size and the partitions inside – to make offices, etc. – were subject to change at short notice as different needs developed. The huts' internal layouts sometimes changed during working hours. One Wren describes a character called Commander Mackenzie, an ex-stage scenery expert, who was "always shifting the partitions about. Once I was typing and suddenly his saw came through the partition I was facing and narrowly missed my head." Bob Watson, a carpenter employed by BP, recalls, "It wasn't a rush putting up the huts, it was a panic. The contractors whacked them up and we all went along behind them sealing and lining them out.

Then Hubert [Faulkner] came round with whoever was going to be in charge of the hut and marked out partitions. Then the coffin makers[23] went berserk putting partitions up and bashing on – you could get them up in one weekend with 20 or 30 people."

Because no paperwork was retained after the war, no one is entirely sure how many huts there were on site. Some estimates suggest that over 50 were built, expanded, replaced and/or demolished in a constant flurry of construction and destruction. However, certain huts remained fairly static. Hut 1 initially housed the Wireless Station but later became an admin office and a Bombe maintenance workshop. The very first Bombe, called "Victory", was housed there. Hut 2 was a recreational hut – the NAAFI – where staff on down-time could have a beer or a cup of tea and relax. It also housed a lending library. Hut 3 was involved in translation and analysis of Army and Air Force decrypts, while Hut 4 and Hut 8 (Alan Turing's hut) worked on cracking Naval Enigma and *Hagelin*[24] ciphered messages. Meanwhile, Hut 6 worked on Army and Air Force Enigma, Hut 5 studied Italian, Spanish, and Portuguese military ciphers, and Hut 7 concerned itself with Japanese Naval codes and intelligence. Huts 9 and 18 were the domain of ISOS (Intelligence Section Oliver Strachey), so named as Strachey, a veteran codebreaker from WWI, handled intelligence from captured or surrendered Nazi spies who were "turned" so that disinformation could be passed back to the Germans; the section was nicknamed "Illicit Services by Oliver Strachey". Hut 10 was home to the Secret Intelligence Service (SIS) – what would become MI6 – and people studying Air Force and meteorological transmissions. Hut 11 was the Bombe building, Hut 14 was the communications centre, and Hut 15 housed SIXTA, paradoxically standing for "Hut Six Traffic Analysis"; often a hut's number became so strongly associated with the work performed inside that even when the work was moved to another building it was still referred to by the original hut designation. SIXTA worked on analysing the content of radio messages. Hut 16 was ISK (Intelligence Service Knox), Dilly Knox's team that deciphered messages from the Abwehr, Germany's intelligence gathering network. There was no Hut 13 due to a belief that the name would bring bad luck.

The population of Station X soon became too great to be housed on-site, and so staff were billeted in nearby towns and villages; 8,902 of them in total. As they were unable to talk about their work, innuendo, spicy rumour and spurious theory soon filled the void. After seeing the eccentricities exhibited by some of the older men, some even came to believe that it was some sort of mental hospital. Among those men were Peter Twinn, Alan Turing, Gordon Welchman and John Jeffreys, who all reported to BP the day after war was declared. Later recruits included mathematicians Derek Taunt, Jack Good, Bill Tutte and Max Newman, historian Harry Hinsley, and chess champions Hugh Alexander and Stuart Milner-Barry.

On January 23rd 1940, Knox, Jeffreys, Twinn and Turing broke the German Army Enigma settings. A short while later they broke the Luftwaffe's. The fact that Enigma had been broken became a secret of the highest priority. All references to such decoded messages were, from that point on, referred to simply as Ultra. Meanwhile, to cover up the truth of how the Allies appeared to have successfully second-guessed enemy plans on several occasions, a story was constructed and "leaked" to the Nazis that intelligence reports had reached Britain via an MI6 network led by a spy codenamed Boniface.[25]

At Station X itself, the staff were constantly reminded of the need for secrecy. One security notice said, "Do not talk at meals. Do not talk in the transport. Do not talk travelling. Do not talk in the billet. Do not talk by your own fireside. Be careful even in your Hut."

"The compartmentalisation of knowledge was particular to Bletchley Park," adds cryptanalyst Oliver Lawn. "The workers knew nothing about what anyone else did." No one ever went into a hut that they didn't work in.

"It just became second nature," says Jean Valentine. "We only had half an hour to eat during an eight hour shift so I got to eat at the Mansion as it was too far to walk to the canteen by the main gate. And you met people from other huts and you had no idea who they were. You talked about the weather and where you came from; anything to pad out the conversation because you simply could not talk about your work. It was the same with our social life, such as it was. Bletchley wasn't a very attractive place and we only had two plain clothes passes a week. We went to the village hop on a Saturday night and we saw a picture occasionally in somewhere like Aylesbury. But when you left the hut you were working in, that was it. You didn't speak about the work to anyone. You didn't even discuss it with the people you worked with." And, of course, no one could tell their loved ones what they were up to. "I couldn't tell my mother where I was, but she assumed I was all right," says Barbara Abernethy, PA to Alastair Denniston. "She put her trust not in the Lord, but in the Foreign Office. For some reason she told people her daughter was in a place called Ashby-de-la-Zouch. Never heard of it."

The codebreakers were now working around the clock in shifts to decode as many intercepted messages as possible. One major breakthrough was made by a young woman who had been recruited to BP from University College London, where she'd been studying German literature. Mavis Lever, better known to us today by her married name of Mavis Batey, had been at Zurich University doing research when the threat of war became very real. "I got out just in time," she says. "And because I spoke German I was then employed during 1939 in what they called the Phoney war – trying to stop the war from escalating by tracking and, if possible, stopping commodities being stockpiled by the Nazis and their allies." It was while doing such work that Mavis was asked to look through reams of Morse code messages to try to work out patterns. "One location had everyone stumped," she says. "I'd been told to look for a location called something like St Goch so I was chasing all around the world looking for it. And then, I suppose out of ignorance really, I asked someone, 'How do we know when there's a capital letter in Morse code?' and was told that, 'We don't'. So I said, 'Then how do we know it's Saint something?' I then wondered if looking at it differently would help so I wrote the letters down on a piece of paper – STGOCH – and it suddenly occurred to me that it might mean Santiago, Chile. Everyone was slightly taken aback, as was I. It was just one of those spur of the moment things, like when you suddenly see the answer to a cryptic crossword clue. And I suppose they thought, 'Here's a bright young thing', and that it was the sort of thing that Dilly Knox would like. At any rate, I found myself packed off to Bletchley Park to work with him."

Mavis became part of Knox's team in one of the cottages. "When I first arrived and met Dilly for the first time, he looked up at me through wreaths of pipe smoke and said, 'Have you got a pencil? Because we're breaking machines.' Of course I had no idea what he was talking about and I'd never heard of Enigma. He then said, 'Here look, have a go,' and passed this huge bundle of gibberish to me. I recall saying something about it 'all being Greek to me' and he said, 'I wish it were!' It turned out that he was a scholar and a linguist and he knew his ancient Greek."

Knox had four brilliant women codebreakers on his team: Mavis, Margaret Rock, Ruth Briggs and Joan Clarke. Clarke would eventually become Deputy Head of Hut 8 under Alan Turing, one of only a handful of women in management positions on the estate – but more on her later. Little is known of Ruth Briggs other than that she was a "talented code-breaker". But Margaret Rock has been described by historian and author Kerry Howard as "the fourth or fifth best of the whole Enigma staff and quite as useful as some of the professors, yet was only ever referred to as a 'linguist', never a codebreaker. Her love of numbers and talent for code breaking during the war years led to a long and successful career at GCHQ."

Between October and December 1941, Dilly's team broke the Abwehr Enigma cipher, which allowed the allies to be one step ahead of the German spy network in Britain and feed misinformation back to Hitler. Dilly Knox gave Margaret and Mavis all the credit for the break.

"He was a courteous and kind man and he was always concerned for our welfare," says Mavis. "As our unit began to expand, he surrounded himself with young and often attractive women and many people misinterpreted this. After all, when he'd started, all he'd had were mathematicians like Turing, Welchman and Peter Tring. Some Whitehall wags suggested that GC&CS actually stood for the 'Golf, Cheese and Chess Society' but that was because they weren't aware of the gravity of the secret work being done. Dilly was always an absolute gentleman – I called him my White Knight – and it turned out that he'd chosen his staff not by looks but by CV. Far from selecting beauties for some kind of harem, he hadn't seen any of them before they arrived. We were all interviewed by this dreadful Miss Moore, a fierce lady in the Foreign

Office. Dilly chose people who were language oriented. There was an actress and some girls who'd been at drama school and they were quite glamorous but they also understood rhythms and patterns of speech. Dilly was always looking for rhythms and patterns. There were linguists like me and one girl was a speech therapist. We were always referred to as 'Dilly's Girls' or 'Dilly's Fillies', even in places like Whitehall, but he chose us because he liked the fact we were intelligent, made good coffee and we could pick up his ideas and work on them while he came up with more. It was no use asking the mathematicians because they were too busy with their own ideas. But we could give him the attention he needed and try to pin down his ideas and try them. Some worked, some didn't, but he was never short of them. He was an extraordinary man."

Mavis' biggest breakthrough came in early 1941 when she successfully broke the Italian Navy Enigma codes for the first time and deciphered a message about manoeuvres near Greece. "Like Dilly said, we were 'breaking machines' with a pencil and using just the code books," she explains. "We did have a small Bombe machine later on to help us. Knox had worked on decoding for many years and Alan Turing used his methodology in his own work, to mechanise the decoding. But, to begin with there was just pencil and paper and hours of concentration."

The first Italian message that Mavis translated was the rather ominous: "Today is the day minus three". Further deciphering revealed that a fleet of Italian ships was gathering and preparing to attack allied convoys near the Matapan Peninsula. A suitable cover story was arranged – in this case despatching a reconnaissance aircraft to the area to make a "lucky" sighting – and a taskforce of Allied warships was secretly positioned to intercept the unwary Italians. The resulting Battle of Matapan was the Italian Navy's worst defeat of the war.[26]

The codebreakers rarely got to see the results of their efforts but, on this occasion, a mistyped telegram was sent through congratulating "Dilly and his guts". The telegram was subsequently corrected to "girls not guts". A few days later, the commander of the victorious British Naval task force, Admiral Andrew Cunningham, visited Bletchley Park to personally congratulate "Dilly's fillies" on their work.

"Our sense of elation knew no bounds when Cunningham came down in person to congratulate us," recalls Mavis. "It did wonders for morale."

By the end of the war, Dilly Knox's team had deciphered over 140,000 messages. But they were just one team among many.

12

The campaign gains momentum

Things were really starting to take off. I'd spoken to so many people about Bletchley Park now that I was used to it being my main topic of conversation, wherever I was and whomever I was with. I started receiving lots of offers to speak about Bletchley Park and the campaign at conferences and events. My piece in the *Telegraph*, "Save Bletchley Park: why I am ashamed to be British", received 135 comments, which showed me that there really was public interest.

I and many others carried on tweeting requests for everyone to sign the petition asking the government to help Bletchley Park. We were all hoping that it would reach the number one spot and then receive a response from the government. I wrote on my blog:

> People on Twitter have been absolutely fabulous and extremely supportive of the campaign, I actually think that Twitter in a way will save Bletchley Park.

Since the start of the campaign less than nine months before, so many people, the vast majority of whom I'd never met, had taken up the mantle themselves, writing, tweeting, speaking, and generally getting the message out to a wider audience. On the social media front, I was particularly pleased that 217 people had almost instantly joined the "Save Bletchley Park" (changed in 2013 to "We love Bletchley Park") group on LinkedIn that I'd set up. Isn't social media wonderful? In just a few moments I had created a space where 217 people interested in saving Bletchley Park could interact with each other. PR people had started noticing us too. The campaign was being used as an example of how to use social media for online marketing and engaging an audience. I felt like we really were gaining the traction and support we needed.

I was also now in regular touch with Jerry and Mei Roberts. Mei let me know that Jerry was going to be giving a keynote talk at UCL, following on from the talk that @sizemore, Jamillah and I had attended the previous month. I was delighted. Jerry played such a key role in getting across the importance and gravitas of the achievements at Bletchley Park and, as he had actually been there, was an absolute mine of information on what it was like during World War II.

Sue Black
@Dr_Black

Capt. Jerry Roberts (UCL German 1939-41)… ticket details here: http://www.ucl.ac.uk/german/aboutus/ events.htm #bpark I'm going :)

4:23 PM – 25 Feb 09

I signed up for the talk straight away and encouraged everyone else on Twitter to do the same.

Meanwhile, Tuttle was still enabling me to meet lots of really interesting and social media-savvy people. I was making great friends from all over London and the south of England. Every week I would chat to a few more people about Bletchley Park, aiming to first get them excited about the place and its importance and then to get them to actually go and visit.

It's great to look back at my tweets from that time and see tweets to people that I now count as friends. At the time I was only just getting to know them.

Sue Black
@Dr_Black

@cliveflint have a great time at #bpark! Let @bletchleypark know ur going.

9:46 AM – 21 Feb 09

Sue Black
@Dr_Black

@marksimpkins hey! Didn't realize u were at #tuttle yesterday, we could have had a chat. Ah well. Next time :)

8:55 AM – 21 Feb 09

Sue Black
@Dr_Black

@benjaminellis meant to chat to u @ #tuttle yesterday, hopefully next time. Have a great weekend :)

8:53 AM – 21 Feb 09

Through Tuttle I was spreading the word and getting to know lots of people who were really interested in Bletchley Park. Several people asked me to speak about Bletchley Park at their events. Mike Sizemore introduced me to a guy called Toby Moores (@Sleepydog) who ran an organisation called Amplified, which was all about using social media, blogging and technology to amplify messages. Toby asked me to speak at their next "unconference", and I happily agreed – it seemed like it would be right up my alley.

Amplified '09 was a great event. Every single person that I spoke to there had something interesting to say. Looking back, it really was a time of early adopters from all different backgrounds finding each other through social media, mainly Twitter, and getting together to discuss what was important to us. We were all intelligent and curious about the world, and it was as if we had all been given access to another dimension of communication which connected us and brought us together. It felt like a very exciting time to be alive.

Sue Black
@Dr_Black

Phew. Home at last from #amp09. If I didn't talk to u
abt Bletchley Park pls visit savingbletchleypark.org
#bpark follow @bletchleypark

11:56 PM – 24 Feb 09

Building with Pride

One of the great things about Twitter is that once you have built up
a community, you can spread a message really quickly. I was starting to
appreciate this fact; I was also learning that sometimes, if you're looking,
amazing opportunities just come along and present themselves. One of
these opportunities was the Building with Pride competition, which was
run by Wickes in 2009 to find the building in the UK that people felt most
proud of.

When the shortlist was announced, we were thrilled to find out that
Bletchley Park was on it, and we immediately started tweeting about it,
asking our community to spread the word and, crucially, to vote.

Sue Black
@Dr_Black

RT @bletchleypark: http://bit.ly/10w7XS please click &,
if you agree, vote Bletchley Park as the building Britain
is most proud of. #BPark

8:47 PM – 24 Feb 09

We tweeted over and over and over. I remember spending several
lengthy sessions on Twitter, Facebook and everywhere else I could think of,
trying to get people to vote for Bletchley Park.

Our efforts resulted in a thrilling few days when we were neck and neck with The Cavern Club in Liverpool, where the Beatles had played, and the Needles Old Battery on the Isle of Wight. It was a great team effort. I'd only really been using Twitter for the campaign effort for a few weeks, but I already felt that I was a part of something very exciting: a movement of people who felt the same way that I did about a cause. We were all passionate about Bletchley Park and desperate to make sure that it was both appreciated and given the respect and funding it deserved.

In March, The National Museum of Computing received a great boost when Bletchley Park Capital Partners and its associates donated a grant of £100,000 to the museum. That month we also learned that our efforts to get people to vote for Bletchley Park as the building Britain is most proud of had not been in vain: Bletchley Park had won the 2009 Building with Pride award! This was one of the earliest examples of the people that cared about Bletchley Park working together via Twitter to both spread the word about something *and* actually get something concrete to happen. People had been voting for two months, the rankings had changed several times, and it had been neck and neck at various points. Many of us had put in lots of time and effort into getting everyone tweeting about the competition, asking our followers to retweet a link to the web page and to vote for Bletchley.

It was awesome to see such a positive result. Twitter is a great medium for finding people or organisations who have shared interests or common goals and starting a dialogue with them – but there's also a very fine line between asking people to help with a cause and pissing them off. I'm always conscious of this and have asked a few times if my behaviour on Twitter annoys anyone. A few people, including friends, have said that it does from time to time. But in general, most people have been happy with my sometimes ridiculously excited ubertweeting. It was certainly gratifying to know that, in the case of the Building with Pride competition, all of that tweeting had helped make a tangible difference! In response to the result, Matthew Critchley of Wickes said:

"The public have really taken this search to heart and have chosen a building that holds an incredibly important place in the British psyche.

Bletchley Park has come to signify British ingenuity, courage and pride. I can't think of a more worthy winner of the first 'Building with Pride' award."

Help! We need your MP

I now quite often had people contacting me via Twitter asking me what they could do to help with the campaign. It wasn't always easy to know what to say to them. Although I seemed to have become a campaigner over the last few years, I didn't really think of myself as one. I'm very passionate about certain issues that matter to me, so I suppose I have always been a campaigner at heart, but I don't think that in 2009 I would have identified with the term. As with my interest in raising the profile of women in computing, which led to me setting up the BCSWomen and other online networks for women, the Bletchley Park campaign still seemed in many ways like a (very time-consuming) hobby to me. Campaigning wasn't something I had ever learned about or thought of investigating – I just got carried away with wanting change to happen and started doing whatever popped into my head as a good idea. In terms of organising and planning, I did almost nothing at all; I just followed my gut feeling about the best way to achieve my goals.

So when anyone asked me what they could do to help with the campaign, my answer would usually be to tell them what we wanted to achieve in big picture terms and then ask them if they could think of something that they could do to help achieve that aim. It may not have been very planned or strategic, but it did mean that we got the best out of people, and also that no one was under any pressure to do anything they didn't want to do – they just came in and contributed in whatever way they could, and in so doing became part of the push to raise awareness that gradually started to build up and permeate the public consciousness.

A good example of this is the letter to MPs that Chris Campbell produced. Chris had contacted me saying that she really wanted to help with the campaign. I told her all about what we were trying to achieve and she suggested putting together a letter that anyone could send to their MP , asking them to help. Chris also sent me the link to add to my blog post so that we could point people towards their MP's contact details if necessary. Every little helps!

The first John Ivinson award

In September 2009 I was delighted to receive the first BCS John Ivinson award for my contribution to supporting women in computing and Bletchley Park. John Ivinson was a previous president of the BCS, and also a friend and mentor, so it was especially poignant to receive an award in his name.

First BCS John Ivinson Award Goes to Dr Sue Black

6 October 2009
BCS

BCS, The Chartered Institute for IT has presented its inaugural John Ivinson award, which recognises the outstanding services of an individual member, to Dr Sue Black.

Dr Black is a founding member and immediate past chair of the 1,200-strong BCSWomen specialist group, which practically supports women working in IT. She is also a member of BCS Council and is a BCS Fellow and member of BCS Elite. Earlier this year Dr Black, currently Head of Department of Information and Software Systems at the University of Westminster, fronted a national media campaign to help preserve the fabric of the buildings at Bletchley Park Trust. Last week it was told it had been awarded a heritage lottery grant of £460,500 to help it develop its £10m restoration plans. Dr Black was also instrumental along with others in supporting a special BCS ceremony at Bletchley in 2007 that recognised the contribution of the Bombe WRNS operatives and the role they played in helping the park's cryptographers during the Second World War.

In March 2009 I sent 519 tweets

13
Churchill visits

"Sweet Boadicea chariot, swing low
To waft Miss Wingfield where she has to go."
—FROM A COMIC POEM
BY PATRICK WILKINSON
ABOUT PERSONALITIES AT BP

Following his election to Prime Minister in May 1940, Winston Churchill received a buff-coloured box of decoded messages from Bletchley Park every day. These messages allowed him and a very small and select group of confidantes to make strategic decisions about troop deployments and future planning of offensive operations. As far as everyone else was concerned, the information that Churchill was privy to came from a brilliant MI6 network led by the spy codenamed Boniface. So valuable was the intelligence coming out of Station X that Churchill decided to pay the site a visit. And so, in September 1941, he did just that.

Details of the day are sketchy – naturally, there were no press reports, no photographs and no publicity – but we know that he made a tour of the huts, met various staff members and then gave a morale-boosting address to a representative group of people outside Hut 6. "You all look very innocent – one would not think you knew anything secret," he said. He then went on to describe them as "the geese that lay the golden eggs – and never cackle".

It was after this visit that Gordon Welchman, Alan Turing, Stuart Milner-Barry and Hugh Alexander wrote directly to Churchill to ask for more resources. Staffing levels grew rapidly from that point on.

Every day, the workforce would be bussed into Bletchley Park from their billets, many in requisitioned country houses such as Woburn Abbey and Crawley Grange. And at the end of their eight-hour shifts, they'd be bussed home and the next shift would take over, three per day, seven days a week. The work was so demanding that many of the staff worked voluntary, unpaid overtime on occasions, just to keep on top of it. "I recall being desperately tired most of the time," says Margaret Broughton-Thompson, a Colossus operator. "It was very hot with the blackout and electric lights. We had meal breaks but the food, especially at night, the reheated meals were revolting." Sometimes there were not enough vehicles available to take the staff home and they would hitch-hike. "It helped being in uniform," say teleprinter operators Eleanor Mulligan and Iris Rattley. "The lorry drivers in those days were marvellous. They'd stop and buy you a cup of tea and never a word out of place."

But the effort was starting to pay dividends. Week after week, the successful decoding of messages aided the Allies in their efforts. The cracking of German Naval codes in 1941 led to victories against German U-boats in the Battle of the Atlantic. "We know that in that second half of 1941 their shipping successes were cut back to 120,000 tons a month average," explains Harry Hinsley. "That has to be compared not with the monthly average of 280,000 tons a months in the four months before June '41 but with the sinkings they would have achieved with their greater number of U-boats. It has been calculated that the Ultra saved about one and a half million tons in September, October, November and December '41." Elsewhere, Rommel's plans were scuppered on the eve of the Battle of Alam el Halfa in 1942; BP code breaking helped destroy the German war effort in Africa. Work by Station X also helped the Russians win a decisive victory at the Battle of Kursk in 1943, halting the German Eastern advance. It has also been said that D-Day might not have happened, or would have had far less a chance of success, without intelligence provided by Bletchley Park.

Life at the park was sometimes tough. The huts were poorly heated and ventilated, and the staff worked long hours. Some were very cold. Others, like Hut 11A – a concrete add-on – quickly earned the nickname of "the hell hole" because of the heat being created by the decoding equipment. In the huts where machines like the Bombes were operating, there was the additional discomfort of noise. On the BBC *People's War* website, Sgt Carol West, a WAAF, describes work in the teleprinter section: "There were 30 to 40 teleprinters back-to-back to a hut, with a moving belt above to take out the enormous volume of work coming in. We worked in Huts 3, 4 and 6; the noise was deafening and the amount of paper spewed out unbelievable. My memory is of working underground but the huts probably had blacked-out windows and we worked in artificial light. We certainly had sun lamp treatment to combat this." There are stories of people's health – both physical and mental – being affected. "We did hear a story about a man who drew ducks on a blackboard and then started feeding them. He had to be carried off," says Margaret Reardon, a wireless operator. "The work really got to you. You had to put your hand up if you wanted to go to the loo or if you wanted something to eat. It was all about discipline." Anne Wyndham describes the work as hell: "I remember the smell. It was oil. Hot oil. There were at least six machines in there, very poor light, frightful noise. And we were there for eight solid hours. You can't say that was fun. It was like factory work."

The staff, though isolated by the very nature of their work, were often kept apprised of events at the front by way of bulletins and messages written on chalkboards. Occasionally, the visceral realities of war became all too real. "Most of us among the lower ranks never knew what went on at BP," says WAAF Sgt Gwen Watkins. "The only time I realised what we were actually doing was when I was shown a codebook which had just been captured and rushed to Bletchley from a captured plane. Of course we had no plastic envelopes or anything then, the poor thing was just given to me as it was and I was horrified to see the stains on it. The blood around the edges was drying but the blood in the middle was still wet. And I realised then that somewhere was this German aircrew bleeding, still bleeding while I was writing their codebook out in modern German. And that did bring the war very close."

The war also came very close on the 20th and 21st of November 1940, when three German bombs fell on Bletchley Park. One of them was so powerful that it shifted Hut 4 by two feet. However, work inside the hut continued even as it was being winched back onto its hard standing. And, as it turned out, the bombs had probably been intended for the nearby railway station.

But that isn't to say that there wasn't some fun and a social life at BP. Morale was important. The difficulty was that, although some staff were housed on-site, many more were living in isolated billets all over the Buckinghamshire countryside with little or no opportunity to get together. Therefore, an assembly hall was built just outside the perimeter of Bletchley Park to encourage off-duty activities such as dances and concerts, plays and variety shows.

Bombe supervisor Nigel Forward recalls: "We had one Christmas review in which I mimed the part of Johnny in *Frankie and Johnny* to gramophone records. I was the hapless Johnny who was caught with Nellie Bligh. You know 'I don' wanna tell you no story/ I don' wanna tell you no lie/ I saw your Johnny about an hour ago/ with a girl called Nellie Bligh.' I was in a very satisfactory clinch with Nellie Bligh. She was a girl called Olivia whom I've not been in touch with since. I was really a dreadful rookie, rather unskilled in the amorous side of life."[27]

"Bletchley Park civilians from time to time put on plays and I still have a photograph of the full cast on stage when I was in *Saloon Bar*," says Carol West. "One of the WAAFs was Kate Karno[28] who put on musicals, drilling us like a professional stage director. The Glenn Miller Band was stationed at a US Army camp near Bedford and a few of us were invited to the dances they gave. The US Army, of course, had much better and more plentiful food than we. Those invited to the dances would take 'doggie bags' along to fill up and take back to share with the others living in the same hut."[29]

It was quite common for string quartets and other small orchestras to visit BP to put on a show. The musicians were, of course, told nothing at all about their destination, often arriving in windowless vans and lorries and going away in the same clandestine fashion.

Boredom was a constant enemy, but people found ways to amuse themselves. Naida Bentley and Brenda Laing (Naval section) recall that there was a Chief Petty Officer called Southey who had been a teacher of music and got people to sing: "We had a wonderful choir and used to go down to Woburn Abbey church." Dilly Knox would write humorous poems, often spoofing his favourite author Lewis Carroll.[30] Ann Lavell, initially a typist but later PA to Josh Cooper, head of the German Air Section, recalls that the Beer Hut (NAAFI) was "quite a haunt". She and her friend Julie Lydekker wrote comic verses about life on the estate.[31] However, the poems had to be passed around from hand to hand within BP; the collection was classified for years as top secret, even though most of them were about entirely mundane issues such as the size and quality of food portions. It's curious to think that lines like: "Now what is this upon my plate, of microscopic size?" might technically be coded as "Ultra".[32]

Japanese codebreaker Hugh Foss was an accomplished Highland dancer and organised a very popular social club for those who fancied learning. The dancers would perform in the long hall of the manor or, in good weather, on the croquet lawn near the lake. And while Ann Lavell recalls with horror "early morning performing physical jerks to the strains of 'Teddy Bears' Picnic'," Margaret Ross has happier memories of playing rounders on the lawn in front of the house during lunch hour.

One of the most popular facilities were the tennis courts, built at the express orders of Winston Churchill himself. "In May 1941 he visited us and thanked us for our work and told us that we had just sunk the Bismarck, the biggest boat of the German fleet. It was a key turning point in the war when Hitler changed his ideas of invading England. I had only been at Bletchley for a few months. 'It's just another boat,' we thought. It just shows we knew nothing of what was going on," explains Naval Section translator Gwen Paxton, who was recruited after graduating from Cambridge. "By the lawn where we were standing, Churchill could see some of the men playing basketball and he said, 'Basketball? An American game? Fancy playing that here. They must have some tennis courts.' So he arranged for us to have two tennis courts built that are still there now. And that's typical Churchill."[33]

Many staff were placed with families or at places like local vicarages. "In those early days I was billeted with a Mr and Mrs Bunce who lived about eight miles away," explains Anne Pease. "Mr Bunce was a retired railway worker and his wife was a very kind, homely little lady. It must have been an upheaval for them to have me and another Wren, also called Anne [Marcel], invading their home and having to produce meals for us at strange times. I particularly remember breakfast when Mrs Bunce would give us huge doorsteps of fried bread like nothing I'd ever had before. They were delicious. At Christmas, the first one I'd ever spent away from my family, the other Anne must have had leave, and I must have been on evening or night watch, because I remember that while Mrs Bunce cooked the Christmas lunch, Mr Bunce took me to the pub – another first, for me. When he asked me what I would drink I hadn't a clue what to ask for, so ordered something I knew my mother sometimes drank, gin and orange. After several of these I don't think I remembered much about Christmas lunch." Nigel Forward found himself billeted with a brickmaker and his family: "The brickmaker knew I was working at the Park; it was a kind of mystery enclave for him that was meant to have some hairy eccentrics. But he knew nothing else."

Other billets were less homely, being inside stately homes and manors. If asked by their families, the Wrens would say that they were posted to HMS Pembroke V and would quite often name parts of the houses they were staying in after places you'd find aboard a ship. It was a way to ensure no slips of the tongue when talking to people outside of work. "I was living in Gayhurst Manor, a Tudor house, talking about sleeping in a cabin and going to the fo'csle and down to the galley," says Bombe operator, and later supervisor, Sylvia Bate. But living in a country house didn't mean that the lifestyle was cushy. "We had household chores. You were watched like a hawk, doing all the dirty jobs," she explains. "They would see how willingly you did them and so on, scrubbing long, long corridors."

But it wasn't all hardship. "I was lucky because I was billeted at Woburn Abbey and it was quite lovely," says Margaret Hamlin, a Colossus operator. "The grounds were vast and we were able to enjoy ourselves and go for walks. There were deer and in the spring the rhododendrons all came out and we'd have picnics. I really enjoyed it there. Mind you, the house itself was a huge building and it was cold and not such a nice place to stay. We slept in the old servants' quarters. And there were mice everywhere. I trod on one in the dark one night which was horrible. I didn't know what to do with it so I flushed it down the toilet." Colossus operator Lorna Fitch agrees: "There were plenty of mice. We tried to entice the ship's cat up there but it was so well fed that it just wasn't interested." She goes on to say that, "Conditions in Woburn Abbey were very cold, not much comfort. I had to sometimes take my clothes to work and dry them over Colossus." She and her colleagues were eventually given better quarters in some wooden huts that they built in an area called the quadrangle.

Joan Bailey found herself living at Crawley Grange among all sorts of people: "We were Navy, Air Force and civilians all mixed together. We'd see the boffins sometimes smoking pipes in their tweed jackets. Some were very famous although we didn't know it at the time. I've seen them since on TV and thought 'I was at BP with him!' It was a strange environment but we got used to it. We made good friends and the sense of camaraderie was very strong. But even off-duty there was some degree of discipline though. There was an ablutions block but the Petty Officers had their own bathrooms. My sister got in trouble because she kept borrowing one of the Petty Officer's bath plugs as it was missing from our block. And they were very strict about lights out and curfew times. We slept in rooms in two-tiered bunks. We were on the ground floor and anyone who was late in climbed through the window. I'm pretty sure some other people climbed in the windows too..."

The birds and the bees were not halted at the gates of Bletchley Park, and in any population of several thousand people, many young and single, there will always be a certain number of, let's say, courtships. At least one Bletchley veteran has said that when she walked back to her digs in the dark after a late shift – and it was very dark due to the blackout – she was "always tripping over bodies". Certainly, registrar Rosamond Case says, "There were certain goings on... quite a lot actually." There must have been a generation of unexpected "Bletchley babies".

But romances blossomed, too, many resulting in lifelong marriages. Arthur Bonsall, who worked in the German Air Section at BP for most of the war, met his wife Joan while stationed at Station X. "After my arrival at Bletchley Park, I soon realised that many of the staff were billeted in the attractive countryside around Bletchley. If one had a car and agreed to convey some of them to and from Bletchley Park on a regular basis, one would be given petrol coupons and a mileage allowance, both highly desirable," he explains. "I bought an old car for £10, a 1931 20-horsepower Chrysler Coupe called Boadicea with a soft top, a bench seat in front and a rumble seat for two in the dickey. I first met Joan when I called at the vicarage in Stewkley to transport her and two other women to Bletchley Park one morning in January 1940. Our nearness of age and the fact that Joan was a linguist and came from Yorkshire led us to finding things we had in common."

Joan Wingfield worked in Hut 4 once it was built built, but at the time she met Arthur she was working in the library in the Manor House. An atmospheric photograph exists of her taken by her uncle, codebreaker Claude Henderson, who also worked in her section. He wasn't allowed to take photographs, of course, but has been described as someone who "wasn't a stickler for the rules".

"We spent any free time we had together," continues Arthur. "We had lunch together in the very unromantic canteen, sometimes at a nearby restaurant, and I remember we played chess there on my portable chess set. It was always very easy to talk to Joan. We worked a six day week and holidays were rare. We were entitled to a week off every three months but this was subject to the 'exigencies of the service' which often arose. We were eventually married in November 1941 at Stewkley Parish Church. We decided to have no guests at the wedding, not even our parents. One reason for this was the secrecy; we had not been allowed to tell anyone, not even family, where we worked. Another factor was cost; we were very short of money and Joan earned even less than I did. Thirdly, it was the pressure of work. We took only two days off to get married."

Codebreaker Geoffrey Tandy's story is slightly less romantic but fascinating nevertheless, if only for the curious coincidences that surrounded his secondment. In 1939 he received notice that he was required to report to Station X. He dutifully did so and was told that he had been recruited by someone at the War Office because he was an expert in cryptograms. Nothing unusual there, of course; Bletchley Park was keen to engage people with a penchant for unravelling cryptic messages. However, Tandy was then obliged to point out that he knew very little about cryptograms but quite a lot about *cryptogams* – plants that reproduce by spores, like algae, ferns, mosses and lichens.[34] He was, at the time, the British Natural History Museum's seaweed expert and Head of Botany.[35]

But embarrassment quickly turned to happy accident; shortly after Tandy arrived at Station X, a number of sea-sodden documents that had been recovered from sunken U-boats arrived at BP. Among them was an Enigma codebook. The documents appeared to be unrecoverable, as any attempt to open them resulted in them falling to pieces. However, Tandy knew how to dry them out by using special absorbent papers because he regularly used the same process to preserve marine algae specimens. And it transpired that the U-boat notebooks contained useful information that aided the deciphering of German codes.

Tandy was to stay on at Station X in the rank of Lieutenant-Commander (RNVR), firstly in Hut 4 and later as Head of Technical Intelligence (Naval Section 6) with responsibility for captured documents. It is curious that he is rarely mentioned in books about Station X. Admittedly he didn't play as grand a part as Turing, Knox, Flowers or Batey et al. However, it may also be because of the kind of person he was.

According to contemporaries and biographers, Tandy was something of a drinker and a womaniser and would disappear for days on end, supposedly on work-related business. The advent of war allowed him to contrive even more absences. Quite what his wife Doris – nicknamed Polly – made of these absences isn't recorded, but it must have put a strain upon her and their three children, Christopher, Anthea and Alison. Interestingly, Anthea's godfather was the poet T S Eliot, with whom Tandy had worked and become friends. Tandy had a third string to his professional bow in that he was an occasional announcer on BBC radio. His Christmas Day 1937 on-air reading of Eliot's *Old Possum's Book of Practical Cats* was the first time the poems were made public – Eliot's book would not be published for a further two years.[36] He was also the co-narrator of the groundbreaking 1936 short film *The Way to the Sea*, featuring the poetry of W H Auden and music by Benjamin Britten.

Eliot developed a deep affection for "Pollytandy" and wrote her many letters, some of which were recently unearthed in her attic – along with some previously unknown Eliot poems. "When a Cat adopts you," he wrote, "there is nothing to be done about it except to put up with it and wait until the wind changes." Eliot's unrequited love also expressed itself in the addresses he wrote on the envelopes, sometimes referring to the Tandys' Hope Cottage in Hampton-on-Thames as Hopeless Cottage or even Hope against Hope Cottage.

As the war ended, so did the Tandys' marriage. Geoffrey Tandy started a new family in 1946 and left the Natural History Museum in 1948 to take on a new role in intelligence gathering at the Foreign Office. He retired in 1954 and died in 1969.

It is a fact that many people found true love during their time at Bletchley Park and many marriages took place as a result. Rosamond Case met her husband Peter Twinn at BP due to a shared love of music: "A girl who'd just come down from Oxford knew Peter and offered to introduce me. He was this unshaven green-faced creature… night shift is not the best time to meet your future husband." Mavis Lever met her husband Keith Batey there. Arthur Bonsall met his future wife Joan Wingfield. There must have been a great many private liaisons going on, both openly and illicitly.

But for some – those people whose sexuality drew them to people of the same gender – such liaisons were not just illicit, they were illegal. In her book *Bletchley Park People*, Marion Hill cites several veterans who recall people who "acted differently". For many of the staff, having a mix of academics, other civilians and personnel from many different branches of the military all working together would have felt quite strange. It was certainly more casual than life in barracks, or aboard ship, or even at some universities. One veteran remembers that, "One of the first things I heard when finishing a late shift in the dark was a group of Naval men frolicking in the lake nude with shrieks and giggles. Apparently this happened quite often and the gorgeous officers – some very blonde – were homosexual." The writer Angus Wilson, who worked in Hut 8, made no secret of his sexuality, despite the prevailing prejudices of the time. He was hugely flamboyant, and one BP memoir states that, "He used to mince into the room, swaggering, and wore what were outrageous clothes in those days – a bright yellow waistcoat, red bow tie and blue corduroy trousers. His nails were bitten down to the quick, he chain-smoked and he had a horrible cracked sort-of maniacal laugh." Wilson would go on to be awarded a CBE and a knighthood and would win many literary honours. However, not all of the gay staff at Bletchley Park were quite so comfortable in their own skin.

14

A celebrity visit to Bletchley Park

11th May 2009 was a significant one for the campaign: Stephen Fry was going to be visiting Bletchley Park. Yippee!

Three months earlier, Stephen Fry had very kindly tweeted in support of Bletchley Park – this had made a big difference to the campaign, and he'd been invited to visit.

 Stephen Fry
@stephenfry

#bpark You might want to sign the Save Bletchley Park petition. Read @Dr_Black's reasons why on http://is.gd/ikEh – BP won us the war!

10:11 AM 4 Feb 09

He took his involvement with Bletchley one step further, and not only visited Bletchley Park but also tweeted the highlights to his almost half a million followers on Twitter. (As an aside, it's interesting to note that in February 2009 Stephen had 220,000 followers on Twitter, in May 2009 he had 500,000, and at the time of writing, in 2014, he had 6.8 million. Amazing.)

After Stephen had agreed to visit Bletchley Park for the day, I had managed to keep the visit a secret, as instructed, though it wasn't easy, considering how excited I was. Still, for two months I had managed not to tweet or say anything about Stephen's visit to make sure that he could have a relaxing day walking around and getting the real Bletchley Park experience. Bletchley Park grows on you as you wander around the site and hear the incredible stories, sometimes from people who actually worked there during WWII. I wanted Stephen to have the opportunity to experience that too.

So, with that in mind, on the morning in question I got up, said goodbye to my lovely family and started the journey up to Bletchley. I'd been quite a few times now, so I did it almost on automatic pilot.

When I was on the train in to London I noticed a tweet from Rory Cellan-Jones (@ruskin147) saying that he was on his way to Bletchley Park to meet Stephen Fry. I was outraged – I so wanted Stephen's day at Bletchley Park to be relaxed and enjoyable, and for him to have the experience of a "normal" visitor. I was really worried that any publicity might mean that wouldn't happen. I actually told Rory off when we met up at Euston to travel up on the train together (sorry Rory!). When we arrived, I checked Twitter, and noticed that after all that, Stephen himself had just tweeted saying that he had arrived at Bletchley Park. (Needless to say I managed not to tell him off!)

After some brief introductions Stephen chatted to one of the Bletchley Park trustees who had come along to meet him. It turned out that they had been at school together, which led me to wonder why the trustee, who knew Stephen, hadn't invited him along before and asked him to get involved. I was more grateful than ever for the power of Twitter.

Stephen Fry was exactly as he appears on television: friendly, charming, interesting and interested in learning new information. He spoke to the trustee, saying that his tie was "positively refulgent!"! I Googled "refulgent" on my phone under the table, and saw that it meant... well, actually, go and Google it yourself and you will find out. Two minutes into the meeting and I had already learnt a new word. Excellent stuff.

After more introductions and background information, it was time for lunch. We chatted about everything Bletchley Park and Simon showed Stephen an Enigma machine.

Stephen Fry and one of the Mansion House griffins

After lunch Stephen unveiled the new griffins at the front of the Mansion House and we then we had a great time touring Bletchley Park and talking to many of the fabulous people that work there, like Tony Sale, seen below demonstrating Colossus.

We also met a lovely lady, Dorothy Richards (née Blake), who had worked at Bletchley Park during WWII and was visiting for the first time since the 1940s. Amazing to think that there are still over 1,000 Bletchley Park veterans alive. If only we could record all of their fascinating memories. Wouldn't

Tony Sale demonstrates Colossus for Stephen Fry

Bletchley Park veteran Dorothy Richards and Stephen Fry

that be great? I've heard many interesting and exciting stories since I've been involved – and I've only met a few of these wonderful people.

On the day I wrote this on my blog:

> It was a truly wonderful day. Stephen Fry so obviously enjoyed himself and was of course extremely knowledgeable and very quick to pick up everything that he had not known beforehand. A genuinely lovely person and now a great supporter of Bletchley Park.

Stephen Fry with Enigma

> Thank you so much @stephenfry you made my day and that of everyone at Bletchley Park. I think Bletchley Park will hopefully be safe now that you are involved. Thank you from the very bottom of my heart.

Oh, Lord!

On 16th February 2009 I'd written a piece for the *Telegraph* entitled, "Why I'm ashamed to be British", asking the UK government to stump up the £10 million needed to save and restore Bletchley Park.

> Bletchley Park needs sustained government funding to preserve it. But then of course we're in an economic downturn – so how could the government afford it?
>
> Well, here's a comparison. In the short term Bletchley Park needs £10 million, which is a pittance compared to how many millions, or is it billions now, that have recently been given to the banks? And how much more than the original estimate is being spent by us on the Olympics?

It was gratifying to learn, therefore, that on 21st May 2009 there was a question in the House of Lords from Baroness McIntosh of Hudnall, asking Lord Davies of Oldham:

"...what support the UK government will give to the restoration and development of Bletchley Park."

Baroness McIntosh of Hudnall was joined by Lord Clement-Jones, Lord Eden of Winton, Baroness Trumpington, Viscount Montgomery of Alamein, Lord Selkirk of Douglas and Lord Lea of Crondall in asking for substantial funding to support Bletchley Park. Alas, the reply from Lord Davies of Oldham was, in a nutshell, that the government was already doing enough. I wrote about this on my blog, commenting, "What utter rubbish."

I was, needless to say, annoyed. There was fantastic support from the Lords, with several saying that they had strong connections to Bletchley Park, but the government position was clear: some money had been given to Bletchley Park by English Heritage and Milton Keynes council, and that would have to suffice. What a disgrace! What was the point of us having a House of Lords, I wondered, if their opinions were so easily brushed aside?

So I did the only thing I felt I could do: I blogged, asking people to write to their MP to complain. I pointed out our online draft letter, to make it quick and easy for people to participate. I also pointed everyone to the international petition that had now been set up asking people to help save Bletchley Park. The government was definitely not doing enough, and I wanted them to know it. If the voice of the Bletchley Park supporters was loud enough, I reasoned, it couldn't be ignored for long.

Recognition at last

In spite of the government's seeming lack of concern about Bletchley Park's financial situation, a great announcement came on 12th June 2009: Bletchley Park veterans were to be formally recognised by the UK government and given service medals "for their efforts".

It was great that the Bletchley Park veterans were finally and rightly being recognised for the crucial work they had carried out during the war – even better that they were now being called "heroes", which they absolutely are. Heartening news indeed.

Bletchley Park Enigma heroes to be honoured by Government
12 June 2009
James Kirkup
The Telegraph

Up to 5,000 surviving codebreakers and other staff who worked in top secret conditions at the centre and its outlying stations around the world will receive a service medal for their efforts.[...]

The decision will be a boost for Bletchley Park which is now run by a charitable trust but which has struggled to raise funds to prevent the buildings where the war was decided from falling down.

EuroPython

The campaign was continuing to garner attention, and I was continuing to speak at events and conferences whenever possible. On a very hot and sunny day in July 2009, Simon Greenish and I were invited to give a keynote talk about Bletchley Park at the EuroPython programming conference in Birmingham. It would be the first time I'd spoken in front of so many people – there were around 450 attendees in the audience.

Simon spoke first about the history and impact of Bletchley Park. I then spoke about my campaigning efforts to help save Bletchley Park. I talked about how Twitter had really made a difference to the campaign and how, although I had started the campaign using traditional media, I had realised quite quickly that with traditional news channels it was very hard to keep something in the public eye for long. Social media had given us the opportunity to find our audience and interact with them over a period of time, gradually building up a larger and larger presence and following.

Social media had also given us the opportunity to connect with key influencers in a way that that simply hadn't been possible previously. My aim was to get people to visit Bletchley Park, as I always kept in mind what Simon had told me: the site's main revenue was from visitors to the Park. So I spoke about the campaign's achievements to date, then highlighted some of the cool artefacts in the museum and urged everyone to visit.

I thought it was important to talk about the physical artefacts at Bletchley Park because it really underlined the importance of actually going to the site. I pointed out that there was a real Nazi swastika badge in the Toy Museum at Bletchley; I remember being amazed on seeing the Nazi badge for the first time. I had felt an immediate and direct connection with a time in history that had previously seemed very distant. Seeing the badge in the Toy Museum at Bletchley connected me viscerally to what had happened more than sixty years previously. In fact, that's what visiting Bletchley Park did to me each time I went there. It gave me a powerfully strong connection to recent history. And it wasn't just me that it had that effect on – every visitor described a feeling of "stepping back in time" or not wanting to leave. The amazing aura of the place just gets under your skin and won't go away.

I hoped that I had managed to give the correct impression of what it was like to visit Bletchley Park. I was a little worried that people in the audience might misconstrue my enthusiasm for the Nazi badge – sometimes things that sound great in your head don't always sound that great when they come out of your mouth, and I didn't want anyone to think that I was pro-Nazi! – but everything seemed to go fine. At the end of our talk we unveiled an Enigma machine on stage. The audience loved it and asked questions for about an hour afterwards. It was such fun and encouraging to have such an enthusiastic audience.

Lady Geek – ah!

Things were really starting to move along with the campaign, and I was being asked more and more frequently to give talks about Bletchley Park, its importance, the campaign, and how social media, especially Twitter, was playing a large role in our success. Social media was just starting to become a hot topic in certain circles, and there was a dearth of good examples of social media being used in practice to make many kinds of constructive changes happen. This, along with the fact that Bletchley Park is such a fascinating and emotive place, helped to ensure that lots of people wanted me to speak at events and meetings across the country.

In May 2009 I was invited to give a talk at OpenTech (an informal, low-cost, one-day conference on approaches to technology, democracy and community) about women in technology. Here's what I posted on my blog about it:

> Last weekend I gave an invited talk at the OpenTech conference in London, this time about women in tech. I had a nice surprise when I introduced myself. I said as part of my intro that I campaign for Bletchley Park and got a round of applause and some cheers. Popular support for Bletchley Park and the campaign is growing :)

One of the most entertaining speakers of the day, in my opinion, was Ben Goldacre. He is so clever and funny and really knows how to work an audience. At the end of the day we all hung around and had a few drinks. I did my usual thing of asking everyone I spoke to if they had been to Bletchley Park, if they could help Bletchley Park and if they had any suggestions for ways to raise the profile of the campaign and garner support. I remember feeling a bit apprehensive approaching Ben Goldacre and asking him about Bletchley, but I needn't have worried – it turned out he already knew about and supported what we were doing!

 ben goldacre
@bengoldacre

@Dr_Black i love Bletchley Park, already linked campaign prevsly, happy to help, give me tasks http://savingbletchleypark.org

1:36 PM – 7 Jun 09

Our chat that night was unfortunately cut short, but I was delighted that, when prompted for his favourite female tech hero on Ada Lovelace Day, Ben named me his "top lady geek". I was extremely honoured.

I was noticing a real change. In just a year the audience response to a mention of Bletchley Park had gone from one of quiet interest to one of active applause. People were starting to hear about Bletchley Park more frequently and appreciate its fundamental place in our history.

That month I also met up with the wonderful Professor Barry Cooper from Leeds University, who was planning a year of celebration for the 100th anniversary of Alan Turing's birth in 1912. Barry had kindly invited me to join the Turing Centenary committee, and I happily accepted. We chatted about Turing and his impact, and I told Barry how successful social media had been in our campaign. I had become such a massive fan of Twitter and couldn't stop talking about the amazing impact it was making. I talked about what we had done with Twitter and urged Barry to use it too.

It's early days

On one of my usual scouts around on Twitter I ended up following a chain of tweeters that led me to Phil Willis MP. At that time he was Minister for Universities and Science. I looked at his Twitter profile and thought to myself that he might be interested in Bletchley Park and would therefore be a good person to start tweeting with. He was reasonably new to Twitter and didn't have that many followers, so there was a reasonable chance that he might actually respond to me.

I was starting to notice something that probably is common sense: people with loads of followers and who had been on Twitter for a long time were much less likely to engage with me than those who did not have that many followers and were quite new to Twitter. I was always on the lookout for influential people who might have some relevance to Bletchley Park and the campaign, especially those who were new to Twitter and didn't have many followers yet – I was learning that that was the profile of someone most likely to engage in a discussion with me. That doesn't mean to say that you can have a chat about just anything. You need to tweet on a topic that is relevant to you both, in a friendly way. It's actually just like being at a party – we've all met those people who start talking and are only really interested in themselves. It's easy to spot these people on Twitter because they won't be engaging with anyone. If you look at their tweet stream, you can see that they are just broadcasting stuff about themselves and they don't @ reply anyone.

Imagine a different person at a party, someone who comes over and starts chatting to you about stuff that you are both interested in. After a while you forget that you have only just met because you have had such an interesting discussion. It's the same on Twitter.

As I got more comfortable with using Twitter as a campaign tool, I realised that there were certain ways of approaching people that were much more effective than others. In my experience, if you want to be successful at finding and engaging with interesting people on Twitter you need to be:

- Authentic – first and foremost, you need to be yourself;
- Friendly – don't be overly pushy or reticent, just imagine what you would say if you were approaching someone in a relaxed and friendly environment, like a drinks party;
- Engaging – there's no point chatting to someone if you don't really have anything to say to them;
- On topic – look for common areas of interest and start there. If you get along, the conversation will develop naturally;
- Cheeky – OK, you don't *have* to be cheeky, but if you have a sense of humour why not use it? Many of the wonderful friends that I have met through Twitter are people I have really bonded with through a shared sense of humour and just having a bit of fun. It goes such a long way in terms of discovering shared interests and making the getting-to-know-you process enjoyable.

I realise, too, that I'm really lucky in that I absolutely love meeting and talking to new people. I enjoy finding out all about other people's lives, what they are interested in, what they have done, and what makes them tick. I think that's partly why I love Twitter so much: it allows me to look for new friends and people to chat to whenever and wherever I am. I love knowing that there is always someone to talk to. I was pretty nerdy when

I was younger, and also painfully shy. This meant that for most of my life, until I was in my 30s, I didn't have many friends – and therefore not many people to talk to. I'm really making up for that now, though. Things started to change when I went to university in my late 20s; later, being encouraged by Professor Robin Whitty, my PhD supervisor, to talk to people at conferences, I gained more confidence and gradually overcame the fear of speaking to strangers. In fact, I actually started *enjoying* talking to strangers, and now I actively look forward to meeting new groups of people. I guess that just shows that your character can change as you get older. Some of the things I do these days, like speaking in front of hundreds of people or appearing on live TV in front of potentially millions of people, are things that not that long ago I wouldn't have dreamt in a million years that I would be able to do.

So... back to Phil Willis. When I saw that he was quite new to Twitter, and that his tweet stream showed that he did tweet with people that he didn't already know, I decided that there was a good chance he would engage with me. It was worth a try, at least!

I sent him a few tweets about Bletchley Park, its importance, its financial situation – the usual stuff. I was hoping that he would be interested and might possibly be able to give some advice or open some doors for the management at Bletchley Park. Thankfully he responded and we had a nice chat. I asked him if I could have a ten minute appointment with him at his convenience to tell him more about Bletchley Park and the situation they were in.

Bingo! He agreed.

The next week I went along to meet Phil at his office in Portcullis House. I had a great chat with him and one of his researchers. I explained the situation and asked them if they had visited Bletchley Park. When they said no, I asked them to visit. Phil said he could visit in a few months' time and got his researcher to add it to his schedule.

When I asked Phil what he could do to help, he told me that he would set up an EDM – he was very happy to do so, and he thought it would have a good effect. I said:

"That's wonderful! Thank you so much."

And then, slightly sheepishly,

"So... what's an EDM?"

We all laughed and then Phil explained that an EDM is an Early Day Motion – a standard government process for drawing attention to particular issues and finding out who is interested in the same issues as you. A statement is made which MPs across all parties can sign to show support. Phil said that it was a good way to make MPs aware, if they weren't already, of the situation at Bletchley Park. He asked me which particular issue at Bletchley Park it would be best to focus on. From my recent discussions with Simon Greenish, I knew that they needed a contribution towards operating costs. Simon had said that the operating costs were around £250,000 per annum and that if we could raise that amount through external funding for the next 5 years, he would no longer be worried about Bletchley Park being able to survive financially. It wouldn't solve all the problems there, but it would mean that there would no longer be a threat of Bletchley Park having to close. I told Phil about this; he agreed it was the right sort of thing to focus on and asked me to write a few sentences that he could use as the statement for the EDM.

My ten minutes went very quickly, but I was happy: I had a result. I went home that day feeling that I'd achieved something, and just a week or so later the EDM was up! I was delighted and of course tweeted about it to everyone asking them to encourage their MP to sign it – in the UK everyone has access to their local MP through the "Write to Them" website. I also blogged about the EDM, giving instructions on what to do and how, pointing at the relevant websites. I really wanted the EDM to get as many signatures as possible.

The women of Bletchley Park

I've met some really great people during my campaign – people that I never would have met if I hadn't followed my heart and started doing what I felt I really must do. Suw Charman Anderson is one of those people.

I met Suw on Twitter, where else? We hit it off right away. We both care passionately about women in tech, amongst other things, so had lots to talk about. Suw is the person responsible for setting up Ada Lovelace Day, which celebrates Ada, who worked with Charles Babbage on the analytical and difference engines and is known as the person responsible for the idea of software. Ada Lovelace Day is also more generally a day to celebrate women in computing and their achievements, so as you can imagine that's something I'm totally up for doing!

In August 2009, Suw organised a Women of Bletchley Park Day at Bletchley Park as a follow-up to Ada Lovelace Day that year. Suw and I both gave talks, as did the amazing Jean Valentine, a Bletchley Park WWII veteran who was also our guide around the Park. Jean was the absolute star of the day, as she always is. She was a Bombe operator at Bletchley during

John Chapman speaking outside the Bletchley Park Post Office

Jean Valentine with a BOMBE

the war and went to Sri Lanka after the war to carry on with her work. She is such an inspiration.

In the Bletchley Park cinema, we watched the Women of Station X film, which had been produced by BCSWomen in 2007. It was a really heart-warming and emotional experience for me, as the film was one of the main outputs of the Women of Station X project, which I'd got funded after my very first trip to Bletchley Park.

The cinema itself is incredible. It seats about sixty people in an intimate setting and boasts a plethora of film and camera equipment in showcases at the back. I spent some energy when I was campaigning trying to get Secret Cinema and other clubs to do some screenings there, as there's a definite atmosphere of history and excitement about the place.

It was a great day of celebrating women, technology and Bletchley Park, three of my passions. But at the end of the day, on a sobering note, I took a photo of Hut 6, the hut that I'd stood outside in 2008, a year previously when I was interviewed by the BBC, right at the beginning of my campaign. Hut 6 was deteriorating rapidly.

Time was running out. Bletchley Park must be saved. I blogged, asking everyone again to "donate, talk to everyone you know, write to your MP, support the campaign in any way you can. Thank you."

A slap in the face

A couple of weeks later, in August 2009, the government responded to the Save Bletchley Park petition, which had been signed by almost 22,000 people. The government acknowledged the contribution made by Bletchley Park, but failed to offer financial help to secure its future. I was disgusted by the response, as my blog post from the day, "Government response a disgrace", shows. But far from making me want to give up on the campaign, I was spurred on to keep trying to find a way to save Bletchley Park.

Government response a disgrace

Thursday 27 August 2009

10 Downing Street's response – or lack of response – to the Save Bletchley Petition, signed by almost 22,000 people, is a disgrace and a slap in the face to the thousands of people that worked there. Bletchley Park not only saved countless British lives and shortened the war by two years, but it is also the birthplace of modern computing and a vital site in the UK's 20th Century wartime and scientific heritage. If the Government truly acknowledge the contribution made as significant why are they failing to help secure its future?

The funds already allocated to the park will go some small way to fixing a tiny number of problems, but the whole site, and particularly the huts where the most important work was done, are in a dire state of repair. This setback will not stop us campaigning – despite this response, we still believe that investment in saving Bletchley Park would be hugely beneficial to the UK, in terms of saving incredibly important history, knowledge and fantastic stories for the nation.

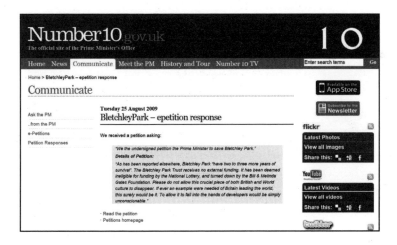

The Enigma Reunion

In September each year Bletchley Park hold the annual Enigma Reunion. It is an opportunity for Bletchley Park veterans to visit the site and meet up with old friends. I was delighted that this year I had been invited to the dinner the evening before the reunion to have a chat with veterans and get to hear some of their stories about their time at Bletchley. I do love the history of Bletchley Park, and of course I'm interested in its contribution to computer science, but what I felt was missing from the campaign was the human face of Bletchley Park. I wanted to know what it had really been like for these, mainly young, female veterans. What had it been like when they first arrived? What did they do in their spare time? Where did they live? What did they do for fun?

With these sorts of questions in mind, I drove up to the hotel near Bletchley in September 2009. I put my bags in my room and then went downstairs to mingle and chat to some of the veterans. I was so excited to find out more about what it was like to be a young woman in the 1940s, arriving and then working at Bletchley Park during the war.

I walked into the dining room, which was full of old ladies with white hair, probably about 80 of them, and a few old men too. I wondered what stories they would tell me. I went over and sat down at a table with seven or eight women and started chatting to them. I told them that I was an academic computer scientist with a love of Bletchley Park, that I'd started a campaign to raise awareness of Bletchley Park, and that I'd love to know more about their time there. I wanted to know what it had been like working there, but also what it had been like outside of work. What had they done socially? Had they got into any scrapes?

They were all lovely. We started talking about how they had ended up at Bletchley Park and what their first impressions were. Most had been about 18 years old when they went to Bletchley and had not really known where they were going. Some had been recommended by schoolteachers or head teachers, others weren't really sure who had put them forward. Some of the ladies talked about asking their father's permission to go and help with the war effort and of being excited about what they were going to be doing, whilst at the same time having not much idea of what that might actually be.

Most were asked to arrive at Bletchley station but not given much more information. The ladies were mostly billeted out at Woburn Abbey, a stately home down the road from Bletchley, and bussed in and out according to their shifts. They spoke of working in the huts, so freezing cold in the winter that they worked wrapped in blankets, so hot in the summer at times that it was unbearable. No heating and no air conditioning. Eight hour shifts around the clock. No chatting during work hours and definitely no discussion of any of the work that they were doing. I've not spoken to anyone who worked at Bletchley at this kind of level who knew anything about what anyone else was doing. They had all signed the Official Secrets Act on arrival and there was no way that they would even think of breaking it.

It sounded like the ladies at Woburn Abbey had been better off than others who had been billeted with families around the village. At least at Woburn, even though they couldn't talk about what they were doing at the Park, the ladies could have fun and chat about other things together. There were some sad stories of women who had been billeted with families, but they were unable to tell the families anything about what they were doing at work, and they were unable to talk about it at home either. It was never said explicitly, but the impression I got was that some of the women had found this very hard to bear at times, and some had become depressed, possibly even suicidal. Imagine being an 18-year-old girl away from home for the first time, working all day, being unable to speak about it, and then going "home" to a family who ask you what you are doing, but not being allowed to tell them anything. It must have been extremely difficult for many people.

I asked the ladies what they did for fun. They must have had some laughs. One of the ladies said to another, *Do you remember that time we nicked the vicar's bicycle to go to a dance?*

We all laughed and I thought to myself, "This is exactly the sort of thing that I was interested in finding out!"

There was a discussion about going to dances in London and catching the last train back to Bletchley, getting a few hours' sleep and then going back to work. One of the ladies then told what has become my favourite Bletchley Park story. She said that when she had been billeted at Woburn Abbey, several of the local RAF officers had been getting into trouble for flying low over the Abbey and were called in to see their superior officer to find out what they were playing at. The officers eventually admitted that they had been flying low over Woburn Abbey to try to get a glimpse of the young female WRNS sunbathing topless in the summer months on the roof of the Abbey.

We all laughed at the story. I guess I love it because it shows that wartime or not, people are still people. It gives a sense that despite the awfulness of war and the relentlessness of being a young person working hard under complete secrecy, fun can still be had.

How wonderful to sit with a group of 80-year-old ladies, listening to them telling stories about what they got up to as teenagers during the war. We carried on chatting over dinner, and at the end of the evening I went to bed feeling extraordinarily lucky to have met these amazing women and honoured to have spent time speaking with them. My passion to save

Bletchley Park was leading me to meet all sorts of wonderful people. There was a life lesson for me right there. Always follow your passion: it will lead you to unimaginable wonders and new depths of understanding about people and about life.

Amplified recordings

The next day I got up, had breakfast and drove over to Bletchley Park. I'd had an awesome night chatting to female veterans and hearing their stories, and today we were going to try capture some of those stories for posterity.

A few months previously, I had given a talk at the Amplified unconference in London. I had been introduced to Amplified – an organisation that encourages people to share ideas using social media – by Mike Sizemore, who had, I'm sure you will remember, been the first person to get in touch with me via Twitter wanting to talk about Bletchley Park. Over the ensuing months I had got to know various people connected to Amplified. I'd subsequently met both Toby Moores, who had set up Amplified, and Steve Lawson, a talented solo bass player amongst other things, at the Tuttle club. I'd had a few conversations with Toby, Steve, Mike, and Christian Payne about the Bletchley Park Enigma Reunion and how I really wanted to record as many of the veterans' memories as possible before it was too late. The veterans were all over 80 years old, and each time I saw any of them I worried that it might be the last time I did. That might sound morbid, but I really wanted to make sure that we captured as much information about what went on at Bletchley as possible, and I knew that once the veterans were gone all of that knowledge would be lost forever. That really didn't bear thinking about.

Thankfully Toby, Steve, Mike and Christian were all up for interviewing and recording veterans, with Toby and Amplified funding some additional people to help us out. In the end we had quite a team working together on the day, including many people that I now hold really dear to my heart for being there with me during our first attempt to capture the veterans' memories on a large scale. They include Hannah Nicklin, Benjamin Ellis, Maggie Philbin, Matt Rawlinson, Kate Day, Julia Higginbottom, and Julia's husband, Nat.

On the day itself, we all met up at around 10am in a designated room in the Mansion House. There was a programme of events scheduled for the veterans across the day, including talks. I told everyone about my chats with them the night before, including the stories about the vicar's bicycle and the topless sunbathing on the roof of Woburn Abbey. We decided that it was probably best to just take in the day, wander around, and interview people that looked or sounded interesting – they certainly wouldn't be in short supply.

 maggie philbin
@maggiephilbin

RT @Dr_Black OMG!! WRNS sunbathing topless at Woburn Abbey causing havoc bcos RAF pilots flying low to have a look!! #bpark70 #bpark

10:36 PM – 5 Sep 09

We all spent the whole day interviewing veterans. Maggie Philbin alone conducted 19 interviews, Benjamin Ellis took loads of photos, and Julia and Nat set up an interview room in one of the cottages and had a stream of people come through. Xander Cansell from Amplified cleverly pulled all of our content together and put it on a website created especially for the occasion. I spoke to a couple of veterans, but my main role was to find interesting people and connect them with our expert interviewers. I also spent a lot of the day tweeting about what was going on, including links to the interview content that everyone was posting, and generally sharing my immense enthusiasm for everything that was going on all around me.

Not only did we interview many veterans, but I also got to revel in the joy of introducing a really smart and fabulous bunch of social media-savvy people to Bletchley Park and of seeing how excited they got about the amazing conversations they were having.

In September 2009 I sent 1168 tweets

15
Turing's treasure

"Mathematical reasoning may be regarded rather schematically as the exercise of a combination of two facilities, which we may call intuition and ingenuity."

—ALAN TURING

There has been so much written about Alan Turing, and several TV dramas and feature films have been made, most recently *The Imitation Game* (2014) starring Benedict Cumberbatch. Turing was a complex, brilliant and deeply troubled man, but his achievements at Bletchley Park and beyond, for which he was awarded the OBE in 1945, were extraordinary. Station X purposely looked out for people who saw the world through different eyes than the rest of us do; puzzle-setters, lateral thinkers, conundrum solvers and cryptographers. Famously, during his morale-boosting visit in 1941, Winston Churchill remarked to Alastair Denniston: "I told you to leave no stone unturned to get staff, but I had no idea you had taken me so literally."

From the earliest of ages, Turing displayed an obsessive dedication to achieving the results he wanted. On his very first day at Sherborne School in Dorset, the 1926 General Strike put paid to his attending. However, the 13-year-old Turing was so fixated upon getting there that he cycled the 60 miles from his home in Southampton, stopping overnight at an inn. Despite this level of enthusiasm, he didn't always do well at school because he put his efforts into the things that interested him rather than the work that his teachers wanted him to do. His English teacher wrote that he produced "slipshod, dirty work" and that he could not "forgive the stupidity of his attitude towards sane discussion on the New Testament". Sherborne's headmaster described him as "the sort of boy who is bound to be a problem for any school or community". He was nearly stopped from taking the School Certificate – the equivalent in those days of O-levels or GCSEs – but after studying mathematics in the Sixth Form, he began to excel and eventually won himself a place at Cambridge.

In 1934 he graduated from King's College with a first class honours in mathematics. Having demonstrated a very high level of competence and understanding, he was elected as a fellow in 1935 at the age of just 22. His first real sorties into the world that would later become programmable computing started there, with the creation of hypothetical "Turing Machines" that could perform any conceivable mathematical calculation as long as it could be represented as an algorithm. He also considered the possibility of a "Universal Turing Machine" that could perform any function run by a "Turing Machine". What he was proposing, in fact, was a computing device that could run many different computer programs all performing different functions. He had predicted the shape of all computers to come, at least ten years before it was possible to build such a thing. He continued to explore the possibilities of computing machines when, between 1936 and 1938, he worked at Princeton University in New Jersey, USA. After gaining his PhD, he returned to Cambridge but also began to work part-time for the GC&CS.

At the outbreak of war, he and several other mathematicians were moved to Station X. Turing was initially posted working with the brilliant Dilly Knox. This marked a major shift in code breaking thinking; until Turing's appointment, cryptography had been the province of Classicists and experts on language. Turing and his colleagues brought a wholly different set of skills to bear and heralded the age of mathematical and mechanical analysis.

Most biographers seem to agree that Knox and Turing got on quite well despite the differences in their ages and backgrounds. This might have been because both were somewhat eccentric in behaviour. Turing – known to his colleagues as "Prof" – famously turned up for work during periods of high pollen count wearing a full-face, service issue gas mask and, later, when he moved into Hut 8, he would chain his tin mug to a radiator to prevent it being used by anyone else. A champion runner, who only just missed out on representing Great Britain in the 1948 Olympics due to an injury, he would sometimes run the 40+ miles from Bletchley to London for important meetings. He also favoured using a bicycle, although his chain had a habit of regularly slipping off. Typically, Turing didn't get it mended. Instead, he worked out the frequency of chain slippage and would stop the bike just before he believed it was about to happen so he could fit the chain back into the worn teeth of the cogs.

A natural loner, Turing would often disappear up into a nearby hayloft to work alone on a problem and didn't take his meals in the canteen or the Mansion. Mavis Batey tells a story of how two women, Claire Harding and Elizabeth Grainger, set up a pulley system to winch meals up to him in a basket during breaks. Knox wrote at the time: "Turing is very difficult to anchor down. He is very clever but quite irresponsible and throws out suggestions of all sorts of merit. I have just, but only just, enough authority and ability to keep his ideas in some sort of order and discipline. But he is very nice about it all." It's possible that the brilliant Dilly Knox didn't recognise that Turing's way of "throwing out suggestions" was very similar to his own behaviour. But despite his love of solitude, Turing did make some good friends at BP. He was a frequent dinner visitor to Max Newman's house and regularly played chess against his son, William. Amazingly, Turing would often play with his back to the board, able to keep the positions of all the pieces in his head. William also tells a story about how Turing once popped in on them while they were out and couldn't leave without somehow telling them that he'd been. His solution was to scratch a message into a leaf and post it through their letterbox.

Turing's first major contribution to the work at BP was producing, with Gordon Welchman, the functional specifications for what became the Bombe machines. Turing's groundbreaking idea – and how the machine differed from the Polish *Bomba* – was that it searched for contradictions. By inputting a stretch of ciphertext and some corresponding plaintext, such as a crib, it could search through all possible settings of the Enigma machine and discard all of those that couldn't possibly have led to the encipherment. This allowed the Bombes to bypass all the least likely Enigma settings for that day and focus on the most probable. While this was going on, Turing was also working as a top-level intelligence officer liaising with the USA. He visited several times to share new cryptological developments.[37]

His next big success came in 1942 with the breaking of the hugely complicated German Naval Enigma system. He apparently took it on because no one else was tackling it and he would "get it all to himself". The breaking of the code, which meant working out the Indicator, allowed the Admiralty to track the U-boat "wolf packs" in the Atlantic that were preying upon allied ships bringing in vital supplies from America.

The Naval Enigma was tougher than other Enigmas to decode because, firstly, the Navy had added two additional rotors to the machine, bringing the total to five and pushing the number of possible rotor combinations from 60 to 336. They also introduced a new system for the Indicators, super-enciphering them by using something called bigram and trigram tables.[38] It was no longer possible to use the usual code breaking methods to work out the possible rotor combinations and the Indicator, so Turing invented a new code breaking technique called *banburismus*, a punch card system that allowed parts of messages to be compared to find common features. *Banburismus* was a way of identifying the right-hand (fast) and middle rotor in use, thus reducing the possible rotor orders from 336 to as little as 20. His punch cards, or "banburies", created in the nearby town of Banbury by a small army of workers, helped the code breakers look for common bigrams and trigrams that would provide a possible method of attack on the cipher.

Turing is sometimes called "the father of computing" and his name is often mentioned in the same breath as Colossus, the ancestor of pretty much every programmable computer that we have today. However, Turing had little to do with computers themselves and was only involved in a peripheral way with Colossus. He is, perhaps, more rightly called "the father of computer science".

Colossus was actually designed and built by a brilliant Post Office engineer called Tommy Flowers to tackle the fiendishly complex Lorenz cipher.[39] Although Turing wasn't directly involved, he was the man who suggested Tommy Flowers for the job, and he contributed tools for calculating probability that could be used by Colossus in cryptoanalysis. It could be said that Turing created the language that Colossus would use in answering complex mathematical questions.[40]

Once the various Enigma and Lorenz ciphers were being decrypted as a matter of course, Turing became a kind of all-purpose troubleshooter for the whole Station X network, going where he was needed to solve problems. He spent much of his time learning electronics and, with Donald Bayley, designed and built a functioning portable voice "scrambler" communications machine codenamed Delilah. But he was also preoccupied with an extraordinary idea: that it was possible to make a physical, working version of his hypothetical Universal Turing Machine.

Turing had been fascinated and obsessed by the idea of artificial intelligence for many years and, while at Princeton, had contributed to the building of several binary multiplying machines, the forerunners of computers. However, his interests lay not in the physical building of a computer, but in the idea that, one day, scientists would be able to "build a brain", an electronic machine that could mirror the faculties of the human mind. In other words, his Universal Turing Machine. The idea was groundbreaking. His work at the National Physical Laboratory (NPL) in South West London led others to build ACE – the Automatic Computing Engine – recognisably a modern computer using coding rather than mechanical processes to perform tasks. Frustratingly, the development of computers at NPL was held back because Turing could not talk about what had been achieved at Bletchley Park during the war. The computer had to, quite literally, be re-invented from scratch for the benefit of uninitiated colleagues.

Turing would later move to Manchester as a reader in the Mathematics Department and, later, as deputy director of the Computing Laboratory where, in 1950, he published the influential paper "Computing Machinery and Intelligence" in which he proposed what we now call the "Turing Test" – a "test of a machine's ability to exhibit intelligent behaviour equivalent to, or indistinguishable from, that of a human". Since 1991, an annual competition called the Loebner Prize has existed to find a machine that can pass the Turing Test. The Bronze Medal is won every year but, to date, no machine has won the Silver or the Gold Medals. But with the increasing complexity of computers, it cannot be long before both are awarded.

It is now well known that Alan Turing's life ended in tragedy. The shabby "Prof" with his bitten nails, awkward manner and voice that always sounded like it hadn't quite broken properly, spent his short, brilliant life with the knowledge that his homosexuality wasn't just frowned upon, it was illegal.

Turing was always aware of the dangers of openly declaring his sexuality but it didn't stop him from having relationships or confiding in close friends. During his time at Bletchley Park, he grew so fond of his deputy, the codebreaker Joan Clarke, that he misguidedly proposed to her and she gladly accepted. However, he was unable to live a lie and withdrew the proposal, admitting his homosexuality to her. After the war, he spoke more openly, encouraged by the growing gay rights movement. However, in March 1952, he was arrested by the police over his alleged sexual relationship with a young man from Manchester. At his hearing, Turing stated that he saw no wrong in his actions. With no defence offered to counter the allegation, he was found guilty. Rather than go to prison, he opted for the cruel process often called "chemical castration", a year of regular injections of oestrogen to supposedly suppress his libido. To add insult to injury, the man who had done so much to help the war effort and who had never breathed a word about his work at Station X was stripped of his security clearances and was no longer allowed to be involved in code breaking because he was seen as a "risk".

Turing spent his last few years using logic and mathematics to return to a childhood fascination with form in the natural world. He was particularly interested in morphology, the way that living things grow and the forms that they grow into. He became fascinated by foetal growth and questions such as, "How can biological matter assemble itself into enormous patterns using such tiny building blocks?" and "Can mathematics explain how asymmetry can arise from a symmetrical starting point?" He became the first scientist to use an electronic computer (a Ferranti Mk 1) to model natural processes. His studies led to the paper "The Chemical

Basis of Morphogenesis" in 1951 and he was elected to Fellowship of the Royal Society. His work on pattern formation explained how plant stems grew and why the Fibonacci number series appears in the leaf patterns of plants and in the spirals seen in sunflower seed heads. His calculations led to what we now know as Turing Systems, and they explain and predict the growth of stripes on a tiger and the spots on a leopard. Rather than random growth, they are all created by mathematical process.[41]

Turing was never to see his biological theories proven and adopted. On the 8th June 1954 he was found dead in his house by his cleaner. A half-eaten apple laced with cyanide was beside his bed.[42] Despite the fact he left no note, the coroner's verdict was suicide. Those who knew him spoke of his desperation and loneliness in those final years and of his hatred for the enforced medication that robbed him of a normal life.[43]

In 2009 Prime Minster Gordon Brown offered a posthumous apology to Alan Turing in response to a public petition that had collected thousands of signatures. "It is thanks to men and women who were totally committed to fighting fascism, people like Alan Turing, that the horrors of the Holocaust and of total war are part of Europe's history and not Europe's present," he said. "So on behalf of the British Government, and all those who live freely thanks to Alan's work I am very proud to say: We're sorry, you deserved so much better." The apology was welcomed by campaigners, although some felt that it had not gone far enough. Peter Tatchell of gay rights group OutRage! was keen to point out that, while the Turing apology was deserved and significant, he was just one of an estimated 100,000 British men who suffered similar treatment, none of whom have ever been offered an apology. Turing later received a Royal Pardon in 2013. This too was received with mixed feelings; a pardon suggests that he did something wrong by being gay. However, some argue that, whatever the rights and wrongs of the legal system, he did nevertheless break the law as it existed back then and a pardon was therefore the appropriate response.

There is a curious footnote to the Alan Turing story. It concerns the whereabouts of his personal fortune. As the war progressed, and Alan, being unsure of its outcome, he drew as much of his pay as he could in silver half-crowns, which he melted down into two large ingots and buried somewhere near the village of Shenley. When he returned to the site in 1944, it had changed greatly and many of the landmarks he'd recorded to ease the bars' recovery had gone. He made two further attempts to find them in 1946 and 1952 but failed. They are now, presumably, somewhere under the housing site that covers the area. As far as anyone knows, they have never been found and his buried treasure is still out there waiting to be discovered.

16

Devastating news and an apology

Although the campaign was continuing apace, August 2009 had been a very difficult month for me. Late in the evening of the 11th August my mobile rang. I could see from the display that it was my sister Sarah calling. It was about 11pm, so I knew straight away that it was important, and probably something bad, because she never rings me at that time of night. I answered the phone with great trepidation.

"It's only me, have you got someone with you? You need to sit down," said Sarah.

I started crying and sat on the sofa. I somehow knew what was coming and it felt like my heart was being ripped apart.

"I'm sitting down, Paul's here," I replied.

"It's Stephen, he's dead. Rachel found him in the garage this evening."

I started howling. I find it very hard even now to put into words how terrible it feels to find out that your younger brother has committed suicide. I felt like I was falling into a deep, black abyss.

Fast forward a month: on the 10th of September 2009 I was out for one of the first times since my brother's funeral. I was at my second Twestival. Twestival is held as a celebration of Twitter and its users. It brings together Twitter lovers from all over to one space where they can hang out together, drink free beer and discuss Twitter, social media and much more.

I was really looking forward to Twestival. I knew that quite a few of my Twitter friends would be there, some of whom I knew in real life and some whom I'd only ever chatted to online. It's always great meeting up with someone you've only interacted with online for the first time. I've never had any surprises from people, they have always been the same in person as they are on Twitter – something I've not found to be true with other online communication channels like email. My theory is that on Twitter you often have real time conversations, and that in real time you are who you are.

So, I was looking forward to meeting up with lots of friends, and I was also looking forward to letting my hair down a bit for the first time since my brother Stephen had died. I'd not felt like going out for a while, but that night I really did. I needed company, invigorating conversation and a few drinks.

When I arrived, I could hear the music inside and could see people standing around in the entrance in front of me. I was invited to write my Twitter ID on a white label with a marker pen and stick it on my T-shirt, which I did. Looking up, I recognised my friend Jamillah Knowles. I went over and said hi.

I spent the evening meeting up with friends new and old and having a few beers – quite a few, actually. It was one of the few nights in my life that I really felt like getting very drunk rather than just a bit tipsy.

At around 9.30pm I got a text from Kelsey at Bletchley Park saying, "What is Stephen Fry talking about?"

I replied: "What do you mean? What is Stephen Fry talking about?"

"On Twitter, what is Stephen Fry talking about on Twitter? He is making coded references to Bletchley Park, what does he mean?"

I had a look at Stephen's Twitter stream. Here is what he had tweeted:

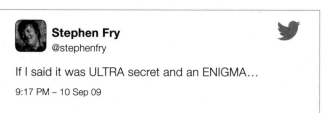

Stephen Fry
@stephenfry

If I said it was ULTRA secret and an ENIGMA…

9:17 PM – 10 Sep 09

I had no idea what he was referring to.

I sent Stephen a direct message saying that Bletchley Park were worried because they didn't know what he was tweeting about. Could he tell me?

He replied saying that Bletchley were not to worry and that all would be revealed at 10pm. I texted Kelsey to let her know and told my friends that were with me that something exciting was going to happen at 10pm, but I didn't know what it was...

At 10pm I checked my phone again. I saw that Stephen had tweeted:

 **Stephen Fry**
@stephenfry

Alan Turing, breaker of the Enigma code receives belated apology from UK Govt – http://www.number10.gov.uk/

10:00 PM – 10 Sep 09

Wow! I couldn't believe it. The UK Government had issued a posthumous apology to Alan Turing. I was amazed and, of course, delighted. I told all of my friends the great news. We had a few more beers to celebrate and I went crazy on Twitter, letting everyone know what had happened. Within a few minutes my Twitter stream went crazy too. So many of the people that I'd connected to on Twitter were massive fans of Bletchley Park. It was a rush seeing how excited everyone was.

An hour later we were all celebrating away, both online and offline, when my phone rang. It was Kelsey from Bletchley Park.

"Hiya, I've just had the BBC on the phone, they want someone to go on *Breakfast Time* tomorrow morning to talk about the government apology. Simon is away in Paris at the moment, can you do it?"

I thought about it for a moment. I had a meeting in Central London the next morning at about 10am, so yes, I could do it.

"Yes, I can!"

I got off the phone and told my friend Lynn, who was still there. Quite a few people had gone home by then. I probably should have done, too, but it hadn't even occurred to me. We had another beer to celebrate and carried on chatting and drinking.

At about midnight I had a phone call from the BBC. They asked if I was OK to go on *Breakfast Time* in the morning. I replied that that was fine. They said that they would probably interview me twice, once around 6.20am and again around 8.30am, was that OK? I said yes, that was fine. They said that they would send a car to pick me up from home. Wonderful!

"The car will pick you up at 5am outside your house, is that OK?"

"Yes, that's great, thanks very much."

5am! Ah well, I was sure I'd be fine.

After that conversation my phone rang a few more times. The BBC Radio 4 *Today* programme phoned and asked if I could go on the show at around 8am; luckily their studio is very near the *Breakfast Time* studio, so I said that would be fine. They said they would come and find me at the appropriate time. I also had calls from other radio stations; I told them about the timings for *Breakfast Time* and *Today*, and they said that they would try to fit in with the other timings. I was going to have a busy morning!

I told Lynn all about the calls and how excited I was that I was going to be on *Breakfast Time* in the morning. After a discussion all about it and another beer we had a look at the time. It was after 1am – I had missed my last train home.

 Sue Black
@Dr_Black

Oh man I'm not home yet and need to b up t 4.30am!! Not sure I'm going to n coherent on breakfast tv at 6.20am. I'm not a morning person!

12:46 AM – 11 Sep 09

We went outside to see if we could find a couple of cabs to take us home. Luckily there were some waiting, so we said our goodbyes and off we went. By the time I got home it was nearly 2am and I was slightly the worse for wear. I had phoned Paul to tell him the news and when I got home he was in bed but awake, wanting to hear more about my evening. I got undressed as I told him everything. I was wearing a trouser suit and zip-up ankle boots. I took my jacket off and hung it up, then unzipped my right boot and took it off.

When I tried to unzip my left boot, the zip bust. It broke right in the middle of the zip, on my ankle bone. I yanked it up and down but couldn't make it budge. Paul had a go and he couldn't get it to move either. I could think of no other solution than cutting the boot off my foot. I made my way downstairs, one boot off, one boot stuck on, to find some scissors. As I was walking downstairs I started thinking:

If I can't wear these boots tomorrow what am I going to wear? I need to wear my suit because I need to look smart on TV. I haven't got any other boots that go with my suit. What other clothes could I wear that look smart and are clean?

I couldn't think of any. It came down to the fact that I needed to wear my trouser suit, and I only had the boots that I had been wearing that would go with it. I was going to have to wear them, broken or not – otherwise I was going to be wearing clothes that didn't match on primetime TV.

I walked back upstairs with my one broken boot on. I took the rest of my clothes off and got into bed, still with one boot off, one boot on. I slept with my booted foot outside the covers, feeling vaguely ridiculous.

Reboot

My alarm woke me up two hours later. It was 4.30am already. I felt pretty groggy, to say the least. I got out of bed, pulled my suit out of the wardrobe and found clean underwear and a top to wear with it. I went into the bathroom, turned on the shower and started brushing my teeth. The usual morning ritual, only this morning I was somehow going to have to shower with one boot on. I decided that the best way to do it would be to leave my booted leg outside of the shower, so that's what I did. It wasn't that easy, but I managed without falling over. After my shower I got dressed and put a bit of makeup on. I checked the time – it was almost 5am. I said goodbye to Paul, went downstairs, picked up my stuff, got into the car and we were away.

We drove through the quiet London streets and after about half an hour arrived at the BBC TV studios in White City, West London. I went into the building, gave my name and was taken around to the green room, which by the way wasn't green, and was shown a seat. A friendly producer greeted me and told me that I would probably be on at about 6.45am and again at 8.30am or so.

While I waited, I read a bit about Alan Turing; I had printed out his entry on Wikipedia so that I could brush up before going on television to talk about him. I wrote down a few key facts. He was born in Maida Vale, went to Sherborne School, his parents left him and his brother in the UK and lived in India for much of his childhood. How hard that must have been! I loved the stories about how he rode his bicycle 60 miles to Sherborne School for an interview at the age of 12 because there was a train strike. It didn't occur to him not to go. What a great character; I would have loved to have met him.

I read about his work at Bletchley on the Bombe and being head of Hut 8. He was called "Prof" at Bletchley and had a close friendship with Joan Clarke, a fellow codebreaker in Hut 8. Another great story involving a bicycle was that he used to cycle around Bletchley wearing a gas mask in the summer to stop his hay fever. He was also a great runner and almost qualified for the Olympic team in the marathon. He was obviously a man of great intellectual and physical prowess – someone to be admired.

After Bletchley he went to work for the National Physical Laboratory in Surrey and then Manchester University. It was so sad to read about how he had been treated by some of the people around him, and especially the circumstances of his untimely death. It was an absolute tragedy.

As I was reading, the producer came into the room to let me know that I would be called through in about five minutes. When I was called, I left my notes in my pink handbag in the green room and went through. We entered the studio and I was asked to sit on a chair just at the edge of the studio behind a black curtain. I could see the *Breakfast Time* sofa with two presenters and a rather good-looking young man, who turned out to be David Miliband, sitting on it. I think that's the first time I've ever thought of a politician as cute! I couldn't quite make out who he was at that point. I was told that they were interviewing him now, they would soon cut to a piece of video, and then someone would come and take me over to the sofa.

Sure enough, after a couple of minutes David walked past me, and I was asked to go over and sit on the sofa. Over I went. I could feel my heart pounding away strongly in my chest. I was trying to keep calm and not to feel scared, but it wasn't easy. The presenters were really friendly and obviously used to putting people at ease quickly. I relaxed a bit. A minute or two later the video finished and the cameras turned on. I had the sudden urge to run out of the studio and wondered why on earth I had agreed to go on live national television, especially considering I'd drunk so much beer the night before.

Joy at PM's codebreaker apology

11 September 2009

BBC News

Gordon Brown has said he was sorry for the "appalling" way World War II codebreaker Alan Turing was treated for being gay.

In 1952 Turing was prosecuted for gross indecency after admitting a sexual relationship with a man. Two years later he killed himself.

Dr Sue Black, from the Saving Bletchley Park campaign, said she was delighted at the prime minister's apology.

I was asked questions, and I answered them, but because of my lack of sleep and my panic at being on national TV talking about a subject I didn't know in great depth, I found it quite hard. Nevertheless, I just tried to do my best. I spoke about how, when Turing was faced with a choice between prison and chemical castration, he chose chemical castration, which caused him to grow breasts. What an awful choice to have to make. Soon it was all over; someone came over and got me and took me back to the green room. Phew! I sat down and looked at my notes. Oh dear, I had got a fact wrong. How embarrassing. Ah well – I would get it right at 8.30am, when there would probably be more people watching.

I had a call from BBC Radio London on my phone, so I went out of the room to be somewhere quieter while I was interviewed by them. The interview went well and I went back to the green room, and soon enough it was time to do it all over again: I went through to the studio and, after a short wait like last time, went over to the sofa again. I apologised to the female presenter for getting my facts wrong the previous time. She was very kind and said it was fine. The interview went more smoothly the second time and I think I answered all the questions correctly.

After my second appearance on *Breakfast Time*, I was taken over to the BBC *Today* programme studio. I sat in the anteroom and was then taken through and shown a chair opposite John Humphrys. After a minute or two he said something about Gordon Brown and Turing and the apology and then said: "So, Mrs Black, what is the significance of this apology, does it really matter?"

I was so surprised at being called Mrs Black that for a few milliseconds I didn't know what to say. But then the adrenaline kicked in and I replied, feeling a bit more relaxed than I had an hour or two previously. As with the interview on the sofa, just a minute later it was all over. I was shown out of the studio and to the front desk where I sat watching *Breakfast Time* on the large TV screen while I waited for a car to take me into London to start my work day.

I sat there thinking, remembering the night before at Twestival. The text from Bletchley Park, the exchange with Stephen Fry, the call from Bletchley and then the BBC. Going to bed late and then getting up early and trying to absorb as much information as possible from Alan Turing's Wikipedia page. So much had happened in the last 12 hours.

I looked down at my boots. I'd not taken my boot off since the previous morning. One boot was properly zipped up and the other just had the zip stuck halfway down with the top gaping open. Luckily it was hidden under my trouser leg, so I'm sure no one had noticed. Well, it was just going to have to stay on for another eight hours at least, as I had a day's work ahead of me.

 Sue Black
@Dr_Black

Phew. That was all a little bit stressful. But actually I seem to be getting used to it now :) I hope I've done some good 4 #bpark

9:02 AM – 11 Sep 09

My car arrived to take me to a meeting with the civil society group that my friend Lucian Hudson was setting up. We were participating in a half-day workshop run by the Tavistock Centre that I was really looking forward to. I got into the car, and we had just driven through the gates of TV Centre out and down the road towards Shepherds Bush when my phone rang. It was the BBC asking where I was and if I could go and film a piece with them for the lunchtime news. I asked the driver to take me back to TV Centre.

When we got there, there was a cameraman and an interviewer waiting for me. They wanted to film me standing in front of the TV Centre in the small garden area near the front gates. We walked over to the space and I started having flashbacks to what had been my favourite TV programme in the 1970s: *Blue Peter*. I was now standing being interviewed in a place that I remembered seeing Valerie Singleton, John Noakes and Peter Purves standing all those years ago. It was a bit surreal.

It took about 15 minutes to get a reasonable take for the news, as every time we started speaking there would be a loud noise, either from the nearby traffic or from a helicopter overhead. But eventually we managed to record without a major interruption, and then I was back in the car to head into central London. The work day was just beginning.

HLF is gonna fund you

After all the excitement of the apology from the Prime Minister and the BBC interviews, life settled back into a more normal pace. I was invited to view an exhibition called "Gay Icons" at the National Portrait Gallery in London, which included a picture of Alan Turing.

It was so great to see that the public were really embracing Alan Turing as a significant figure. What should have happened in Alan's lifetime was happening more than 50 years after his death. Better late than never, I suppose. But I did, and still do, feel upset when I think of what he did for this country and juxtapose that with the barbaric way that he was treated.

So things carried on as usual. I spent a lot of my spare time tweeting and conversing with people about Bletchley Park, encouraging them to spread the word, and of course to also visit. The number of people involved with the campaign had been gradually increasing and I now felt that every time I went online there were quite a few friends and supporters that I could chat to about how things were going.

And then, on the 28th September, I got a call from Kelsey asking me if I could be at Bletchley Park the next morning as the Heritage Lottery Fund were going to announce that the recent Bletchley Park application had been successful. How amazing! Some substantial funding from an established UK institution. This, to me, was the first real sign that everything was going to be OK. Up until now things had been going well and we had got quite a lot of coverage in the press and through social media. But this funding meant that the British establishment were now finally seeing a future for Bletchley Park. Simon Greenish had told me that he had turned Bletchley Park from an organisation that was losing money to one that was just about breaking even, and that was crucial because no one with any sense would invest in an organisation that was losing money. The funding from Heritage Lottery was £450,000. This was a substantial sum of money, but more importantly it demonstrated that Bletchley Park was now seen as worthy of investment.

Unfortunately I couldn't be at Bletchley the next morning to meet the people from Heritage Lottery and the media, but that didn't matter. Bletchley Park was on the way up. My Twitter stream went crazy, with everyone excited that Bletchley Park had received its first substantial amount of funding. Stephen Fry tweeted that it was the Heritage Lottery Fund's purpose to support exactly this type of organisation. He had tweeted after the Turing apology that getting funding for Bletchley Park was the next goal. Maybe he had had a quiet word with the people involved with Heritage Lottery. Who knows? The main thing was that this was another major turning point.

 Hannah Nicklin
@hannahnicklin

@Dr_Black the @stephenfry quote is right, this is the HLF's purpose. Well done for your tireless efforts. Big buckets of WIN ^_^

12:40 AM – 29 Sep 09

Sue Black
@Dr_Black

@hannahnicklin thx hon, and thx so much for ur help
xxxxxxx

12:45 AM – 29 Sep 09

Sue Black
@Dr_Black

Thk gdness 4 #bpark HLF success :) It means that
@bletchleypark and I don't have 2 chain ourselves 2
House of Commons railings tmoz! ;)

12:47 AM – 29 Sep 09

I blogged about the amazing news from the Heritage Lottery Fund, thanking everyone for their support, saying that this was not the beginning of the end but the end of the beginning. It was great news and a step forward, but I really didn't want everyone to think that it was all OK now and that they could forget about Bletchley Park. I reminded everyone that Bletchley needed £250,000 per year in operating costs for at least the next five years and another £6 million in funding for renovation work, and that without that money it could still close. The Early Day Motion that had been set up in July by Phil Willis MP had gained quite a few signatures; that had perhaps helped persuade the Heritage Lottery panel that there was a groundswell of support for Bletchley, adding to its future viability. But there was still plenty of work to be done.

Paper trip funder

One of the things that I was really keen to do as part of the campaign was to connect Bletchley Park with the international museum network so that they could make contacts with other museums that might be able to offer advice and support. I also wanted to make the international museum community aware of Bletchley Park, its significance and its struggle to survive. I was convinced that getting a paper accepted at the Museums and the Web conference was the best way to do this. A few years earlier I had written a paper on women and museum websites with Professor Jonathan Bowen, a colleague at London South Bank University. We had presented the paper at Museums and the Web in Vancouver in 2005. I had really enjoyed the conference. It had been very diverse in terms of gender and background of participants. It was very relaxed and friendly, yet it was clear that everyone really cared about what they did and felt passionately about getting museums online and finding innovative ways of making that happen. My experience in 2005 led me to believe that this was a great network to connect Bletchley Park into.

I discussed the possibility of writing a paper with Jonathan and with Kelsey at Bletchley Park. They were both interested. I wanted to focus on what we were doing with social media to raise awareness and build up a supportive community around Bletchley Park; I thought it was cutting edge as I'd not seen any other museums doing anything like it at that time. We called the paper "Can Twitter save Bletchley Park?" Here is the abstract:

Bletchley Park is the historic site of secret British codebreaking activities during World War II and birthplace of the modern computer. The work carried out there is said to have shortened WWII by two years, saving possibly 22 million lives. The Park is now a museum, with a 26 acre site, many exhibitions and working rebuilds of machines such as the Colossus, a forerunner of today's computers, invented to mechanize codebreaking. The museum is staffed by a 75% volunteer workforce and is grossly underfunded compared to its historical importance.

After a visit by Sue Black to Bletchley Park in July 2008, a campaign was launched to save it. A letter to the UK broadsheet newspaper *The Times* signed by 97 eminent UK computer scientists was published and highlighted in a BBC news broadcast. Following traditional media coverage, a blog was established, and then social media, (particularly Twitter), which have been used to great effect to raise awareness and support for the campaign. Other Web 2.0 technologies, including

Facebook, have also been used as part of the campaign.

This paper explores the effectiveness of this approach, using statistical evidence as appropriate, highlighting how the use of social media has contributed greatly to campaign success. Since the Saving Bletchley Park campaign started, visitor numbers have increased, along with public awareness of the contribution of the site to world heritage and the history of the computer.

Campaign efforts have received national coverage on television, on radio, and in the press and have contributed to the Park recently receiving £460K funding and a potential further £4 million funding from the UK Heritage Lottery Fund.

Read more: Archives & Museum Informatics: Museums and the Web 2010: Papers: Black, S., et al., Can Twitter Save Bletchley Park? http://www.museumsandtheweb.com/mw2010/papers/black/black.html#ixzz2ZcX5gWPZ

We put the abstract together, sent it off just before the deadline, and waited to see if it would be accepted. It wasn't long before we found out that it had been. How exciting!

However, my excitement at finding out that our paper had been accepted turned to dismay when I realised that I had now put Bletchley Park in the position of having to pay for Kelsey and possibly me to go to Denver to present our paper. Whilst trying to do something good, I had inadvertently done something which in my eyes was very bad: I had added to Bletchley Park's financial worries.

I was quite perturbed and spoke about my concerns on Twitter. I was really annoyed with myself for not thinking ahead and realising that this might happen. My friends on Twitter were very supportive – particularly Paul Clarke (@Paul_Clarke) and Daren Forsyth (@Daren140), who suggested that it would be a good idea to set up a JustGiving account and ask our community on Twitter for financial aid. At first I was hesitant, but they persuaded me that it was a smart thing to do, that people would want to help, and that, frankly, I would be an idiot not to try. I love my Twitter friends!

So, the upshot of our conversation was that, after clearing it with Simon and Kelsey at Bletchley Park, I set up a JustGiving account, asking for £2,500 for Kelsey and me to be able to attend Museums and the Web 2010. Here's what we wrote:

Hi there!

Can you help us to raise awareness of Bletchley Park at Museums and the Web 2010?? Bletchley Park would like to send Kelsey Griffin and me to give our paper at the #MW2010 conference in Denver next April. You probably know the story of how I went up to Bletchley Park, loved it, heard that it might have to shut because they were short of cash, then started a campaign to make sure that could never happen? You don't? OK, please have a read of my blog first then. That'll give you all the exciting details of lunch with Stephen Fry and much, much more :))))

So, Bletchley Park. The place where the codebreakers worked during WWII, shortening the war by approx. 2 years thus saving possibly 22 million lives, *and* the place the first computer was invented. It is a very important place. It's the Geek Mecca!

So, as I was saying, in a nutshell, I went up to Bletchley Park, fell head over heels in love with the place, got upset at the financial situation it finds itself in, and decided to do something about it. I've been campaigning for 18 months now to ensure that Bletchley Park is there for our children, grandchildren and great grandchildren to enjoy. To help them understand what happened there and the massive contribution that it has made to the world we live in today.

Kelsey Griffin from Bletchley Park, Professor Jonathan Bowen from Museophile, and I have had a paper accepted for the Museums and the Web conference 2010 in Denver. It is entitled "Can Twitter save Bletchley Park?" Kelsey and I would really like to go to present our paper, but have no funds to do that. That's where you come in. Could you please give a small amount towards our trip? It is not only about going and presenting the paper. It is about helping Bletchley Park get on the international map with other museums and their staff across the world. It is about helping a ridiculously underfunded museum get out there to talk to others in their field, to get ideas, create a network of contacts, be inspired.

Together we can not only save Bletchley Park, but make sure that it gets the recognition it deserves.

Thanks very much for your time
Sue – @Dr_Black

I set up the JustGiving page a couple of weeks before Christmas 2009 and started tweeting, asking friends to help us so that we could attend the conference, deliver our paper, and connect Bletchley Park with the international museum community. I also mentioned it to everyone that I met.

I needn't have worried about raising the money. Amazingly, in less than two weeks, we had reached our target, though we kept fundraising in the new year – one donor gave a substantial contribution directly to Bletchley Park, which wasn't reflected on the JustGiving website, so it took us a little longer to "officially" reach our target. Sixty-eight amazing supporters gave us money just before Christmas, at a time when many people need every last penny to pay for their Christmas celebrations. The wonderful Paul Clarke even offered to go and take photos of people for free as long as they put some money towards our JustGiving campaign.

 Paul Clarke
@paul_clarke

another few quid raised for http://www.justgiving.com/
sueblack from some of my photography. C'mon, let's
get to 100%, people! #bpark

3:02 PM – 9 Feb 10

Paul also very kindly went and gave a talk about the campaign at a conference when I was ill and couldn't do it myself. So many people, especially those that I met through Twitter, really went out of their way to help the campaign. It was incredible – I really couldn't believe the generosity of the people who had supported us. It was a real lesson for me in how much so many people cared about Bletchley Park

So, we had our paper accepted and we had the money to go. All we needed to do now was actually write the paper! It took some time, and we were all still at it the night before we needed to submit. I had a moment of panic: what if we missed the submission deadline? How would I explain that to everyone who had invested their time, energy and money in making sure that we were able to go?

Finally, at five minutes to midnight, we clicked "submit". Phew! The pressure was off, at least until the time came to actually travel to Denver and present the paper...

In November 2009 I sent 2125 tweets

17
Can Twitter save Bletchley?

In March 2010 I got a call from Simon Greenish. He was excited because Bletchley had just had a call from the UK Government Department of Culture, Media and Sport (DCMS) asking them if they could spend £250,000 in the next week, before the end of the financial year. If they could, then the money was theirs.

How wonderful! Simon said that they could easily spend that and was really happy that it could be used for operational costs that were not very sexy, such as getting the drains and roofs fixed and resurfacing the car park and some of the internal roads. The announcement appeared in the press with Simon saying that the funding was hugely significant:

"This enormously appreciated funding boost will not only enable vital repair and maintenance of this WWII site for the benefit of our rapidly growing number of visitors, but it also represents endorsement by the DCMS that Bletchley Park is a place of national importance which deserves Government support."

Ben Bradshaw MP, the head of DCMS, commended the work of the Bletchley Park Trust, saying:

"The work carried out at Bletchley Park had a huge impact on the course of the war, and the museum does a brilliant job in bringing this alive for people of all ages. But, having doubled its visitor numbers over the last three years, it urgently needs funds to keep it in good condition. I am delighted to announce this grant which will help renovate the buildings and ensure that future visitors enjoy a really high quality experience when they come here."

It was great to see a key government figure talking about "future visitors" in the national press and stating that Bletchley Park had a "huge impact on the course of the war" and was doing a "brilliant job" – three extremely key messages. If I'd had to bet on the viability of Bletchley Park after this announcement, I would have staked my life on it being saved. I realised that up until now, I hadn't really been certain of Bletchley Park's future. Now that the government was recognizing the importance of the site, I had a strong feeling that Bletchley was probably going to be OK.

Things to do in Denver when you're alive

In April 2010 Kelsey and I flew to Denver to present our paper at the Museums and the Web conference. We were funded by the generous Bletchley Park Twitter community, who'd supported us through our JustGiving page. Professor Jonathan Bowen, our co-author, managed to get funding from the Royal Society so that he could also attend. The prospect of taking Kelsey out to Denver to present the paper was exciting – I was so looking forward to introducing her to my friends in the museum community, particularly friends like Sarah Winmill, who is a massive Bletchley Park fan, an ambassador and committee member for the network that I started, BCSWomen, and Director of Information Systems at the Victoria and Albert museum in London.

I had wanted Kelsey to present our paper so that everyone got to know her name and face, but she thought that it would be better if I presented. We were part of a session of about ten speakers. There were about 300 people in the audience – I'd presented to about 400 people with Simon when we talked about Bletchley Park at EuroPython a few months earlier so I wasn't fazed by the size of the audience. I was mainly worried about conveying the importance and historical significance of Bletchley Park as well as its financial situation in the few minutes that we had available.

The audience was fabulous. They obviously really appreciated and enjoyed the talk, and at the end of the session many people came over to discuss what they had heard. Kelsey and I probably spoke to about fifteen or twenty people at the end of the session as well as others throughout the rest of the conference who approached us asking for more information or offering help of some sort. It was great, just what I wanted to happen.

One of the funny things was that many, though not all, of the people who came over to talk to us were from the UK. It's rather ironic that we had flown thousands of miles to meet up with and chat to a bunch of museum people who were also from the UK! But I guess that is what happens at international conferences – you meet like-minded people from all over the world, including the place where you yourself have come from.

Anyway, it was wonderful. There was so much love and support for Bletchley Park and lots of new friends were made, including from the big London museums, the National Trust, the Royal Palaces and The Other Media, a digital agency based in London. We also met people from the Smithsonian and from museums around the world.

But there were other things going on in the world at the same time as the conference, one of which was about to affect us. The Eyjafjallajökull volcano in Iceland had erupted, sending massive clouds of ash into the atmosphere and presenting a safety hazard for airlines. All planes were grounded in the UK – no planes were allowed in or out. We were due to fly home from the conference in the next day or so, along with many other people at the conference, and we were not sure what to do. How were we going to get home?

The conference organisers were amazing. They set up an information point and put out requests for people at the conference to host other delegates that couldn't fly home. We decided in the end that we would be better off going to Washington, DC, to talk to people there about Bletchley Park; it was one step closer to home, and both Kelsey and I had friends there. While we were in Denver a friend of a friend of mine, Lisa Crispin (@lisacrispin), had got in touch with me via Twitter. She was based near Denver and coincidentally had been halfway to the UK to give a talk at Bletchley Park, but her plane had been forced to turn back because of the volcanic disruption. She had seen that I was in Denver, tweeted me and suggested meeting up.

Kelsey and I met Lisa for breakfast at the conference hotel on the day before we were now due to fly to DC. We had a great chat about agile testing – Lisa is an expert on the subject, and it relates to my PhD and other research – and we also know quite a few of the same people. She is also a big fan of Bletchley Park. Then Lisa said, "So what are you guys planning on doing today?" We told her we were thinking of trying to get out of the city for the day to see a bit of countryside. Lisa, being the wonderful person that she is, invited us to spend the day with her at her friend Anna's ranch up in the mountains. We accepted straight away. What a wonderful opportunity.

Lisa drove us to Anna's ranch and we had a wonderful day meeting all of Anna's animals, including several llamas. Anna gave me a horse riding lesson, and we also had a go at driving the donkey cart. It was a real day to remember. After a day of fabulous hospitality from people we had only just met, Kelsey and I said goodbye to all our new Denver Museums and the Web friends and flew to Washington, DC.

We spent a great couple of days there visiting Capitol Hill and some of the fantastic DC museums. We also met up with one of Kelsey's friends, who looked after us wonderfully well, and my friend Mike Hinchey, who at that time was working for NASA. After we had spent couple of days in DC the volcano stopped erupting and flights home resumed. Just a couple of days later than expected, we returned to the UK after having had quite an adventure.

Matt Ball, the UK editor of MSN, is a great supporter of Bletchley Park. He captured the feeling from the community and the spirit behind our use of Twitter well in his blog post about our Denver trip:

Can Twitter save Bletchley Park?

From MSN Tech & Gadget BlogUK

17 April 2010

Guest post by Matt Ball, MSN UK editor-in-chief

(follow on twitter @thisismattball)

Today is the closing day of the Museums and the Web 2010 conference in Denver, Colorado.

I would not normally be overly excited by this event but today, for me and quite a few people I've met through social networking site Twitter, is different.

One of the presentations on the final day is entitled *Can Twitter Save Bletchley Park?* In case you didn't know, Bletchley Park is where Britain's codebreakers cracked enemy codes such as Engima during World War II, thereby helping to shorten the war by about two years and save millions of lives. It is also the birthplace of modern computing and shares its location with The National Museum of Computing. In short, it's geek and historian heaven rolled into one.

I visited it in 2006 and had a great time but was surprised at the dilapidated condition of some of the buildings.

As you can see from the photo of one of the huts where the codebreakers worked (taken on a second visit in late 2009) the problem – due to a lack of funding – remains. The Bletchley

Park Trust aims to raise £10 million to secure the venue's long-term viability and transform it into a world class heritage and educational centre. It is a big target but the future is looking increasingly bright for a place that played such an important role in the war and that is so inspiring when you visit.

Last month the Department for Culture Media and Sport announced a grant of £250,000 for urgent repairs at Bletchley Park. That announcement came after the Heritage Lottery Fund announced a first round pass for the Trust's application for museum development funding and awarded £460,000 to work up detailed plans. These will be submitted early to mid 2011 in a bid to secure the £4.1 million needed and subject to the Trust raising the £1 million needed for match-funding the bid. The Trust will then work on raising a further £5 million to complete the development.

I am certain that it would have been far less likely for the Trust to have attracted these two awards without the significant publicity that Bletchley Park has achieved in the past 18 months which has raised its profile, spread the word about its cause and helped to attract record numbers of visitors.

The Twitter campaign
A campaign on Twitter has played an important role in this success. The two key pages have been the official twitter.com/bletchleypark page run by Bletchley Park's director of operations Kelsey Griffin and twitter.com/dr_black run by Dr Sue Black, head of computer science at the University of Westminster, who began campaigning for Bletchley Park in 2008.

Their use of Twitter highlights the various ways the platform can, and should, be used by those seeking to achieve worthy aims:

1. They establish credibility and trust by participating in the social networking aspects of Twitter. They follow almost everyone who follows them, they join in other discussions, share personal anecdotes, retweet etc.

2. They use it as a medium for broadcasting their campaign and corporate messages.

3. They use it to contact influential people (celebrity Stephen Fry's well-publicised visit to Bletchley Park last year is one such example of success here).

4. They willingly meet offline the people they have first met through Twitter (including me).

Their success in building a community of interested followers is best demonstrated by how they have funded the costs of travelling to Denver to present their paper at the conference today. Encouraged by some of her Twitter followers, Dr Black set up a page on the Just Giving website (http://www.justgiving.com/sueblack) seeking donations. More than 60 people chipped in, raising more than £2,300 which has covered the majority of the trip's costs. Looking at the names of the donors, I could find almost every one of them on Twitter.

Their work also proves that you do not need a million followers on Twitter before you can achieve meaningful, ongoing influence. They each have fewer than 4,000 followers and some of those are common to both.

To learn more about their campaign and their use of Twitter you can read their paper Can Twitter save Bletchley Park? on the Museums and the Web 2010 conference website.

Enigma Reunion Day 2010

The Enigma Reunion 2010 was another fabulous day full of interesting conversations. Kate Arkless Gray and Benjamin Ellis came along again to interview veterans as part of the Amplified social media crew, this time along with Britt Warg, A L Ranson, Drew Buddie, Gordon Tant and Graham Johnson.

There were around 2,000 people there that day – I think it was probably a record turnout. We interviewed veterans and sometimes their relatives as well. Kate interviewed Christopher Hughes Reece, who was there looking for anyone that remembered his mum, Joan Dodderidge, also known as "Fougie" – she had worked at Bletchley and then gone to work in Ceylon

(Sri Lanka). He really wanted to know more about what his mum had done there. She hadn't talked much about her experience at Bletchley, and unfortunately she died before Christopher was able to find out much about her role during the war.

Kate also interviewed Sir Arthur Bonsall, who had been a veteran at Bletchley Park and had gone on to be Director of GCHQ. Sir Arthur was recruited from Cambridge University, where he had just finished a degree in languages. Having been turned down due to a heart murmur by the army doctor when he tried to enlist, Sir Arthur was delighted to be asked by Martin Charlesworth, proctor of St John's College, Cambridge who recruited many of the now-famous people to Bletchley Park, if he was interested in confidential war work. He was recruited alongside another man, Harry Hinsley, who went on to become well known in naval intelligence and later as a war historian.

Shortly after the meeting Sir Arthur was sent a letter asking him to report to Euston railway station, take a particular train and get off at

Sir Arthur Bonsall

Bletchley Junction where he would be met by someone. He was told: "Don't tell your parents or anyone else where you are going!"

Sir Arthur did just that. He was met, taken to Bletchley Park, asked to sign the Official Secrets Act, given an address of a place to stay and told to report back the next morning at 8am. When he came back the next day as requested, he was taken to Hut 4, now the Bletchley Park canteen, where he met Josh Cooper, Head of Section, who explained that he would be working on the radio communications of the German Air Force. He worked in radio telephony, on the voice messages of German aircraft pilots intercepted by WAAFs. The information gleaned from the pilots was used to put together reconstructions of the battles afterwards and was very useful in understanding how the pilots worked.

"Within minutes I was seated at a trestle table copying out coded messages on to large sheets of paper," he said. Sir Arthur worked his way up until he was in charge of German code breaking in Bletchley Park's Air Section. He played an important role in the breaking of Luftwaffe codes

L to R: Me, Gordon Tant, Kate Arkless Gray and Benjamin Ellis

Chatting to Daisy Bailey, wonderful Bletchley veteran

and ciphers during the Battle of Britain and the strategic bombing of Nazi Germany from 1942 until the end of the war. Unfortunately, Sir Arthur died in 2014 at the great age of 97.

Other veterans interviewed that day included Joan Farmery, who was 23 when she worked at Bletchley. Her work included plotting the waters around Nagasaki in Japan and producing and looking after a box of cards containing information about Japanese Navy movements gleaned from the code breaking effort. Joan was billeted out at Woburn Abbey and ended up having her morning wash in the room that Queen Victoria had stayed in many years before.

Another story with a royal connection was told by Audrey Wind, who was one of the many Bombe operators working at Bletchley. Audrey remembered going into London on a day off with one of the other WRNS. They were standing in uniform on a traffic island in the middle of the road in Central London when the Royal Family came past. They were amazed and delighted when King George VI of England saw them standing there and waved at them. What a story to tell your grandchildren!

Bletchley Park veterans at the annual Enigma Reunion 2010

It wasn't all fun, of course. There were many stories told to us of how hard it was keeping everything secret all of the time. Most of the people working there were very young and away from home for the first time. Some people unsurprisingly found that they were unable to cope and went off the rails.

On Enigma Reunion Day 2010 there was an awesome flypast by a Lancaster bomber, a marching band and much more. Sir Arthur unveiled Churchill's stone, a stone which Churchill had stood on outside of the Mansion House at Bletchley and from where he addressed the entire workforce to let them know that the war was over.

At the end of the day we all made our way home, excited by the interviews that we had captured and people that we had spoken to.

Turing film at Information Pioneers event

I've been involved with the BCS for many years now, since around 1992 when I was studying for my degree at London South Bank University. My colleagues and friends at the BCS have been very supportive of my campaigning for Bletchley Park and I've had many an interesting discussion around Bletchley Park and its importance to the nation. The BCS had also gave me, or more correctly my organisation BCSWomen, funding to run the Women of Station X project, so that we could record the oral histories of some of the women that worked at Bletchley. My involvement with both the BCS and Bletchley Park over the years has taught me a lot about the ten thousand people who worked at Bletchley, as well as about others such as Tommy Flowers, who did not work at Bletchley Park per se but invented and built Colossus, the world's first programmable computer, which was used at Bletchley Park to mechanise and industrialise the codebreaking effort.

In January 2010 I was invited to be on a panel for the BCS Information Pioneers campaign. The BCS wanted to emphasise the role that information technology has played over the years by highlighting key figures in the field and getting the public to vote for the most important. We were given a long list of pioneers by the BCS and asked to choose our top five about whom short films would be made. I was determined that there would be at least two women in the final five and that people connected with Bletchley Park should also be represented.

At the panel meeting to discuss who should be included, I noticed that the suggested shortlist that we were presented with, and asked to consider, did not include Tommy Flowers, and it only included one woman, Hedy Lamarr, overlooking Ada Lovelace.

The panel were a great group of people who were obviously very passionate about the pioneers and about making sure that we chose the right people. After preliminary welcomes and introductions we got stuck straight in. We were told that the aim was to find a set of five pioneers that we were all happy with, and that the shortlist we had been given was not prescriptive but suggestive. A discussion commenced. When it came to the appropriate point in the discussion I said that I thought we should choose Ada Lovelace over Charles Babbage. It was quite a difficult argument to make, especially as at that point in time not that many people knew about Ada Lovelace and her contribution, whereas everyone had heard of Charles Babbage. But, fortunately, the rest of the panel listened to my reasoning and agreed that we should include Ada Lovelace.

I then spoke up for Tommy Flowers, who I also felt should be included. The panel, however, felt that we *must* include Alan Turing, and that to have two people from Bletchley Park would seem a bit skewed. I could see their point and demurred.

After a very long and lively discussion, our final list was as follows: Ada Lovelace, Alan Turing, Hedy Lamarr, Sir Tim Berners-Lee and Sir Clive Sinclair. We were interviewed about our choices and I said the following about the women that we had chosen:

"I am delighted that BCS is highlighting and celebrating key Information Pioneers and am particularly glad that these two great women Ada Lovelace and Hedy Lamarr have been chosen. These great films show us that women have made really fundamental contributions throughout history, let's make sure that we encourage and support women to continue playing a key role in this exciting area."

and about Alan Turing:

"Not only did Turing play a key role in the code breaking work carried out at Bletchley Park during World War Two, he also made fundamental and insightful contributions to computer science and elsewhere. Last year's very welcome government apology highlighted his lasting contribution and acknowledged his persecution and abhorrent treatment as a consequence of being gay, at a time when homosexuality was illegal. Honouring Turing as an Information Pioneer gives us a chance to celebrate Turing's life and legacy and promote him as a role model for information pioneers of the future."

I was happy that even though I hadn't completely got my way and managed to get Tommy Flowers included, I had managed to make sure that everyone on the panel now knew about Tommy – and we had 40 per cent representation from women!

A few weeks later I was invited one evening to a preview screening of the films near Goodge Street underground station. Five short films had been made with five celebrities, one for each pioneer; I couldn't wait to see them.

I met up with Kelsey, who had come down from Bletchley for the evening, and we went in together. Luckily I knew quite a few people there as

I had been involved with the BCS for some time and I'd also been on the judging panel. After picking up some drinks we circulated and chatted to various people. I introduced Kelsey to anyone that I thought might be useful to Bletchley Park. I felt that my role was to be like a warm up act for Kelsey or Simon whenever we were together at events. I would start or move a discussion to the topic of Bletchley Park, say what an amazing place it was, ask if had they visited, then introduce Simon or Kelsey to take the discussion further as they saw fit. It was an arrangement that worked well.

Kelsey Griffin and me at the Information Pioneers film preview

After a while it was time for the film previews, so we all trickled into the small cinema and took our seats. I sat with Kelsey behind Ortis Deley from *The Gadget Show* and Kate Russell from *Click*, two of the film stars. We watched the five films in succession: Ortis Deley spoke about Ada Lovelace, Kate Russell about Alan Turing, Miranda Raison about Hedy Lamarr, Phil Tufnell about Sir Tim Berners-Lee and Dom Joly about Sir Clive Sinclair.

James Thellusson from Glasshouse, who had spearheaded the initiative for the BCS, gave a short talk about the process, the panel and the films and then the lights were dimmed and the films began. They were all very good – entertaining, well written and interestingly presented and put together. I felt very proud to have played a small role in making them happen. When all five films had played we had a general discussion, with the director and writer answering questions about who had been chosen and why. It was very clear that everyone had really enjoyed the films and that they were excited to see what the public thought of them. It was a great evening.

© Lynda Freely at BCS

With Ortis Deley and Sarah Blow from GirlGeekDinners

Shortly afterwards the films were put up online, and featured in the media, and the public were asked to vote on their favourite over a period of a few weeks. The voting vacillated between the different pioneers during the voting period, but in the end there could only be one winner... who do you think it was? Who is the greatest information pioneer ever? It's a tough question to answer. (In case you're still wondering... the winner was Alan Turing.)

Initiatives such as BCS Information Pioneers may be seen as fluffy in comparison with the roles that these groundbreaking scientists played in our history. But I believe that this type of initiative, which gets information across in a way that is palatable and entertaining to the general public, is a great way to honour our pioneers. It is an important role of both traditional and social media to present important information in a way that helps us all to understand our history. Alan Turing, Ada Lovelace, Hedy Lamarr, Clive Sinclair and Tim Berners-Lee have all made important contributions to the world of technology, and campaigns such as the BCS Information Pioneers serve to help us all understand and be inspired by these contributions.

You can still see the films on the BCS Information Pioneers page: http://pioneers.bcs.org/

18

Colossus, Tutte and Flowers

"At the time I had no thought or knowledge of computers in the modern sense, and had never heard the term used except to describe somebody who did calculations."

—TOMMY FLOWERS

In November 1941, Bletchley Park experienced something of a panic.

The cause, as unlikely as it sounds, was a new detective novel called *N or M*, written by the world's greatest crime novelist, Agatha Christie. In the book, her plucky heroes, Tommy and Tuppence, are on the trail of Nazi spies working inside Britain. That in itself was hardly a problem for the staff of Station X. However, when this paragraph appeared at the end of Chapter 1, all kinds of alarms went off:

> "I always introduce my guests," said Mrs Perenna, beaming determinedly at the suspicious glares of five people. "This is our new arrival, Mr Meadowes – Mrs O'Rourke." A terrifying mountain of a woman with beady eyes and a moustache gave him a beaming smile. "Major Bletchley." Major Bletchley eyed Tommy appraisingly and made a stiff inclination of the head.

Mention of the name Bletchley in a book about spies was just too worrying a coincidence. To make matters worse, it was known that Christie was friends with Dilly Knox. MI5 immediately opened an investigation and sent agents to see Knox, suspecting that someone had perhaps been talking a little too openly about the work going on at BP. However, Knox was convinced that this was not the case and agreed to sound her out.

He therefore invited Christie to his home in Naphill in Buckinghamshire and, over tea and scones, asked why she had named her character Major Bletchley. She replied, "Bletchley? My dear, I was stuck there on my way by train from Oxford to London and took revenge by giving the name to one of my least loveable characters."[44]

This event happened at a time when Knox's cancer had started to take a serious toll on his health. When Christie visited him he was already so frail that he'd been forced to spend most of his time working at home with only very occasional trips to BP. He was never to see the allied victory he'd so brilliantly supported as the cruel disease finally claimed his life in February 1943. Knox's passing marked the end of an era for code breaking, an era that had relied heavily on linguistics, intuition and knowledge of human behaviour in which Dilly Knox and codebreakers like John Herivel excelled. Not that such work stopped; there were still plenty of the "old school" achieving extraordinary results and his colleague Peter Twinn took over the day-to-day management of the team, now known as ISK or "Intelligence Services Knox".

By 1943 the computer age had arrived. It was in answer to the hugely increased traffic in coded messages – far too many for pencil and paper-based "breaking machines". The most important ciphers that need to be cracked at this time were those used by the German High Command to relay messages between Hitler in Berlin and his commanders in the field. "We knew nothing about this cipher machine; the Germans had kept it completely secret," explains Tony Sale. "We first began to intercept radio transmissions in 1940. It was actually a group of policemen on the South Coast of England; they were listening for German agents' transmissions from within the UK – of course there weren't any as we'd captured all the agents – but they heard these weird signals and they sent them to Bletchley Park."

This was the fiendishly complex Lorenz cipher, generated by a machine attached to a teleprinter that cleverly used the teleprinter's binary language to produce a complex code. The codebreakers referred to these machines as "Fish". Individual models were then given specific fish-related names such as "Sturgeon' (the Seimens & Halske T52) and "Codfish" (the NoMo1). The Lorenz SZ40 and 42 models were codenamed "Tunny" and the places identified as transmission and receiving sites for Tunny messages were also given fishy names e.g. Bream (messages sent between Berlin and Rome), Mullet (between Berlin and Oslo) etc. Because Lorenz was so complex – it used twelve wheels compared to Enigma's three – it quickly became the High Command's cipher of choice. It therefore became paramount that the code be broken as soon as possible.

Efforts to break the Lorenz cipher using traditional methods were eventually successful, largely due to the efforts of three codebreakers: Brigadier John Tiltman, Major Ralph Tester and Cambridge graduate Bill Tutte. It was Tiltman who first recognised the importance of these messages and that they were coded using a letter substitution process known as the Vernam System. This fact became apparent after a German operator made a big mistake. On 31st August 1941, the operator sent two versions of the same message without resetting the machine in between. Because both were sent using the same key, it enabled comparison and analysis, which led Tiltman to the fact that Vernam was involved. A section was set up at BP, headed up by Tester and which became known as "The Testery", to work on breaking the system. But it was Bill Tutte, working meticulously through pages and pages of squared graph paper, writing out line after line of characters, who found the answer. Using a technique called Kasiski Examination, he built up a huge matrix of letters in which he could spot repetitions of sequences of characters that were more common than could be accounted for by chance alone. Over the course of several months, Tutte spent every working hour adding to the matrix – some of his colleagues even accused him of slacking off work to "fiddle with letters" – until, one day, the system revealed itself and the codebreakers could now crack the Lorenz cipher. To put Tutte's extraordinary feat into perspective: it's been calculated that without his efforts, it would have taken an operator 500,000,000,000 years to crack a message coded using Lorenz. As the result of his dogged perseverance and professionalism, that time was reduced to just four hours. It has rightly been called one of the greatest intellectual feats of World War II.

The Testery carried on attacking Tunny for the next twelve months and broke over 1.5 million coded messages. From mid-1943 onwards, the Testery is credited with breaking over 90 per cent of Tunny traffic and saving thousands of lives. For example, they were able to warn the Russians of the impending German assault on the city of Kursk allowing the Russians to prepare. The resulting tank battle – one of the largest in history – was a decisive victory for the Russians and has been called the turning point in their war. It would have been a very different story had the Germans retained the element of surprise.

Ralph Tester, Captain Jerry Roberts, Major Denis Oswald and Captain Peter Ericsson headed up a team that eventually employed nine cryptanalysts, 24 ATS[45] and a total staff of 118. However, even if they had taken on hundreds of extra staff, it would have been impossible for the Testery to keep up with the volume of intercepts and translations. Just as Turing had done with Enigma and the Bombe machines, the decoding of Lorenz needed to be mechanised. The man to whom this problem was passed was Professor Max Newman, a mathematician from Cambridge University. Taking Bill Tutte's findings on board, Newman and his team in "The Newmanry" began designing an automated version of Tutte's graph paper method, comparing ciphertext and key to look for departures from randomness.

The first machine they designed was nicknamed the "Heath Robinson" by its Wren operators due to its rather thrown-together arrangement of wheels and belts looking remarkably like one of the famous illustrator's gadgets.[46] Construction began in January 1943 and the first prototype was operating by June. Newman, Donald Michie, two engineers and sixteen Wrens kept the machine going. However, the machine was still too slow and the messages were piling up. Plus, having to run two punched paper tapes in unison at 1,000 characters per second meant that the tapes snapped, and the machines frequently broke down or got out of sync.

It was at this point that Alan Turing, who was aware of a brilliant engineer called Tommy Flowers who had done some sterling work in improving electronic telephone switchboard systems with thermionic valves, suggested that he be brought into BP to examine the problem. Flowers was a radical thinker, although he was in admiration of people like Turing who seemed to operate on a different, higher level to everyone else. He once said in a lecture, "You'd be working on a problem and not able to solve it, and sometimes someone would look over your shoulder and say 'Have you tried doing it like this?' and you'd think 'Of course, that's how you do it!'. With Turing, he'd say 'Have you tried doing it this way?' and you'd know that in a hundred years you would never have thought of doing it that way."

Flowers examined the problems with the Heath Robinsons and concluded that there was nothing that could be done to improve them or to decrease the amount of times they malfunctioned. He therefore suggested that maybe a new, different approach was needed. He suggested that the clunky, frequently malfunctioning, mechanical switching units used by the Heath Robinsons be replaced by valves. The valves could also act as memory storage, meaning that only one punched tape would be needed. At first his suggestion was met with scepticism by the codebreakers but he eventually persuaded them that it would work. However, time was against him; Flowers' estimate that a valve-based computer would take a year to build was simply unfeasible; in a war of this complexity and magnitude, the entire direction of the conflict could change in days, let alone a year. The decision was taken to "make do" with the Heath Robinsons and more were built.

But Flowers wasn't ready to give up on his idea yet. He returned to his laboratory and workshops at Dollis Hill in London and set to work. Ten months later, he and his team had built the prototype of his new type of machine. Weighing in at over a ton and filling most of a room, it was quickly dubbed Colossus. And, on the 8th December 1943, the machine was transported to Station X, set up and demonstrated to the codebreakers for the first time.

Colossus was a huge leap forward; it could run through the millions of possible settings for the code wheels on an enciphered teleprinter, such as Lorenz, at a staggering 5,000 characters a second – slow to us now but mind-blowing back then, and five times faster than the Heath Robinsons could ever hope to manage. The codebreakers immediately set about testing its accuracy and reliability. It passed on both counts, test after test after test.

Colossus would go on to make a huge impact in decoding enemy messages, but Flowers didn't sit back on his laurels. Having proven the worth of his concept, he was then asked to build a MKII Colossus with 2,500 valves rather than the 1,500 used in the MKI. He was also challenged to build it before June 1944. Although he wasn't immediately told what it was needed for, Flowers delivered on time and Colossus MKII, which ran even faster than the MKI, was tested and operational by June 1st. Just a few days later, the need for it became apparent when D-Day happened. The messages deciphered by the Colossus MKII proved beyond a doubt that the deception campaign designed by the War Office to throw Hitler off the scent had worked. It meant that the Normandy landings – or Operation Neptune – could go ahead as the Nazis had kept their Panzer tank divisions in Belgium, expecting a landing there.

By the end of the war, 10 MKIIs were operating at full capacity and 63 million characters of high-grade German messages had been decrypted.[47] Like the Bombes before them, much of the day-to-day operational work on both the Heath Robinsons and Colossi was done by women. "There were 1,500 wireless valves or more in each machine," recalls Lorna Fitch. "They looked a bit like light bulbs and the heat was terrific." But, at the close of hostilities, most of the Colossus machines were dismantled and the plans for them destroyed. Only two machines were retained and were moved firstly to Eastcote in West London to the first home of what became GCHQ and then to its current home in Cheltenham, Gloucestershire. One of the machines remained operational until 1960; it's been suggested that it was used to decode Russian traffic during the Cold War as the Soviets undoubtedly captured many of the Nazi's Enigma and Fish machines. It's generally felt among historians that the Russians were the reason that Churchill had everything destroyed when BP was run down.

Tommy Flowers recalls the day in 1960 when he was contacted to destroy the last two remaining Colossus machines: "That was a terrible mistake," he says. "I was instructed to destroy all the records, which I did. I took all the drawings and the plans and all the information about Colossus on paper and put it in the boiler fire. And saw it burn."

After the war, Flowers returned to the GPO and did research that led to the creation of modern day electronic telephone exchanges. He was also involved in creating ERNIE, the Post Office computer that randomly chose the winners in the monthly Premium Bonds draw. For his work during the war, he received an MBE and a paltry £1,000 award which didn't even cover the personal costs he'd accrued in building the first Colossus. As it was, he shared the money with the people who'd helped him build it. Somewhat ironically, he was then refused a bank loan to build another machine like Colossus because the bank didn't believe that such a machine could work. And, of course, he couldn't offer proof of concept as, just like everyone else at Station X, he could not talk about what he'd done during the war.

Tommy Flowers died in 1998, but not before his achievements were finally recognised, unlike so many BP veterans who passed away before their stories became known. What he built was, in effect, the first recognisable ancestor of all modern programmable computers. In time, the valves became transistors and the transistors became microchips but the basic concept has remained fairly constant, based on Turing's logic and Flowers' engineering.

There's a charming story about Flowers that appeared on the BBC's *Timewatch* series in 2013 during a programme about the codebreakers' work. In 1993, he attended a basic IT course at a college in Hendon, North London, and was presented with a certificate to prove it. He would have been 88 years old at the time.

None of his fellow students would have had an inkling that the gentle old man sitting with them in their classroom was the man who'd made modern computing possible.

19
Talk at BCS Wiltshire

I was now being invited to give talks not just around the UK but also overseas. Several BCS branches invited me to talk about Bletchley Park and the campaign that I had started. I had been campaigning for two years. Sometimes that made me unhappy; I got upset that the world, and particularly the UK Government and technology industry, had not come forward to completely sort out Bletchley Park's financial problems. I and now many others were putting a lot of time, effort and love into raising awareness of Bletchley Park's importance and rightful place as a key heritage site, promoting it as the "Geek Mecca". Why did everyone not feel the same way? But it was important to stay positive – things were moving along now and support was clearly increasing.

In June 2010 I gave a talk to the BCS Wiltshire branch in Swindon about my campaign. I always really enjoy giving talks to groups of people that I know will be supportive of the cause, and for a self confessed geek, a geek audience is ideal. The very knowledgeable Nick Miers from Bletchley Park, who knows all about Enigma and the Enigma machine had also been invited to speak. People had travelled from all over, including Pat Galea, who had been one our most active campaigners. Pat also has the most wicked sense of humour so is always a pleasure to interact with on Twitter. I got the train down to Swindon from London and arrived just before the start of the talk. The BCS Swindon Chair met me and introduced me to other members of the branch. What a lovely group of people they were!

I started my talk by describing my first visit to Bletchley Park in 2003. I couldn't believe that it had already been seven years. I then described my subsequent trip in 2008, the Women of Station X oral history project, and being interviewed by Rory Cellan-Jones for the BBC News. The story of the campaign was really the story of my life for the past few years; it was building into quite a long talk.

But then as soon as I had started, it seemed, it was over. The audience had some great questions about Turing, social media campaigning, the actual number of people that had worked there and the current financial situation at Bletchley. It was wonderful to feel the warmth that people who knew and understood the massive contribution made by those that had worked at Bletchley Park felt for the site.

Stay on the scene

Not long after my talk at BCS Wiltshire I gave another talk at OpenTech, which I'd spoken at the previous year. OpenTech is held on a Saturday in June every year. It's a great chance to catch up with the latest thinking in the alternative tech scene. To me the phrase "tech scene" used to conjure up images of middle-aged middle managers in suits doing deals with each other and then going down the pub. OpenTech is absolutely nothing like that. The speakers at OpenTech are free thinkers with innovative and sometimes radical ideas. They are also, in my experience, people who both understand tech *and* want to make the world a better place – people like Bill Thompson, Jamillah Knowles and Chris Vallance from the BBC. At OpenTech 2010 I was on a panel about women in tech with Suw Charman Anderson, Zoe Margolis and Janet Robinson. Later on I gave a talk about Bletchley Park and asked the audience to help in whatever way they could.

What *you* can do...

- Visit Bletchley Park, the "Geek Mecca" (only £10 for an annual pass)
- Have a look around the Bletchley Park website: www.bletchleypark. org.uk
- Pledge 1 days wages: http://www.pledgebank.com/work4bletchley
- Read all about my campaign: savingbletchleypark.org

- Donate money: www.justgiving.com/sueblack

- Watch the BCS Women of Station X video

- Follow @bletchleypark and @Dr_Black on Twitter, search term #bpark

- Check out the Bletchley Park annual reunion site: www.bletchleyparkreunion.info

- Attend the Station X social media cafes, details can be found by following @StationX on Twitter

- Talk to everyone you know about Bletchley Park. Have they been there? Do they know how important it was/is?

I had great conversations that night with the BBC's Bill Thompson, who had always been very supportive of Bletchley Park, and Cory Doctorow, who I had not met before. I spoke to Cory about how Bletchley could improve what they do in order to get more people interested, visiting the site and

Bill Thompson, me and Cory Doctorow at OpenTech

spreading the word. He said that he thought ecommerce was a massive opportunity for Bletchley and that geeks all over the world would love to buy merchandise of all sorts that came from Bletchley, but that frankly, at the moment, their merchandise was "all a bit shit".

After a bit of consideration, I unfortunately had to agree.

My first thought was that this was a trite point. To me it didn't really get to the heart of the matter. It was important to me that people realised the weight of the fundamental contributions that Bletchley had made to society both in terms of shortening the war and by serving as the birthplace of the computer. But, as I spoke to Cory, I suddenly realised that we didn't need everyone to think about Bletchley Park in the same way that I did. We weren't all the same. Some people might never fully understand the implications of what had happened at Bletchley – but they might still be willing to part with some cash to own something with Bletchley Park branding. It was important to reach this market as well. Having come from an academic background, I wasn't the most clued-up about marketing and branding, but the more I thought about it, the more sense it made.

I left OpenTech happy that the geek community knew about and were interested in Bletchley Park, and grateful for their ideas and support.

Papers, please

In 2006 I'd applied and been accepted for a Crucible Fellowship through the National Endowment for Science, Technology and the Arts (NESTA). The whole experience made me love NESTA, so I remained on the NESTA mailing list in the years that followed and quite often attended events there. In November 2010 I noticed they were holding an event as part of the Silicon Valley comes to the UK (or SVC2UK) programme. It sounded interesting, so I signed up and went along.

I was particularly happy to see that there was a female Google vice president, Megan Smith, speaking. She made some good points in her talk and I was glad that I had gone along to the event – it would have been worth it just to hear from her.

At the end of the event I went to get a drink and chat to a couple of friends. One of them was Karen Barber, who I'd met previously at Tuttle club – she was one of the people who had realised the potential of Twitter and social media before most other people had even heard of it. We spoke about the event and we were catching up on how everything was going in general. Of course the conversation turned to Bletchley Park and how the campaign was going. I told Karen that some of Alan Turing's papers had come up for auction at Christie's and that a journalist called Gareth Halfacree had set up a JustGiving account to try to raise the money to buy the papers for Bletchley Park. I wanted to help. The papers were up for auction for £300,000, and even though Bletchley didn't have that sort of money, I couldn't imagine a better place for them to be. Gareth had raised over £10,000 very quickly, but the auction was the following week and I couldn't see how he would make it to £300,000 in that time.

I remarked to Karen that I would really like to ask the Google VP who'd just spoken if perhaps Google could help with buying the Turing papers, but I was scared. Even through I was used to asking people to help Bletchley Park, I wasn't used to approaching top-ranking US Google executives and asking them for large sums of money! I desperately wanted to talk to her, but I was completely in awe and suddenly felt very shy.

Luckily, Karen persuaded me to go and speak to Megan. I gathered up my courage, approached Megan, and started up a conversation. Megan hadn't heard of Bletchley Park or Alan Turing, but when I started telling her more about them she seemed interested. I then asked her if Google would be interested in helping Bletchley Park to buy the Turing papers. She said that she would like more details and asked me to send her an email outlining what I was asking for with appropriate links so that she could check it out. After thanking her, I walked back to Karen to tell her what Megan had said. Although the conversation seemed to go well, I wasn't totally convinced that Megan had been genuinely interested – perhaps she was just being polite. After approaching hundreds of people over the last few years I had got very used to people asking me to send them an email, and then sending them an email only to never hear from them again. But, I was proud of myself: I'd asked a Google VP for help. It couldn't hurt to try – this was becoming my constant refrain for the campaign. That night I put together an email to Megan about Bletchley Park, Turing's papers and the auction I and sent it through.

I'm feeling lucky

The next day I got a direct message from someone at Google who was following me on Twitter. His name was Simon Meacham. Simon said that he had been meaning to get in touch with me for ages to offer to help with the campaign to save Bletchley Park but had been a bit busy. He was a Brit who had lived in the US for a long time, but he was was currently based in London at Google's offices in Victoria. We had a direct message conversation via Twitter during which I told him that I had met Megan Smith the day before. I told him about the Turing papers, the auction at Christie's and that I had sent Megan an email telling her all about the situation. Simon told me to send him the same email, and he would see what he could do. I felt excited – maybe Google would help out after all!

The next day I heard from Simon again. He had been in touch with Megan. He had also been in touch with the head of the UK office and he was really hoping that Google might be able to help.

Subject:	Google
From:	Simon Meacham
To:	Dr Sue Black
Sent:	18 November 2010

I have communications under way with Matt Britten (UK Country Manager for Google) and Megan Smith. Will keep you posted.

Best –
Simon

Meanwhile we were getting closer to the day of the auction. It was now Thursday evening and the auction was being held on the following Tuesday in London. Simon and I exchanged mobile numbers and many phone calls as he kept me updated on how things were progressing. I remember being in a car park on the Saturday taking a very excited call from Simon. He was calling to tell me that the Google UK office had approved some funding to help Bletchley Park buy the Turing papers. I was astounded. *This might actually happen*, I remember thinking. Incredible.

The next thing Simon needed to do was to get the funding amount approved by the main Google board in the US over the weekend. I had no idea how hard or easy that was going to be. Simon said that on a regular weekend, it might be fine, but this weekend was Thanksgiving, so chances were it might not happen. The Google board needed to convene an extraordinary meeting to approve the funds on Thanksgiving weekend. Simon said that he was really hoping that it would happen and that the funding request would go through, but this was probably the worst weekend of the year to try to make it happen.

I was desperately hoping that it might work out, but also trying not to get my hopes up too high as it seemed that time and public holidays were against us.

I spent Sunday wondering how things were progressing, hoping that the Google board were meeting to give the go ahead, and then thinking, *but why would they?* I was obviously very caught up in what was happening with the Turing papers, but how much did the Google board know or care about Bletchley and Turing? I went to bed Sunday night thinking that it probably wasn't going to happen.

On Monday morning my mobile rang. It was Simon.

"Hello Sue, good news! We got the money! The board met and they have approved $100,000 to go to Bletchley Park to put forward for the purchase of the Turing papers."

"Oh my God! Simon, that's amazing! I can't believe it, thank you SO much."

It was incredible news. $100,000 from Google towards the purchase was a substantial amount of money. I couldn't believe that the board had met up on Thanksgiving to make sure that it happened.

I phoned Kelsey at Bletchley Park. She was so surprised by the news that she thought it might be a scam. I persuaded her that it wasn't. We were one step closer to securing the papers.

Subject: $100,000 Grant Approval for the purchase of the Alan Turing papers

From:	Simon Meacham
To:	Dr Sue Black
Sent:	22 November 2010

Bletchley Park Trust
Attention: Sue Black
The Mansion
Bletchley Park
Milton Keynes
MK3 6EB

Dear Sue,

I am pleased to inform you that we've completed our review of your proposal and will recommend funding by the Google Inc. Charitable Giving Fund of Tides Foundation to the Bletchley Park Trust in the amount of $100,000 USD, as well as the use of our name, in order to support the purchase of the Alan Turing papers at auction (Christie's Lot 60 Sale 7882). This is a one (1) time grant. If for whatever reason you are unable to purchase the lot referenced above, Google will not recommend the grant to Bletchley Park Trust.

Your query returned 100,000 results

That day I wrote a blog post called "Bletchley Park needs you!", telling everyone what had happened and asking them to help make up the shortfall in funding between the amount that Bletchley Park now had and the amount that was needed to purchase the papers.

I had a chat with Gareth, who had started the JustGiving account; he said that there was now £18,000 from the public to help Bletchley buy the papers. So Bletchley had approximately £18,000 + $100,000. This was fabulous, but still nothing like the £300,000 needed to buy the papers. Both

Gareth and I phoned Christie's to ask them if anything could be done to somehow help Bletchley in this situation. Christie's told us:

> "At this late stage, Christie's would only consider withdrawing the lot from sale if the appeal were to make a serious offer. This would have to be at the high estimate, £500,000, and any offer made would be subject to Christie's buyer's premium (25% of the bid price up to and including £25,000 and 20% of the excess of the hammer price up to £500,000)."

I wasn't impressed with their response. I suppose looking back on the situation now, what else did I expect Christie's to do? They are in the auction business to make money. But at the time I thought their statement was absolutely outrageous. I ended my blog post thus:

> Hmmm… thanks very much Christie's.
>
> So, over to you… can you help? We have until 2pm tomorrow to raise the money to save Turing's papers so that they can be housed at Bletchley Park where they belong. I can't bear to think of them being taken overseas and held in a private collection. Can you?
>
> Please help Bletchley Park to buy these papers, to keep them where they belong, in the UK, at Bletchley Park, where we can all go and see them any time we want. Where Newman and Turing worked side by side, day after day, helping to save millions of lives.
>
> We owe it to them, don't we?

My blog post was linked to and quoted widely in the press and tweeted and retweeted on Twitter. I had a huge number of views on my blog that day, second only to the time a couple of years before when Stephen Fry had tweeted a link to my blog and caused me to get eight thousand hits. This time it was around five thousand. Incredible. There was obviously a lot of support for what we were trying to do. But would Bletchley actually get the Turing papers? All would be revealed at the auction the next day…

That's a lot, we'll give it a shot

The day had finally arrived. The auction began at 2pm at Christie's auction rooms in Mayfair, London. I had never been to an auction before, so I was very excited to see what it was actually like.

Once I'd got to Christie's and found the auction room, I went over and sat down next to BBC technology correspondent Rory Cellan-Jones at the front of the room. What really struck me was how fast everything moved and how much money was changing hands. I guess that is to be expected, but it wasn't until I was sitting right in the middle of it all that I really understood how exciting – and nerve-racking – it could be. There were lots of people standing at the front and side of the room on their mobile phones and at laptops bidding on the lots that were coming up. I felt a bit like I'd walked on to a film set.

The auction was Sale 7882, the sale of valuable printed books and manuscripts, including an album of Faraday's "Deflagrations of Gold, and other metals, on vellum", which sold for £32,450, and an Enigma machine, which sold for £67,250.

The Turing papers were Lot 60, which were due to come up at about 3pm. I had been keeping in touch with everyone on Twitter throughout the day about the auction and it was starting to feel like we were all going crazy with excitement together. I was so hyper-excited by the time the lot came up that I thought I was going to pass out!

The auctioneer at Christie's

When it came to Lot 60, the Turing papers, the auctioneer described the lot to the audience and then said something to the effect of:

"...and bidding starts at £170,000..."

I was horrified. I knew that Bletchley Park only had about £87,000 in the kitty, so the fact that bidding had started at £170,000 meant that Bletchley had no chance at all of winning the lot. My mind went into a bit of a tail-spin. I don't know what I had expected, but being out of the game before it had begun hadn't featured in any of the scenarios that I had imagined. I was still coming to terms with what had happened when, after only a few seconds... it was all over. It had been so fast that I didn't even know what had happened. I knew that the bidding had stopped at £240,000, but I didn't know why. Had the Turing papers been sold? Thanks to friends on Twitter and Rory sitting next to me, I found out that the seller's reserve price had not been met. But what did that mean for the papers and for Bletchley Park? I had no idea.

While I was sitting with my mind whirling away, an Apple-1 had been selling for £133,250, and well known Apple co-founder Steve Wozniak had been sitting at the back of the room.

Steve Wozniak at Christie's

But in spite of the excitement and the atmosphere around me, I left the room feeling quite depressed. I found someone to talk to from Christie's who gave me the details of an administrator to contact regarding the non-sale of the Turing papers. I then went back upstairs to see what was happening. There were a lot of press setting up their cameras in an ante room, waiting for Steve Wozniak to join them for a press conference. I stayed and watched and then did a quick interview with Rory before leaving and making my way to the Google offices in Victoria.

I wanted to go over to Google to say thank you, especially to Simon Meacham and Megan Smith, for supporting Bletchley Park in their bid. I arrived expecting a cup of tea and a quick chat, but was whisked into a large meeting of Google software engineers, given a microphone, and asked to tell everyone what had just happened. I was surprised, but it was nice to be able to share the news, and I really felt from the software engineers in the audience that they cared about the Turing papers and about Bletchley Park. It was a great moment in the midst of a stressful day.

After I had finished speaking Simon took me to the Google canteen and we sat for about two hours chatting about what had happened over the last few days. Looking back on it I realised it had been quite crazy. We had only known each other about six days, and just through Twitter at that, but we had shared a bit of a roller coaster ride. That kind of experience can be very bonding, and after we had debriefed about the Turing papers, our conversation turned to ourselves. We chatted for ages about life, the universe and everything. Simon was also really hoping that I would be able to meet up with Megan again. It turned out she was not only still in the UK, but also in the building that day. Luckily Megan had time to come and say hi, which was great as it was my conversation with Megan less than a week previously which had kickstarted this whole thing. Megan is, like me, passionate about getting more girls and women interested in science, technology, engineering and mathematics (STEM) and in empowering everyone through technology. We also of course talked about Bletchley Park, and Megan said that if she and Google could help Bletchley when they spoke with Christie's, they would be very happy to do so. I thanked Megan and said that I would let Simon Greenish at Bletchley know about this kind offer.

After a few hours I made my way home. What an exhilarating day. The auction had been so crazily exciting, and the story wasn't over yet. I wondered what was going to happen to the Turing papers.

In November 2010 I sent 1731 tweets

20

The USA at Bletchley

"The 6812th reached a degree of efficiency far above the greatest expectations. When operations ceased on VE day the Detachment was averaging in output runs per day approximately 38% above that of the British units engaged in the same work. This seems almost incredible when it is understood that the British had the benefits of four years of experience. From the beginning of operations to VE Day the 6812th Signal Security Detachment found the solutions to a total of 425 German Enigma Keys."

—FROM A 1945 REPORT[48]

People are often surprised to hear that the Americans had a presence at Bletchley Park. After all, the "special relationship" that now exists between the UK and the US didn't really exist back then. In fact, despite their last conflict being the War of 1812, both countries still viewed each other with some suspicion up until WWI. While most historians report that Churchill and Roosevelt got on very well, the military commanders from both sides didn't see quite so eye-to-eye. In both wars, it took an act of aggression against the USA, rather than a plea from the UK, to bring America into the conflict. But while things may have been frosty beforehand, WWII was what brought the two nations together as friends and allies.

From a time before the opening of hostilities, the UK and US had an agreement to share whatever intelligence they had that might benefit the other. It is known, for example, that Alan Turing went to America during wartime to act as a liaison and to pass on tools and techniques in person rather than by transmission. According to Bletchley Park's own official

history: "In the British archives there is no intelligence of any importance that was not available to the Americans." So when the US entered
the war in 1941, it was only sensible that a contingent of US codebreakers
and communications staff come to Bletchley Park to learn all they could,
especially about the Japanese use of ciphers. It wasn't the Americans'
first visit to meet the codebreakers; a full year before in 1940, a small
team of four cryptographers had come to Station X to look at how the
place worked. The Scottish dancing Hugh Foss and Oliver Strachey had
broken the Japanese diplomatic codes back in 1934 and John Tiltman had
figured out the Japanese military ciphers in 1938. With trouble brewing in
the Pacific, America was watching Japan very closely.

The codebreakers all got on splendidly by all accounts. However,
the visit did end on a sour note. The American government was willing to share the decryption machine they'd built, called "Purple", with
the British, but British Intelligence and Alastair Denniston were unwilling to share Alan Turing's Bombe. It is not known precisely why the
UK was unwilling to reciprocate, particularly as they'd already handed
over a great deal of code breaking knowledge and experience. Consen-
sus among historians seems to suggest that it was simply that American
security – they were not yet in a state of war – was more lax than British
security, and it was known that enemy spies were operating in the USA.

But while, at a diplomatic level, things would remain frosty for a
while, the codebreakers continued to enjoy a close, working transatlantic
relationship and even friendships. As previously mentioned, Alan Turing
went over to America in 1942 to share some of his knowledge and to
make new contacts that could prove useful to the work at Station X.

The situation did eventually resolve itself – partly due to the American people's great respect and liking for Winston Churchill – and the
British and American security agencies signed an agreement to share
information. America could now build its own Bombes, based on Turing's designs. The first two were called Adam and Eve and were built in
Dayton, Ohio.

Meanwhile, it seemed practical to send a contingent of US troops
and codebreakers to work at Bletchley Park. The first wave was under
the command of Captain William Bundy. He went on to join the CIA,

become President Dwight D Eisenhower's staff director at the Commission on National Goals, and become foreigner affairs advisor to John F Kennedy and Lyndon B Johnson. He was a major player in planning the Vietnam War and in trying to prevent its escalation. Despite a glittering career, in a 1999 BBC interview he stated: "Although I have done many interesting things and known many interesting people, my work at Bletchley Park was the most satisfying of my career." His and his colleagues' journey to the UK was not without incident; not only were they wary of attracting the attentions of the U-boat "Wolf Packs", but their cover story – that they were messenger pigeon experts employed by the Signal Corps was sufficiently outlandish to have raised the suspicions of an officer checking their papers. "They asked us if we'd passed the Army General Classification Test because they couldn't find our scores on our records," explains maths graduate and cryptographer Arthur J Levenson, selected by Bundy to be a member of the 6811th Signal Company and posted to BP. "They said, 'Would you mind taking the test?' and we said – there were five of us – 'No, we don't mind.' So we took the test and this sergeant graded them and he came back to us and said ,'Holy raccoon! What scores! You guys ought to be in Intelligence!'"

Levenson worked on Enigma and Tunny in Hut 6 and, after the war, was part of a joint British and American team who were sent to Germany to find and secure any leftover cipher equipment and to question their German cryptographer counterparts. In a 1999 PBS documentary called *Mind of a Codebreaker*, Levenson says, "I don't think I'd ever met an Englishman in my life until that point. I'd been full of stereotypes, that they were distant and had no sense of humour. But these were the most outgoing, wonderful people. They fed us, it was quite a sacrifice for them, and there were just enough screwballs there to be real fun."

The arrival of the Americans and their ease in joining existing teams was surprisingly smooth. In his memoir, *Top Secret Ultra*, Head of the Air Section Peter Calvocoressi wrote, "A Colonel Telford Taylor was introduced into Hut 3, the first of our American colleagues. He already knew a great deal about Ultra and it seemed to take him no more than a week to master what we were up to. Others of similar calibre followed. They too were temporarily mobilised civilians and their backgrounds were roughly comparable with our own except that there were rather more lawyers among them than among us. They were slotted into our various sections and in next to no time they were regular members of those sections". He goes on to say, "The addition of the American contingent was so smooth that we hardly noticed it. Presumably this was in part due to the sense of common purpose but it must also have owed more than we realised at the time to the personalities and skills of the first Americans to arrive and of the head of Hut 3 and his peers elsewhere in BP." And Colonel Telford Taylor later wrote, "I cannot adequately portray the warmth and patience of the Hut 3 denizens in steering me around and explaining the many aspects of the work. I take pride at the ease, goodwill, and success with which the merging was accomplished by Britons and Americans alike." Taylor later caused a scandal by having an affair with a married British cryptographer called Christine Brooke-Rose (who later became a very well-respected experimental writer).

It was almost inevitable that the glamorous new visitors would be attractive to the young staff of Station X, many of whom had only ever seen or heard Americans on the Big Screen. And the Americans weren't oblivious to the charms of the female BP staff either. One of Tommy Flowers' colleagues on the building of Colossus, Harry Fensom, told an Enigma symposium in 1992: "A visiting American lieutenant said that the buildings contained marvellous machines and many attractive ladies. The machines were made by the British Tabulating Company and the ladies by God." But that's not to say that this was always an excuse for bad behaviour; the work was hard, the world was more repressed than it is today, and contraception wasn't as freely available. People tended to be more reserved and faithful. In Marion Hill's *Bletchley Park People*, she quotes an unnamed American soldier, who says: "We were 100 American men, at least half of whom worked side by side with the natives, many of them female. In the community at large, there was a shortage of men, many of the local lads being away in the service. Consequently, Americans were always invited to dances. At least half of us were married, but there is little evidence we forgot it." The fact that the British and the American staff got on very well is evidenced by there having been only one major falling out. Barbara Abernethy recalls a bat and ball game played with a broom handle and a ball. Both teams went in to bat but, at the end of play, there was some confusion. "We all clapped each other on the back and the Americans said 'We're sorry we beat you,'" says Barbara, "But then the British captain said, 'I'm sorry but we beat you.' So the Americans asked what rules we played by. And we said, 'Our rules.'" It is entirely possible that, during the match, the Americans were playing baseball while the British were playing rounders.

The Americans became very good at their job. Arthur J Levenson claims that sometimes the teams at BP deciphered the German messages before German forces in the field could read them. In one instance, on the eve of D-Day, a message from Rommel stated that German tanks were being sent to a location in Normandy where US paratroopers were due to land. "They were going to drop one of the airborne divisions right on top of a German tank division," says Levenson. "They would have been massacred."[49] Once again, brilliant work by the staff at BP prevented a tragedy.

For the Americans, the breaking of the Japanese ciphers was a major factor in their eventual victory. At the Battle of Midway, one of the most decisive battles of the war in the Pacific, the Japanese fleet intended to lure US aircraft carriers into a trap, believing that a second damaging attack – Pearl Harbor having been the first – would demoralise and weaken the US military. However, because American codebreakers had discovered the plot, the American fleet led by Admirals Chester W Nimitz, Frank Jack Fletcher, and Raymond A Spruance were able to set up an ambush of their own. The result was that a heavy cruiser and four Japanese aircraft carriers, the *Akagi, Kaga, Soryu* and *Hiryu*, all of which had taken part in the attack on Pearl Harbor, were sunk. The Americans lost just two ships. Midway was the turning point in US fortunes as Japan was unable to recover from its losses.[50]

The American codebreakers were also helpful to the Allies in Europe too. Before the breaking of the German high command's Lorenz cipher, there was a short period in which Britain was in the dark. However, the Americans were deciphering messages from the Japanese high command and discovered that the Japanese ambassador in Berlin was reporting home whenever he spoke to Hitler and his closest confidantes.

Consequently, many German secrets were given away third party. In one memorable instance, the Japanese military attaché was given a tour of the defences in Normandy shortly before Operation Neptune in June 1944. His subsequent report to the ambassador – which included a very detailed description of the size and extent of the German defences – was transmitted to Tokyo and, without them knowing, to Bletchley Park.

It was staggeringly useful intelligence for the forthcoming D-Day landings.

21

A relationship with Google

December came and went, and all too soon it was a new year. 2011. I was now a member of the Fundraising Committee at Bletchley Park and was excited about finally being involved in a formal way with helping to secure Bletchley Park's future.

In November of 2010 I had begun speaking with Google about supporting Bletchley Park, and they had given Bletchley $100,000 to put towards bidding for the Turing papers. I knew instinctively that Bletchley Park having a relationship with Google was a good thing, but the Fundraising Committee weren't so sure. At the first meeting I attended, when I suggested that the Bletchley Park Trust (BPT) should build up a relationship with Google, Kelsey and several committee members spoke against the idea, saying that, amongst other things, Google was not a "clean brand" and thus we should not have anything to do with them. Luckily it was not only me speaking for a relationship with Google. Simon Greenish realised the potential power that working with Google would give us, and between the two of us we managed to persuade the rest of the committee to accept and develop the relationship.

Following on from Google's $100,000 donation, Simon Meacham from Google had introduced me to Peter Barron, who was the new Head of Press and PR for Google EMEA. On 17th January 2011 I took Peter up to Bletchley Park for his first visit and a meeting with Simon and Kelsey. Simon gave an overview of the history of Bletchley Park up to the present day and described the current financial situation.

One moment during the meeting that made us all laugh was, when discussing the massive increase in visitor numbers to Bletchley Park over

Simon Greenish, Peter Barron, me and Kelsey Griffin in the Ballroom

the last few years, both Simon Greenish and Kelsey Griffin pointed to me and said, "It's all your fault!!"

I'm very happy to be blamed for that.

We had a good initial discussion about Google and Bletchley Park developing a relationship. Peter asked Simon to send him a list of things that needed funding around the Park for him to have a look through and see what they could do. That sounded very promising.

Simon and Kelsey took us for the obligatory tour around Bletchley Park

Me, Peter Barron and Simon Greenish in front of Hut 6

On the way back to London after a
successful trip to Bletchley Park

and as usual I learned even more interesting facts about the place. I never
tire of touring the Park. There is so much to know and understand about
what happened there and the implications over the years.

When the tour finished Peter and I said our goodbyes and got the train
back to London. We discussed our meeting and potential funding possibilities. It was the first time that I'd met Peter. I really liked him. A smart,
friendly and interesting chap, I found out that he had previously been the
editor of BBC's current affairs flagship programme *Newsnight*.

When we reached Euston Peter and I parted, agreeing to meet up
again once he had received the necessary information from Simon. I went
home feeling very positive about the relationship and the possibilities that
opened up if Google became involved with saving Bletchley Park.

Straight out of Compton Street

One of the really cool people I've met through the campaign is Patrick
Sammon, President of Story Center Films. Patrick is from the US and is a
big fan of Alan Turing – such a big fan that he decided a few years ago
that he wanted to get a documentary made about Turing, his life and his

contributions to the world. I'd first met Patrick at Balans restaurant on Old Compton Street in London in 2010 for a drink and a chat while he was visiting the UK to talk to people about making the documentary. It was obvious that we were kindred spirits who share a love of Alan Turing and great respect for his legacy. This is what Patrick said about Alan Turing and the documentary:

"As you know, Alan Turing was the British WWII code breaker and father of computer science who faced persecution for being gay. In his short life, Turing profoundly changed our world. Historians believe that his WWII code breaking work helped save millions of lives and shortened the war by two years. He also founded three new scientific fields: computer science, artificial intelligence, and morphogenesis.

"In 1952, he was arrested by British police for having a relationship with another man and eventually was forced to undergo chemical castration to 'fix' his sexual orientation. Two years after his arrest, Turing killed himself at age 41. Turing is one of the most important scientists ever, yet his tragic story and lasting legacy remain largely unknown. This film will change that fact.

"Almost 100 years after his birth, an international production team is set to take viewers on a journey to rediscover Alan Turing. Research and development for this feature-length drama documentary is underway, with plans to reach millions of viewers around the world through broadcast and theatrical release. The international production team includes Turing's pre-eminent biographer Dr Andrew Hodges. Funding is currently being lined up for the film, with a goal for completion in mid-2012, to coincide with the centenary of Turing's birth. It's an important story that needs to be told."

I thought that making a documentary about Turing was a great idea and offered to connect Patrick to people and organisations that might be able to help. One thing that I really do love doing is connecting people and organisations to make things happen. It really is true that if you can bring the right people together, incredible things can happen – my work on the Save Bletchley Park campaign had certainly taught me that. I wrote a blog post about Turing, Patrick and the film, and I introduced Patrick to Peter Barron at Google in the hope that he would be interested in helping Patrick make the film a reality. Google ended up hosting the premiere of *Codebreaker* at BAFTA!

Turing papers saved

Between November 2010 and February 2011 I had several conversations with Simon Greenish, Google and others about securing the Turing papers for Bletchley Park. There was a lot of activity going on in the background, some of which I was party to and some of which I wasn't. From my perspective, it seemed like things were reasonably positive and that hopefully the Turing papers would be secured for Bletchley, but there was the dual problem of reaching the funding target and making sure that a better offer wasn't accepted by the seller. All that we knew about the seller was that they lived in Canada and wanted to remain anonymous.

I was delighted, therefore, to get a call from Simon Greenish one day

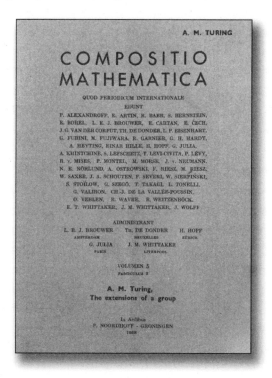

in February letting me know that the Turing papers had been secured for Bletchley Park.

Simon and others had been working quietly away, finding funding from the Heritage Memorial Fund and a private donor to meet the price that the anonymous seller was asking. The local Member of Parliament, Iain Stewart MP, had asked a question about the papers as part of Prime Minister's Questions in December:

> Iain Stewart MP addressing David Cameron:
> "Will my Right Honourable Friend do all he can to secure these important papers for the nation?"
> Prime Minister David Cameron replied:
> "I would certainly like to do that… of course, I hope private donors will generously support the fundraising campaign and I'm happy to work with him to do all I can to make it happen."

It was wonderful to see so many people picking up the mantle.

A few days later I went up to Bletchley Park with Peter Barron from Google to finally get a glimpse of the papers and to meet the other people who had played a role in making sure that they ended up at Bletchley Park. One of the great moments of the day was meeting Gareth, who had set up the JustGiving page and raised almost £20,000 towards the papers. Throughout the build-up to the auction we had been in touch regularly, so it was great to finally meet up and reminisce about the excitement we had felt.

I also got to meet Julian Wilson, who looked after the papers at Christie's, and Iain Stewart MP. Along with Peter Barron, we all had a chat about the parts that we had individually played in ensuring that the Turing papers ended up at Bletchley Park. Gareth had started the whole thing off and set up the JustGiving site, I had brought in the $100,000 from Google, Julian had emailed *The Pink Paper* with the story to try to increase coverage, and Iain had asked the question in Parliament. After we went around telling our stories, I remarked on something that I found very interesting – each of us had said a variation of the same thing: "I didn't know what the chances of success were, but I just thought, 'Sod it!' and decided

Codebreaker Max Newman's family visitors' book

Max Newman's family visitors' book close up,
including Turing's signature

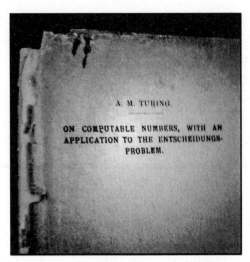

"On Computable Numbers" by Alan Turing

to give it a go." During my years of campaigning to save Bletchley Park, I'd had that thought many times – it just goes to show that it's important to take chances sometimes!

Another highlight of the day was meeting Professor William Newman, son of codebreaker Max Newman, and hearing his stories about Alan Turing, who had beenone of Max's good friends. He told a particularly wonderful story about Turing running ten miles to their house one morning and, on finding no one in, writing a message using a leaf and a twig and putting it through the letterbox in the front door.

I spent some time looking at the Turing papers, which were laid out over a very large table. I walked around the table and took a few photos; a tear in my eye thinking about Turing, his genius, and the awful way that he had been treated. It was wonderful that we had all worked together to bring the Turing papers to Bletchley Park, but everything to do with Turing was always tinged with sadness due to the fact that he was never publicly appreciated in his lifetime for his enormous contribution.

Something else that Julian said during the day really captured my attention. Apparently the massive amount of support on Twitter in November, just before the auction at Christie's, really made a difference to what had happened in the auction room. Christie's were expecting bids of well over £300,000 for the Turing papers, but the bidding stopped under that and the papers did not meet the reserve. Julian said that several of the people who had been planning to bid for the Turing papers held back because they didn't want to take the papers away from Bletchley Park.

I was thrilled that once again the voices of supporters on Twitter had made some tangible difference to the campaign. Acquiring the Turing papers for Bletchley Park was a great example of many people and communities, online and offline, working to achieve a common aim. The spirit of the thousands of people that had worked at Bletchley Park during the war lived on.

Don't halt me now

Over the last few months, a number of people had asked me why Turing's papers were important. What was it about them that made them so valuable, and why was it meaningful for Bletchley Park to have them? I found myself only able to answer in very general terms, so I asked Christie's Books and Manuscripts specialist Julian Wilson, who had handled the papers at auction, if I could interview him to get a definitive answer. Julian agreed, so I set off one afternoon to meet him for a coffee and then interviewed him in his office at Christie's auction house in Mayfair.

Julian's office was up a back staircase and was full of books and other artefacts. I nosed around a little bit; it was obvious from the room that he enjoyed what he did. I thought the best way to record the interview would be on Audioboo (now audioBoom), an audio recording app which is very easy to use and automatically uploads your audio file to your account on its website. I told Julian that I would introduce us and ask him a question about the Turing papers, and then he just needed to answer within about five minutes. Julian explained how extremely rare the Turing papers are, their connection to the leading thinking in mathematics and computer science at the time, and why his scholarly paper "On computable numbers with an application to the Entscheidungsproblem" is of the utmost international importance for the history of the science of computing. As Julian put it:

"This collection of offprints is really important for a number of different reasons. I think the first thing to stress is just how rare these offprints are. There's been quite a lot of confusion surrounding these; a lot of people think that they're manuscript material – in fact they're not, they are actually printed, but they are so rare that they might as well be unique. […] The collection was assembled by Professor Max Newman, who was a very close scientific colleague and one of the true friends of Alan Turing – and of course in connection with Bletchley Park, Max Newman was the co-inventor of the Colossus. So for Bletchley this really does have everything. It has the founding theoretical paper of comput-ers, owned by somebody who I think could and should be seen as the father of the practical application of the computer."

If you are interested in listening to the full interview, you can hear it online - http://bit.ly/1O7ISDn

Riding techie

At some point Robert Llewellyn and I had become aware of each other on Twitter. Robert is an actor, famous for appearing as Kryten in *Red Dwarf*, amongst other things. In early 2011 Robert got in touch with me to ask if I would be interested in appearing on his *Carpool* programme. The format for *Carpool* is an interview by Robert during a journey in his Prius hybrid car. Robert picks you up and takes you somewhere that you would like to go, interviewing you along the way. He has interviewed some of my favourite people, including Jo Brand, Stephen Fry, and many other comedians and techy people. So I was excited when Robert emailed me saying that he would like to interview me for *Carpool* sometime in the spring, and could I please have a think about where I would like to go?

We decided on a trip from my office at UCL to – you guessed it – Bletchley Park, and arranged a date and time to suit us both. When the date arrived, I headed to my office to meet Robert at midday. It was a lovely spring day and all the leaves on the trees in Gordon Square were glinting in the sunlight – perfect conditions for a trip to Bletchley Park.

I saw Robert sitting in his Prius outside my office. He showed me the cameras that were placed around the car to record the interview; they are tiny and after no time at all I had forgotten they were there.

We drove around Gordon Square and up to the Euston Road, then along Edgware Road and up to the M1. There was quite a lot of traffic – I don't know how Robert manages to hold a cogent conversation and navigate through traffic at the same time. It's quite a skill! The interview was completely open in terms of subject matter; I could have talked about any aspect of my career or my passion for encouraging more girls and women to go into computing, but I wanted to focus on Bletchley Park as I knew that this interview would be put online and viewed by a large audience. Although Bletchley Park was in a much better place than it had been in 2008, it still needed support, and I was still in campaign mode.

Robert asked me to tell him how I had got involved with Bletchley Park, and so began a two-hour conversation. Along with recounting my first few visits to Bletchley Park and describing my desire to do something to help, I also told Robert some of the stories told to me by female veterans. One lady from Scotland had been put forward by her school headmaster. She had never left home before leaving for Bletchley Park at the age of 18. She arrived with a group of girls and they were all taken to one of the blocks at Bletchley after being picked up from the station. They had been surprised to find that their block was guarded by a soldier with a gun. The girls worked eight-hour shifts around the clock in huts that were freezing cold in the winter and boiling hot in the summer. In the winter they sat wrapped up in thick blankets, as there was no heating at all. They were teenage girls away from home for the first time, working hard, in complete secrecy and sometimes in poor conditions. And yet they were still able to really enjoy themselves in the evenings, getting up to all sorts of harmless mischief. I told Robert about the RAF pilots flying low over Woburn Abbey to see the topless WRNS – such a great story.

We arrived at Bletchley Park just after 2pm and were met by Simon Greenish who took us for a whistle-stop tour. We got the edited highlights edition as we only had 45 minutes before we had to leave. Simon took us to the canteen in Hut 4 first for a lunch of sausage and mash, then into the Mansion House, up to see Colossus, into Hut 8 for a quick peek at Alan Turing's old office and then down to see the Bombe machine rebuild and the slate statue of Alan Turing. Then we thanked Simon, said our goodbyes

Me and Robert Llewellyn at Bletchley Park

and got back into Robert's car.

It had been a short visit but I felt confident that Robert had got a good sense of the general ambience of Bletchley Park, and I hoped he might come back and encourage others to do the same.

The drive back to London took another two hours, during which time we carried on the conversation about Bletchley Park. Now that Robert had seen it first-hand he was, like most people who actually visit, really excited about the place. It really does have an atmosphere which is palpable when you're there but difficult to put into words. It's clear that something quite extraordinary happened there. How wonderful to still be able to walk around the lake, knowing that Alan Turing, Tommy Flowers, Winston Churchill and so many incredible people had spent a lot of time and energy there.

The video of our trip is on YouTube - http://bit.ly/1RVUw3o

Secret Days

On 15th April 2011 I was invited to a book launch at Bletchley Park. Lord Asa Briggs, who had been stationed at Bletchley during the war, had written *Secret Days: Codebreaking in Bletchley Park* and had personally invited me to the launch in the Ballroom at Bletchley. I was very excited to attend as I had not met Lord Briggs before and was really interested to hear his memories of his time at Bletchley. I was also delighted to find that Lord Briggs had mentioned me in his book, noting that I had led a social media campaign to raise awareness of Bletchley Park.

At the beginning of the event Simon Greenish welcomed us all and introduced Lord Briggs, who spoke for some time about his involvement at Bletchley Park. It was very affecting to hear him talk about how important it had been to keep his work secret:

> "I felt very reluctant to reveal secrets, even after Winterbottom had
> written his book in the 1970s. When I got married in 1955, I didn't
> dare to tell anything to my wife about what I had done at Bletchley.
> Occasionally people would come up to me in the street in London and
> say, 'It's nice to see you back from Hut 6 again,' and Susan [Lord Briggs'
> wife] would say to me 'What in the world was Hut 6?' I could tell her
> that I had been at Bletchley, but I couldn't tell anything about what
> happened in Hut 6. In fact it is most interesting that during the war,

Lord Asa Briggs and me at Bletchley after his book launch

I couldn't tell my mother and father anything about what I had been doing... it wasn't the Official Secrets Act that made me keep secrets, it was a feeling that these secrets had to be kept if we were going to win the war."

Incredible campaign news

Bletchley Park's situation was strengthening by the day, with more interest from the media, higher visitor numbers and a higher profile generally. I was still spending most evenings and weekends raising awareness through tweeting and chatting to everyone I met – looking back now I can see that I was absolutely obsessed, but at the time these things had just become part of my normal routine.

During my talks about Bletchley Park and the campaign to save it, I always asked the audience if they had visited. I was now noticing that more and more people were putting their hands up and saying yes. The demographic of people interested in Bletchley Park was also shifting; it now seemed to be a much younger and geekier crowd.

I was also very happy that the relationship between Google and Bletchley Park had been moving along. I'd had several discussions with Peter Barron and others at Google around what needed to be funded and how Google could potentially help.

In the spring of 2011, Peter and I went up to Bletchley for a regular meeting to discuss Google's continuing relationship with Bletchley Park. We discussed where we were with various issues, and as part of the conversation I used the phrase "saving Bletchley Park". To my surprise, Simon Greenish interrupted,

"Hold on, Bletchley Park is saved! There is no way that we are going to shut now with all the support we have. What we need to talk about now is building Bletchley Park for the future."

A massive smile spread across my face. I had been so caught up in campaigning and raising awareness that I hadn't stepped back and realised that, yes, Simon was right. With the amount of publicity and support generated, the interest from the media, and visitor numbers going up steadily, Bletchley Park was no longer under threat of closure. It was a wonderful moment, and it was amazing how it had snuck up on me. Three years of campaigning, with thousands of people getting involved. And it had actually worked.

I sat there through the rest of the meeting, nodding and interjecting where appropriate, but my mind was whizzing around at 100 miles per hour. Bletchley Park was saved. SAVED! The best way to describe how I felt is that it was like the feeling demonstrated in cartoons when you see a character get hit over the head with something and stars appear around its head. I was shocked. I was over the moon. The words *Bletchley Park is saved*, *Bletchley Park is SAVED* ran on a constant fast tape around and around my head, a bit like the paper tape used in the Colossus. *BLETCHLEY PARK IS SAVED!*

In May 2011 I sent 1819 tweets

22
D–Day

"Without Bletchley, the D-Day landings might well have been a catastrophic failure and the forces could have been thrown back into the sea."

—PROFESSOR SIR HARRY HINSLEY OBE

We've all heard of D-Day.[51] But less well-known is the Pas-de-Calais Gambit of 1944, also called Operation Bodyguard. It was something that Bletchley Park very much had a hand in.

Following the Trident Conference in Washington, DC, in May 1943, plans were drawn up by the Allies for a massed channel crossing of troops into Europe with the goal of liberating France, pushing on to Berlin and ending the war. It was to be called Operation Overlord. But first, there was the tricky business of pulling together the troops and resources needed, picking a date and appropriate landing site, and getting everyone and everything safely across the English Channel without the Germans noticing. The obvious solution was to wrong-foot the German high command by a campaign of disinformation.

The Allies had already had some success with this tactic. "We read all the Enigma signals of the German Abwehr which meant that we captured every spy that arrived in the United Kingdom by having advance knowledge of his arrival," says Harry Hinsley. "Which meant that we could turn such as we needed and use them to send messages we wanted the Abwehr to receive, and monitor the reception and the reaction of the Abwehr. All that signal intelligence underlay the effective use of what was called the Doublecross Operation for the purposes both of stopping

German reception of intelligence (other than false intelligence) and also of creating deception by sending them false intelligence."

What began now was a similar thing but on a much larger scale. German radio operators started to pick up word of a large new military force called the First US Army Group (FUSAG) being assembled in the UK. At the same time, they received intelligence that the British 12th Army was getting ready to invade parts of Scandinavia, Turkey, Crete and Romania. The Allies were apparently planning something very big and very coordinated. And, what was more, there were strong hints that the Allied forces would be landing at the Pas-de-Calais, the closest part of France to the UK.

Of course, it was all lies. The planned landing was going to take place further west, in Normandy. To bolster the lie, five separate sub-operations were set up to support Operation Bodyguard: the first was Operation Fortitude, the aim of which was to convince the Germans that the Allies had more troops and equipment than they actually did. This featured a fictional British 4th Army, based in Scotland, and the fictional FUSAG in the south of England which was supposedly under the command of General George Patton. One of the more ingenious ploys used for Fortitude was the creation and display of hundreds of inflatable tanks that, to a spotter plane, looked just like the real thing. Secondly, there was Operation Graffham. This was a deception aimed at making the Axis Powers believe that Britain was building political ties with Sweden in preparation for an upcoming invasion of Norway. Operation Ironside played on the Germans' fears about a landing at Pas de Calais by suggesting that a secondary force would be landing ten days afterwards. Operation Zeppelin was similar to Fortitude but suggested targets in the Mediterranean. Finally, there was Operation Copperhead which involved the actor M E Clifton James – who looked very much like General Montgomery – making a number of appearances at strategic, but fake, sites to suggest the idea that he was overseeing preparations. This operation formed the basis of the famous 1954 autobiography and subsequent movie *I WAS Monty's Double*.[52]

Supporting all of the various operations was Station X. By monitoring the Axis radio and telegraphy traffic, they were able to check and double-check that the deception was working. Veterans attest to the fact that, during the preparations for D-Day – even though many of them had no idea that such an audacious plan was underway – the work at BP suddenly became much more intense, as did the need for secrecy. A 20-mile travel restriction was imposed, and staff were discouraged from leaving the site. The canteen was shut and people had to eat in their billets or offices. In her book *Bletchley Park People*, historian Marion Hill describes the sense of excitement experienced by one worker who was made privy to the impending Normandy landings: "One morning in June 1944, JH (John Herivel) beckoned me to a corner and whispered, 'We're invading Europe today.' My heart stopped... from then on was a most hectic time for BP."

As the crossing – codenamed Operation Neptune – got under way, Station X went into overdrive. Messages flew about in the ether from U-boat crews and other ships at sea, and from observers in France of parachute landings and mysterious vessels being spotted. As each message was intercepted, decoded and translated, counter-intelligence was fed back the other way to denounce such sightings as insignificant or explainable by other means. "This knowledge of the enemy's ignorance and relative passivity was not only reassuring; it was certain," says Peter Calvocoressi. "Since, by this time, we had from Ultra a panoramic knowledge of the German forces, we could tell that units which could be switched were not being switched. We could therefore confidently assert that the failure of additional squadrons to show up in the new theatre was not due to our failure to spot them there but was confirmed by the fact that they were all positively known to be elsewhere. In intelligence the negative can be very positive."[53]

Churchill contacted Harry Hinsley several times during the crossing to ask if the enemy had figured out what was happening. Hinsley was delighted to be able to report that, as far as anyone knew, the Germans were watching the wrong part of the coast.

Bletchley Park was to continue to provide the same level of support throughout the entire Operation Overlord campaign. Meanwhile, the Germans responded with deadly force, sending wave after wave of V-1 and V-2 rocket-powered bombs to obliterate selected cities and military sites across the UK. Once again, the extraordinary bubble of secrecy around BP kept it safe from harm. To counter the V weapons, BP worked with double agents, feeding information back to Berlin about how successful their bombs were. "At that point, the bombs were falling in Central London so [...] this double agent was instructed to tell his masters that they were falling north of London," says Mavis Lever. "The result of this was that the Germans cut the range back a little and, as a result, the rockets started falling in south London. Just where my parents lived. I had no idea and it is just as well that I didn't. So when I saw the devastation at Norbury, I did not know that it had anything to do with anything I was doing. It really would have been a terrible shock to know that."[54]

As the workloads got ever higher, staff health started to falter.[55] The numbers of people reporting sick started to increase and exhaustion set in. With a sense that the end of the war was getting closer, anyone who decided to take a day off rather than work voluntarily was seen by many as a slacker or, at worst, a traitor. Marion Hill went through the Bletchley Park archives and found a number of diary entries and audio interviews in which Wrens and WAAFs describe how they felt during those months: "You'd have nightmares about setting the machines," says one Wren. "You'd wake up clutching a phantom drum. The work was painstaking and at times soul-destroying. Depending on shifts, you sometimes didn't see sunlight in days." Another described getting "awful boils" by her eyes and under her arms. Yet another: "The strain got me down. I realised I could be dangerous because slipping up on one message meant that some agent may be killed. I became afraid to open my mouth in case I gave away something I'd heard during my work. I was becoming a liability. I got ill with the strain of it all and decided I should walk before I did any real damage." Stories started to appear about attempted suicides: "People who were not suitable just... went. And, of course, other people had breakdowns and they went. The writer Angus Wilson had a breakdown when he was here – he tried to commit suicide in the lake and it was hushed up – but then you heard lots of things..."

VE Day finally arrived but, despite the mass celebrations all over the UK, things were rather more downbeat at BP. After all, there were still rogue Nazi units to be accounted for and the war with Japan was far from over. As one veteran recalls: "We assembled on the grass outside the Mansion to hear that war with Germany was over. There was a huge cheer and great excitement – though our delight was muted as we still had the Japanese to finish before we could go home. So back to our decoding machines." But no amount of discipline could prevent a certain amount of celebration or douse high spirits. Outside one of the huts there was a large brass bell that staff were not supposed to touch. "Quite a lot of us rang that bell," recalls one Wren. "I think the guard officers turned deaf."

That bell was the death knell for Station X.

As the war in Europe finally wound up, staff started to drift away from BP. There was still a great deal of interest in monitoring the communications of other countries – particularly Russia – and the war with Japan was still current, but the huge numbers of people that had been on site were no longer needed. "It was a sort of dribble down," says cryptanalyst Sheila Mackenzie. "The numbers got less. Ten thousand, then eight thousand, however many it was, we didn't all leave at once." In August 1945 word came through that the Americans had dropped the atomic bomb on the Japanese cities of Hiroshima and Nagasaki.

Soon afterwards, memos titled "Re-Distribution of Surplus Staff" and addressed to individuals started to arrive at BP. The memos began: "Owing to the cessation of hostilities, there is no further work for you to do in this organisation. In these circumstances, there is no object in continuing to report here for duty, and with effect from… [date], you are free to absent yourself."

Bletchley Park's war was finally over.

23
A royal visit

Bletchley Park was saved! I was relieved but also excited for what the future held. That summer was a good one for Bletchley – full of celebration and planning.

15th July 2011 was a particularly important day for Bletchley Park. The Queen and the Duke of Edinburgh came to visit. I knew the Queen's visit was happening but didn't receive my invitation until the day before in the post. (It's a good job that mid-July is a reasonably quiet time for academics!) The Queen was at Bletchley to unveil a memorial to the codebreakers that had worked at Bletchley Park during World War II.

It was absolutely wonderful to see so many codebreakers together at Bletchley Park, especially to see them being interviewed by the press.

The Queen gives a speech at Bletchley Park

Codebreakers Oliver and Sheila Lawn

Me, Captain Jerry Roberts, his wife Mei.

The Queen's speech was wonderful, and it included mentions of Alan Turing, the women who worked at Bletchley Park, and the rebuild of Colossus, which is housed there. It was great to be there and listen first-hand to a speech from our reigning monarch about so many of the things that I and many others had been trying for years to bring to the attention of the establishment.

The highlight of my day, though, was seeing Captain Jerry Roberts and other veterans being presented to the Queen and getting recognition for their contribution at Bletchley. The Queen's visit was certainly fabulous for the amount of national press that it generated. Finally, after almost 70 years, the veterans' efforts were being recognised on a national and international scale. Hallelujah!

Twist of fêtes

To celebrate the fact that Bletchley Park was out of danger, a garden party was planned for 3rd August 2011. Having a summer garden party at Bletchley Park was an absolutely inspired idea. Peter Barron at Google said that it was an opportunity to say thank you to all of the people that had been part of the campaign to save Bletchley Park. I loved that idea, as not only would I get the opportunity to give something back to the people who had put so much effort into making sure Bletchley Park was saved, but I would get to celebrate with them at the place that had brought us all together in the first place.

I was also excited about the prospect of finally meeting in person all, or at least some, of the people that I had been tweeting with for the past two and a half years. I had really got to know some people well over Twitter in that couple of years – that had been one of the really wonderful things about the campaign. Not only did it bring lots of people together to achieve a specific aim, but it was also the basis for many friendships and enjoyable human interactions.

I went to the Google offices in London every week to meet up with Peter and three of his colleagues, Lynette Webb, Claudia Baker and Amy Brown, to discuss what we were going to do at the party, who we were going to invite and what needed to be done to make sure that it was a success. We

BLETCHLEY PARK
Home of the Codebreakers

Google is supporting the Bletchley Park Trust with a summer garden party to help raise funds for the restoration of Block C to create a new visitors centre.

Including:
- Tombola prizes
- An auction
- Museum tours
- Afternoon cream teas

When: Thursday 4th August 2011 (3.00pm - 7.00pm)
Where: The Mansion, Bletchley Park, Sherwood Drive, Bletchley, Milton Keynes, MK3 6EB
(Sat Nav reference is Sherwood Drive)

RSVP by 22 July 2011
bletchleyparkparty@gmail.com
Tel: 0207 346 2827

supported by Google

decided that it would be great to theme it around the traditional British village fête. We would have cream teas, tombola, guess the number of sweets in the jar, and all sorts of traditional fête activities. Bletchley Park already had a marquee, so that was handy.

We also wanted to give everyone who came along the opportunity to have a tour of Bletchley Park and TNMOC. With about 400 guests hopefully attending, that was a serious task to organise logistically. We decided that 30-minute tours would be best, allowing us to ensure that everyone who wanted to have a guided look around would get the opportunity.

The Turing papers were going to be on display so everyone would be able to see them as part of the tour. I had seen the papers when they had first been brought up to Bletchley Park. At that time they had been laid out on a table in the library in the Mansion House. Since then a special exhibition area had been put together at Bletchley and I'd not yet seen it.

The cinema was going to be opened up for the afternoon of the fête showing wartime Pathé newsreels all day. I'd always thought that the cinema at Bletchley Park was a completely underused resource, so I was glad that people were going to have the chance to experience it.

I learned that *The Daily Telegraph* were going to be covering the garden party, and as well as featuring it in the paper they were going to make a special edition handout in a 1940s style. The handout would be made

Google code auction prize at the Google garden party

available on the day at Bletchley Park and also distributed as an insert to the paper that week. There would also be an auction to raise money for Bletchley Park and provide another focus for attention during the garden party. Peter knew an auctioneer at Christie's, so he was tasked with asking him if he could run the auction on the day. Lynette was going to sort out the "guess the number of sweets in the jar" and a framed piece of Google code to be auctioned. I was tasked with sifting through about two thousand names from my contacts for the guest list. Because of the campaign, I did have a huge number of contacts who I knew were big fans of Bletchley Park. There were also the many professors and heads of computer science from universities around the UK that had signed the petition to 10 Downing Street in July 2008, and the many contacts that I had from setting up BCSWomen and banging the drum about the lack of women in computing. Most of the actual organisation was done by the extremely capable Claudia Baker from Google, who was really great at keeping us on topic and managing the whole project, as well as being fun to work with.

At the beginning of July, a month before the big event, I was tasked with writing a blog post about the garden party, then tweeting and Facebooking about it to raise awareness of what we were doing. I posted the invitation and details of the day along with some photos of Bletchley Park, train times from Euston and driving directions. I could hardly wait – I was so looking forward to celebrating not just Bletchley Park's hugely important past, but also its bright future.

When, at last, the day of the garden party arrived, I made my way up to Bletchley, excited about the party but anxious about how many people were going to attend. It was a grey day, overcast and spitting with rain – not really the best weather for a summer garden party.

By the time I arrived at the Park, though, it was brightening up a bit, and the view over the lake towards the marquee was as lovely as always. There was a Bletchley Park Trust fundraising committee meeting before the party, so when I arrived I made my way up to the Mansion House and joined the meeting.

After the meeting finished I had a chat with Claudia from Google, the main event organiser, and Simon Greenish, Director of Bletchley Park. We were excited about the party but worried about the weather. We walked over from the Mansion House to the marquee on the lawn next to the lake to have a look at how things were progressing. Yes, it was still raining, but Kevin Hollick and the team from Benguela Events were working away making the inside of the marquee look amazing.

I wandered round to Hut 4 for lunch, where I was joined first by Lynette from Google and her husband Dave and then by some great Bletchley Park

The lake at Bletchley Park

social media stalwarts: Graham Johnson (@Filce), PJ Evans (@MrPJEvans) and Gordon Tant (@125f8) – all fabulous guys who have supported Bletchley Park in so many ways over the years.

After lunch we all walked over to the marquee to see how everything was progressing. We looked up at the sky as we walked. It seemed that the rain was stopping and the sun was coming out. Hooray! Preparations continued and at 2.30pm, despite the weather, guests started arriving. At 3pm the party started in earnest, and by then people were arriving in droves – we needn't have worried about turnout.

The marquee looked incredible. It was set up with 1940s village fête-type games, Enigma machines and more. There were also tours of the whole site including TNMOC running all afternoon. We were keen that visitors had the chance to have a look around the whole site while they were there. It had been my first tour around Bletchley Park that had got me hooked on Bletchley in the first place, so I knew the power of hearing the incredible story of Bletchley, preferably told by a veteran, whilst walking around the site. It was a winning combination.

Throughout the afternoon I felt quite emotional. Hundreds of people that I knew well, either in real life or through Twitter, had come together for the first time to meet in person and celebrate the wondrous place that is Bletchley Park. We had spent hours and hours talking about Bletchley

Park over the last few years, discussing our love and support for the place, what we wanted to do and how to do it. Many of these people had set up their own projects to raise awareness of and funds for Bletchley and had run with them. They had all made a difference in some way to Bletchley Park's fortunes.

It was a day of excited hellos, quick catch-ups and heartfelt thank yous. It was a fabulous celebration of the power of people coming together around a cause and making positive change happen. The excitement and

Simon Meacham chats to Giles Sandeman-Allen whose
grandfather ran Bletchley Park during WWII

Sir John Scarlett speaking at the Google garden party

good feeling that comes from making something like that happen is more powerful than anything I have ever experienced. It's what drives me, and I know from the number of wonderful people who have been involved in saving Bletchley Park that it drives so many others, too.

It is hard to pick a highlight of the party, because there were several, but one of them had to be introducing Simon Meacham, who had flown over from Mountain View especially to attend (he'd started a new role at Google's global headquarters in January 2011), to Gareth Halfacree. Gareth is the guy who started the campaign to buy the Turing papers for Bletchley Park, setting up a JustGiving page to collect donations from the public; Simon is the Googler who took up the mantle of helping Bletchley Park to purchase the Turing papers. Both were instrumental in securing the papers for Bletchley, and it was wonderful to be able to introduce them at the Park.

Another highlight was having a look at the Turing papers, which are now on display in B Block, with Simon. It brought back the memory of lots of frantic telephone calls over a few days, culminating in the very exciting call when Simon told me that the Google board had approved a donation of $100,000 for the purchase.

At the end of the afternoon I was interviewed by Christian Payne. We were both so excited that so many people we knew, especially from Twitter, had shown their support for Bletchley Park. Christian asked me what I thought of the party.

"It's like a dream come true," I said, and I meant it.

Me and Simon Meacham

Me and @documentally

Look to the future now

The campaign had succeeded, but that didn't mean it was over. There was still a lot of momentum and public interest around Bletchley Park, and over the next year or so I saw this interest really blossom. It was heartening to know that exciting things were still happening and awareness was still growing – documentaries and TV shows and art projects were being made, events were organised, talks delivered, exhibitions opened – because there was and is still plenty of work to do to ensure Bletchley Park's ongoing place in our lives. It was as Simon had said when he'd delivered the news that Bletchley Park had been saved: "What we need to talk about now is building Bletchley Park for the future."

Trending Turing

Patrick Sammon's film about Turing was finally produced and appeared on UK TV in November 2011. I had watched and enjoyed it at the UK premiere hosted by Google at BAFTA a couple of weeks previously. It was so great to see it now on television and read everyone's tweets as they enjoyed it too. It was good to see people finding out about Turing for the first time from the film – the programme even got Alan Turing trending on Twitter!

Silicon Brit

In November 2011, I got an email from Megan Smith from Google. Megan was in town again as part of #SVC2UK (Silicon Valley Comes to the UK – an annual opportunity for Silicon Valley entrepreneurs and innovators to come to the UK) and wondered if I could help her arrange a trip to Bletchley Park for the delegates. I was pleased that Megan had remembered Bletchley and wanted to visit.

On the day of the visit, I met up with Megan and some of the other delegates, and we boarded the minibus that would take us to Bletchley Park. There were five of us in the bus: Megan, Julie Hanna, DJ Patil, Reid Hoffman and me. On the journey up to Bletchley Park Megan told everyone how we had met when I approached her at NESTA a year before asking for her help to secure the Turing papers for Bletchley Park. Megan then asked me to tell everyone how I had got involved with Bletchley Park, why it was important, about my campaign and use of social media, and what the situation was there now regarding funding.

I happily told the story, which began with my first visit in 2003, included the Women of Station X project launch and my appearance on the BBC in 2008, and concluded in the present day. It had now become quite a long story, as it spanned several years, and Megan chipped in from time to time with relevant and interesting facts, especially when I started talking about the Turing papers. Megan loves to talk about the fact that at Bletchley Park everyone worked together, regardless of race, background, or sexual orientation. She makes the point that it was because of this diversity that Bletchley Park's work was so successful.

When we arrived we were met by Simon Greenish, taken to the Mansion House and given an introduction to the history of Bletchley Park along with a nice cup of tea. We then spent about an hour touring the site.

The trip was far too short but Simon managed to cram a lot in. It really reminded me of the day that I'd gone up to Bletchley with Mike Sizemore, Christian Payne and Jamillah Knowles three years previously. I had the same feeling of absolute joy at being able to introduce some top quality geeks to Bletchley Park. Everyone had more questions about Bletchley Park now that they had actually been there; it was clear that everyone had really

Looking at the Turing papers. L to R Simon Greenish,
Megan Smith, Reid Hoffman, Julie Hanna, DJ Patil

Inside Hut 8 where Alan Turing worked

Julie Hanna and Alan Turing

enjoyed the visit. Reid even said that the highlight of his #SVC2UK tour that year had been the trip to Bletchley Park. That made me very happy! Reid also offered to organise an event in Mountain View, California, to raise awareness in the US; it was exciting to think that we might be able to spread the message about Bletchley Park even further.

Top tech non-celebrity tweeter

Another thing that happened in 2011 was that I was named top tech non-celebrity tweeter of the year in the *Independent*. All of my obsessive tweeting seemed to have paid off!

Independent voices of 2011: The most influential non-celebrity users of Twitter

22 December 2011

Rhodri Marsden

The Independent

TECHNOLOGY: Winner: Sue Black / @dr_black

As well as being a noted computing academic at University College London, Black has made her name as a digital campaigner – pushing for the advancement of women in technology. She was also a key figure in the successful campaign to save and preserve Bletchley Park, home of the Enigma code-crackers and birthplace of the modern computer. Sue's Twitter feed combines all the above interests, from poor IT teaching in schools to her work and talks. A key voice in an increasingly digital future.

Followers: >7,000

PeerIndex rating: 47

December 2011 I sent 1462 tweets

Did Twitter save Bletchley Park?

At the beginning of 2012 Simon Greenish retired and Iain Standen was appointed as the new CEO of Bletchley Park. Before Iain started we met up for lunch at the Army and Navy Club in London. We had a really good chat about Bletchley Park; I answered all his questions and asked about his life. Iain comes from an army background and has particular interest in battle-grounds. He seemed perfect for the role at Bletchley as he was obviously extremely interested not only in the site as a whole but also in its historical context and where Bletchley fits into the big picture. I left the lunch feeling that Bletchley Park would be in safe hands.

I had been asked some weeks previously by Professor John Clark, head of the computer science department at York University, to give a public lecture about Bletchley Park and the campaign to save it. I suggested that I give a talk loosely based around the research paper "Can Twitter save Bletchley Park?" that Kelsey Griffin, Professor Jonathan Bowen and I had written for the Museums and the Web conference in Denver. But of course I had to bring it up to date; its new title was "Did Twitter save Bletchley Park?". John was delighted with that and we set the date.

I thought it would be a good idea to ask Simon Greenish to give the lecture with me as our previous talk at EuroPython in Birmingham had gone so well. Simon kindly agreed and we got to work on our presentation. After having chatted to Iain Standen it occurred to me that it would be great if Iain could join us, too: Simon could talk about the history and what had happened during his time in charge, I could talk about how I had got involved and the campaigning, and Iain could talk about the present position and his plans for the future. Bletchley Park: past, present and future.

Iain agreed, and the lecture went ahead as planned. In the first section Simon gave an overview of the history of Bletchley Park and the code break-ing work done there. He mentioned that during the war Hitler thought that the messages the German forces were sending were unbreakable – little did he know that people at Bletchley Park were reading most of the messages sent, sometimes even before the intended recipient!

When Simon had finished his section of the talk, I took over. I spoke about the Women of Station X project, and about how it was at the launch of the project that I found out from Simon Greenish that Bletchley Park was having financial difficulties and might have to close. I recounted the whole story: how I started the campaign, blogging highlights along the way; how I first used traditional media to raise awareness, appearing on BBC News and the Radio 4 *Today* programme, and sending a letter to *The Times*; and how, a few months later, I started using social media, particularly Twitter, in earnest, and soon realised how powerful a tool it could be. Twitter helped me to connect with people and organisations who cared about Bletchley Park and wanted to help secure its future, from social media gurus like Christian Payne, Mike Sizemore and Jamillah Knowles through to Stephen Fry, Tom Watson MP and Google. Twitter, I said, was absolutely fundamental to the campaign.

The final section of our talk focused on the vision for Bletchley Park's future. Iain spoke about the grant from the Heritage Lottery Fund, some exciting plans that were in place, and the work that needed to be carried out over the next few years. He ended by asking everyone to help out; the spirit of the campaign lived on.

At the end I asked the audience if they thought that Twitter had saved Bletchley Park. The resounding answer was YES! I thought about this later: I've made so many great friends on Twitter, and it's created so many important opportunities and connections.

Inside D Block

In April 2012 I had the exciting opportunity to go and have a look inside D Block, a disused block at Bletchley Park. It was very exciting and evocative. I absolutely loved walking around, looking at the discarded telephone switching systems, broken chairs, and dead pigeons and absorbing the atmosphere.

I felt strongly that Bletchley Park should be made into a museum that is fit for purpose as a first-class world heritage site, but at the same time, I was sad that not many more people would have the opportunity to walk around the buildings as they were, in some cases left empty for decades. There was something very haunting about seeing this.

I was delighted, therefore, to find out that some of this atmosphere was

D Block

being highlighted and preserved by artists like Maya Ramsey, an installation artist whose work deals particularly with sites connected to armed conflict. Along with a few other artists, Maya created an exhibition called *Station X* which offered a multi-sensory insight into the derelict buildings of Bletchley Park:

> "The exhibition is the result of a unique collaboration between installation artist Maya Ramsay, sound artist Caroline Devine, photographer Rachael Marshall and filmmaker Luke Williams. Together they provide a contemporary interpretation of Station X, by documenting the visual and aural histories imbued in the very fabric of the buildings, before they are lost when planned renovation takes place. This includes work made from surfaces lifted from the walls of the buildings, recordings of sounds produced by and within the decaying buildings, and photographic and filmed documentation of the buildings..."

Marathon man

That same month my partner Paul ran the Milton Keynes marathon in aid of Bletchley Park. It was his first marathon, and it was run on a day of absolutely

Paul just after finishing the MK marathon

torrential rain. I've never been out in such awful weather in my life. He was joined by Bletchley Park CEO Iain Standen, who finished in a great time of 3 hours 37 minutes, and others raising money for the same cause.

We saw Iain enter the stadium and cheered as he ran past. It was about another hour later before we saw Paul enter the stadium. We made our way through the crowds and found him, looking pretty grey, with blue lips. I asked him if he had hit "the wall" during the run.

"I don't think I hit the wall, but I felt like crying at 20 miles," he said.

Poor guy. The weather was absolutely horrendous; I don't know how he and all the others managed to keep going. True grit, but for a good cause: in total they raised about £20,000 for the Bletchley Park Trust!

I become a Bletchley Park trustee

In May 2012 Sir John Scarlett, the new chair of the Bletchley Park Trust, asked me to have lunch with him to have a chat about Bletchley Park. Over lunch I got to know him a bit better and got to share some of the exciting ups and downs of the campaign and my involvement with Bletchley Park. After the lunch, Sir John sent me a letter inviting me to become a trustee of Bletchley Park and join the board. I was delighted to accept, hoping that I would be able to help Bletchley Park move into a new exciting phase of its history. Now that Bletchley Park had been saved, it was time to preserve it, develop it, and turn it into the world-class museum, heritage site and education centre that it deserves to be.

Turing in one word

June 2012 was the centenary of Alan Turing's birth. I had been asked to speak at the Turing's Worlds conference at Oxford University on Turing's birthday, the 23rd June. I spoke about Turing in the public consciousness, calling my talk "Turing 2.0(12)" as a nod to web 2.0 and social media. There was by now so much about Turing in the media, both social and traditional. Over the preceding few years, we had seen a massive rise in interest in Turing from the public, and not just from computer scientists. I talked about the UK Prime Minister's apology, the Turing papers, Barry Cooper's

excellent work in putting together the Turing centenary, and the ACM Turing 100 conference in San Francisco which I had just attended. There was also Patrick Sammon's film, of course. Even George Takei (of Star Trek fame) was now posting pictures of Turing on Facebook with the heading "Share if you've used a computer" – the images received tens of thousands of "shares" and "likes".

I showed the awesome video of the Lego Turing machine that had been built and the petition to put a statue of Turing on the Fourth Plinth in Trafalgar Square in London. I had previously tweeted a short questionnaire, including a question that asked respondents to describe Turing in one word. The Wordle below, which I displayed during my talk, shows that most people think of the word "genius" when they think of Turing. It was good to see so much public interest in and respect for Turing and his work.

A welcome in the valley

During my day at Bletchley Park with the #SVC2UK guys the previous November, Reid Hoffman, founder and CEO of LinkedIn, had very kindly said that he would host an event in Silicon Valley to raise awareness of Bletchley. Megan Smith, Simon Meacham and others had taken this forward and put together a schedule of events for Sir John Scarlett, the chair of the Bletchley Park Trust, and me. Sir John was to speak about his career at an event at the Computer History Museum in Mountain View, and I was to give a talk to Googlers at Google Mountain View.

I flew over to San Francisco in June 2012 with my partner Paul and my daughter Leah. We had a week's holiday together over half term, then I stayed on for a week afterwards.

Unfortunately, Sir John was only able to come over to the Bay Area for a couple of days. We met up with Simon Meacham at Google on the Monday morning and had a good chat together about how the event at the Computer History Museum (CHM) that evening was going to run. We then went over to the museum, which is just down the road from the Google Mountain View (MTV) offices to have a look around.

We were shown around the CHM by the museum director John Hollar. We got to see a working model of Babbage's Difference Engine, which was just stunning. I wish the Science Museum in London would demonstrate theirs running from time to time, it's breathtakingly wonderful. So wonderful that I actually cried (very inconspicuously of course).

There was also an exhibit about Colossus which featured a video including Bletchley Park and The National Museum of Computing hero Tony Sale. It was great to see him represented there, thousands of miles from Bletchley Park, in another geek mecca.

After our tour, a few of us sat down together to have a chat about Bletchley Park and the CHM and whether there was any scope for working together. Megan was keen to start up a mutually beneficial relationship and this was the first step towards making that happen.

After a while, we all said our goodbyes and I went back to Google MTV with Simon Meacham. Simon asked if I wanted to have a go on one of the Google bikes that were sitting around the site. I said, "Yes please!"

Me on a Google bike at Google MTV

Riding around Google MTV campus on a bike in the sun, representing Bletchley Park's interests in Silicon Valley, I thought to myself, *it doesn't get much better than this.* I was supremely happy. When I had been in Denver in 2010 presenting our paper "Can Twitter save Bletchley Park?," I really had the sense that people in the US understood and appreciated how important Bletchley Park is. I had written a proposal to the BPT board when I got back from Denver, asking them to let me go to the US to spread the word and fundraise for the Trust. At the time they had not thought it was a good idea, so I was glad that, two years later, I was able to help take the idea forward.

Before long it was time for the event at the CHM. As I got out of the car, I spotted DJ Patil and Julie Hanna, who I had spent the day with as part of the #SVC2UK trip to Bletchley some months previously. I chatted to Julie and DJ for a while. They introduced me to some other really cool tech entrepreneurs and told them about their trip to Bletchley Park and how much they had enjoyed it. More and more people arrived and then after a while Megan introduced herself and gave a talk about Bletchley Park, about how she had met me at NESTA and how I'd asked for help to secure the Turing papers for Bletchley Park.

At dinner, Megan introduced Sir John Scarlett. John gave a great talk about the history of espionage and the contribution made by Bletchley Park during WWII. We hung on his every word – he is a great speaker. He mentioned me near the end of his talk, saying that Bletchley Park would not be doing as well as it was now if it weren't for people like me, which was very kind. It was a great evening and a great first step in building a relationship and understanding between Bletchley Park and the Bay Area tech community.

I gave my talk "Did Twitter save Bletchley Park?" at the Google MTV campus a couple of days later. One of the members of the audience turned out to be Nigel Sale, Tony and Margaret Sale's son, who (amazingly) worked for Google MTV. It's such a small world!

Sir John Scarlett at the CHM

NOMINET INTERNET AWARDS

One of the fabulous people that I've met through Twitter is Maggie Philbin, who is now a friend. You may know Maggie from her appearances in the UK on shows like *Swap Shop* and *Tomorrow's World*. She is an institution. I first met Maggie at the Tuttle club in London; we had been chatting via Twitter for some time as Maggie was interested in Bletchley Park and had asked what she could do to help the campaign. We got to know each other over the next couple of years, and in 2012 she very kindly nominated my blog "Saving Bletchley Park" for the Nominet Internet Awards in the charity/non-profit category.

I invited several people who had been instrumental in making the blog successful to join me at the awards dinner. My partner Paul has supported me all the way through the Save Bletchley Park campaign, and he is also a computer scientist himself so completely gets why I think it is so important. I also invited Chris Maigler from Brave Media, a friend who encouraged me to set up the blog and kindly hosted it for free, and Iain Standen, the current CEO of Bletchley Park. I also invited Christian Payne and Mike Sizemore, who couldn't make it, and Jamillah Knowles, who did come but was unfortunately called away early on an emergency.

The awards dinner was held at the Saatchi Gallery on the King's Road. I got there early and stood outside in the sunshine for a while, enjoying watching all the people walking around.

The atmosphere inside was electric. Our table got very excited when Bletchley Park was mentioned in the opening speech by Baroness Rennie Fritchie. By the time it got to our category I was so nervous. I was absolutely delighted when I was awarded the runner-up prize in the best charitable or not-for-profit work online category. It was a lovely evening and great to have friends who had helped me to make my blog successful there with me to celebrate my award.

In October 2012 I sent 2578 tweets

As seen on TV

When I first started campaigning to save Bletchley Park I dreamt of the day when I would be able to see programmes on television and go and see plays about Bletchley Park and the people who worked there. That dream has now come true several times over. It's been so wonderful to see *The Bletchley Circle*, *Universal Machine*, *Codebreaker* and other productions on television and in theatres in London's West End. As I write this I'm also looking forward to seeing *The Imitation Game*, a film about Alan Turing starring Benedict Cumberbatch.

One of the things I had tried to do during my time campaigning for Bletchley Park was to find and talk to people about creating a TV programme or film about the women who worked there. It is such an interesting story: all of those young women, working somewhere that probably seemed very alien. It was particularly wonderful to hear in 2012, therefore, that a programme called *The Bletchley Circle* was being made about the women that worked at Bletchley and would be aired later in the year.

Record book book

Many people that I have spoken to over the years have said that I should write a book about the Save Bletchley Park campaign and my experiences. I spoke to several friends about this, some of whom had written books themselves, asking for advice on publishers and on writing. I wondered whether I was actually capable of writing a book. I chatted to a couple of people who worked for publishing houses and, although they were interested in talking to me about it, I was disheartened because it seemed as though it would be a very restrictive process. I wanted to write a book that brought the story alive, through photos, tweets, little digital snippets of the campaign's history – a book that looked more like a blog, maybe, and one that really captured the excitement of social media, particularly Twitter.

At some point I came across the Unbound website. Unbound described themselves as a new kind of publisher, who funded their books through crowdfunding. I found that very exciting, and very much in line with the way Bletchley Park had been saved: through the efforts of a community of like-minded people, many of whom used social media to spread the message.

I got in contact with Unbound, and they were interested in taking the project on. I was thrilled. We assembled all the materials we'd need to put together for the pitch page on the Unbound website, including a short video which was shot at Bletchley Park.

When everything was ready on 25th October 2012 the page went LIVE. I tweeted, emailed, Facebooked and everything else that I could think of, asking people to buy my book.

So many wonderful people not only signed up for my book but also encouraged their networks to buy it too. It was an absolutely remarkable experience. I was completely overwhelmed by the support and excitement that people so obviously felt about me writing the book. To be honest it gave me a lot of much-needed confidence that I actually could write a book and that it was a story worth telling. Thank you so much to everyone who encouraged me and pledged. At the time of writing, we went into the Unbound record books, with *Saving Bletchley Park* becoming the fastest crowdfunded book in history. It took less than five days to raise the money needed to make this book, and all because of a strong and committed community of supporters.

One thing I've learned from this whole experience: it's true that you "get out what you put in" in life. I put so much of my time and energy over the several years I spent campaigning for Bletchley Park into a cause that I completely believed in, and I got back just as much if not more. The campaign and the people involved, especially those I met through Twitter, have been truly wonderful. I've made so many friends, built up my confidence in myself, grown as a person, and I guess, in a way, found myself. Social media has allowed me to be myself, the me that was always there inside but a bit scared to come out. I grew up a shy person, scared to voice my opinions in case I offended someone. Over the years, I've forced myself to speak out when something needs changing.

Social media has shown me that there are many people out there that feel the same way that I do and that it's fine to say what I think in public. It's a simple lesson, but having grown up a girl in the 1960s and '70s, it's diametrically opposed to what I grew up being told. "Don't speak until you are spoken to" was a frequently used phrase in my upbringing, something I have in common with a whole generation of girls. I'm so glad that women are finally finding their voice. It may cause some change that will be difficult for society as a whole to deal with, but in the long run it will benefit us all.

The Duchess of Cornwall visits

The 20th February 2013 was a red letter day for me and for Bletchley Park which, in a way, brought everything full circle.

In my capacity as trustee at Bletchley Park I had been invited to host a table of female veterans at afternoon tea. There was to be a special guest on the day, the Duchess of Cornwall. The Duchess had specifically requested that she meet female veterans at Bletchley and about 60 Bletchley Park veterans from the local area had been invited to talk to her. My role as trustee was to host a table of six ladies, and we would have six minutes in the Duchess' company. I was sent the names of the veterans on my table and some details of their time at Bletchley and their experience. They were an interesting bunch, one of whom I already knew: Jean Valentine, well-known Bletchley Park guide and all round amazing woman. Jean has such energy and enthusiasm, she's an absolute force to be reckoned with.

BritishMonarchy
@BritishMonarchy

On 20 Feb: The Duchess of Cornwall – will visit
Bletchley Park, the home of the Second World War
code breakers . . .

12:15 PM – 19 Feb 2013

I had an opportunity to have a quick chat with all the ladies at our table before the Duchess arrived. I always feel humbled meeting Bletchley Park veterans.

When the Duchess arrived at our table, I introduced each lady in turn by name. The Duchess was very obviously interested in what the women had to say about their experience during the war and in particular at Bletchley or one of the outstations. She told one lady that she had visited a few years ago, but couldn't remember the date. I said that I knew the date of the visit: it had been on 23rd July 2008. I knew this because I had been on the BBC News and the *Today* programme that same day, talking about the letter that I had written to *The Times* along with 97 UK computer scientists, asking the government to save Bletchley Park.

I told the Duchess that if it hadn't been for her and Prince Charles, the whole campaign to save Bletchley Park might never have happened. If the royal couple had not been going to visit the Park on that day, would Rory Cellan-Jones have phoned the editor of *The Times* asking him to print our letter in his newspaper? Possibly not. The Duchess remembered their visit, and she also remembered hearing something on the radio that morning about Bletchley Park. I chuckled at the thought that she and Prince Charles might have heard me speaking on the radio rather than the more likely scenario of me hearing one of them speaking!

The Duchess spoke very kindly to the ladies, taking each one in turn and asking about their experience. My mind drifted back ten years to 2003, when I had first visited Bletchley to attend the BCS Specialist Groups Assembly... I had walked around the site afterwards, bumped into John Harper and his team rebuilding the Bombe machine and had been intrigued by what they were doing. After I had asked all about the Bombe,

The Duchess of Cornwall talks to Bletchley Park veteran Jean Valentine

John had asked me why I was there. When I told him that I was there representing BCSWomen, he asked if I knew that more than half of the people that had worked at Bletchley Park had been women.

> "No, I had no idea. How many people worked here during the war?"
> "About ten thousand."
> "Ten thousand! That's incredible, how come I don't know about that?"

It had been the beginning of a ten-year journey for me. Ten years of trying to fulfill a passionate desire to make sure that not only were the women of Bletchley Park known, but that Bletchley Park itself was recognised as the national treasure that it is. I can't put into words, although I have tried very hard in this book, how important Bletchley Park is to me. I have visited many, many times now, and every time I walk up the road towards the Mansion House, with the lake on my left and the code breaking blocks on my right, I get a tear in my eye. I take a deep breath and think:

> "This place and the people stationed here helped to shorten the war by two years, potentially saving 22 million lives. It was also the birthplace of the computer. What other place in the world could be more important?"

In February 2013 I sent 749 tweets

24
The end of an era

"It looks as if Bletchley Park is the single greatest achievement of Britain during 1939-45, perhaps during the [20th] century as a whole."
—GEORGE STEINER

"Without Bletchley Park, we would have lost World War II."
—LORD CHARLES BROCKET

In the autumn and winter of 1945, Station X was slowly and carefully dismantled. "It was so strange," says one veteran. "It was already nearly empty – a ghost town with just a few removal men shifting furniture. Thousands of people just walked out of the gate never to return." Another veteran recalls the moment when the point of no return was reached: "I remember having to dismantle the Bombes, bit by bit, wire by wire, screw by screw. We sat at tables with screwdrivers taking out all the wire contact brushes. It had been a sin to drop a drum but now we were allowed to roll one down the floor of the hut."[56] All of the other machines were similarly dismantled; the Heath Robinson and Colossus machines were broken up and reduced to boxes of parts.

Winding Station X down wasn't simply a matter of shifting some furniture about and dismantling equipment; due to the ultra top secret nature of the work conducted there, every last scrap of evidence had to be located and destroyed. Absolutely nothing could be left behind. This meant fingertip searches of every hut and building; a surprising number of messages were found that had been crumpled up and stuffed into wall cracks and draughty window frames during the bitter cold of winter. All were removed and, along with every other piece of paperwork, burned in large bonfires. No evidence that Bletchley Park had ever existed would be left behind except for the huts which could possibly be repurposed. What few remaining Bombes and Colossi remained were kept at Stanmore and Eastcote before moving to permanent homes at GCHQ in Cheltenham.

Many of the codebreakers resumed their previous occupations as university dons and engineers. Things were different for the military personnel, especially the thousands of Wrens and WAAFs who had been the backbone of BP. They found themselves posted to new jobs that were often more menial than the work they had been doing. And, frustratingly, due to the intense secrecy, they couldn't produce any evidence of what they had proved themselves capable of. For the women returning to "Civvy Street" things weren't much better. The best that most of them got was a letter of reference that said:

"Miss XXX performed her duties in a very satisfactory manner. She was employed on important and highly specialised work of a secret nature. The Official Secrets Acts preclude giving any information in connection with those duties."

The secrecy surrounding Bletchley Park also meant that they would receive no official recognition for their work; there would be no campaign medals, no reunions, no war memoirs. For some staff, this did lead to resentment and a feeling that they had been forgotten and their efforts unrecognised. For others, the opportunities for women that BP had provided were an inspiration. "You suddenly realised that life was full of possibilities, that a new world was opening for us all," says telegraphist Barbara Mulligan. "Instead of being at home and helping look after the babies and put the flowers in the vases, I could do something else, so I did... never regretted it." She went on to become a police inspector at a time when very few women reached officer rank. Other BP veterans who went on to have notable careers include Sally Norton, a Naval Section operative who became Lady Astor; Alvar Lidell, the famous BBC newsreader; writer and former Wren Rosamunde Pilcher; Jeanie Campbell-Harris, who became Baroness Trumpington; and future MP Roy Jenkins, who worked in the Testery and Newmanry. One veteran also mentions "Audrey Element – the first Western woman ever to enter Tibet on a yak."

The Bletchley Park estate soon fell silent and empty. Disposing of it turned out to be problematic because the government technically didn't own it; the late Admiral Hugh Sinclair had paid for it from his own personal fortune back in 1937 when Whitehall was still umming and erring over whether to fund it. And so, for a while, it was loaned or rented out to various bodies: GCHQ trained engineers there and the GPO, which had become British Telecom, used it as a management school. A teacher training college took over one block of buildings and several small government departments squatted in others. But, in the meantime, the iconic huts were getting colder and damper and the house itself was soon in need of repairs. In 1987, after a 50 year association with British Intelligence, Bletchley Park was finally decommissioned. Talks began with respect to possibly selling off the estate for housing development and/or development of an out-of-town retail and supermarket site.

Meanwhile, the story of what happened at Bletchley Park during the war finally went public in 1974 with the publication of F W Winterbotham's controversial book *The Ultra Secret: the inside story of Operation Ultra, Bletchley Park and Enigma*.

Epilogue

On 18th June 2014, the Duchess of Cambridge, arguably one of the world's most influential women, visited Bletchley Park to open the new visitor centre. Bletchley Park management had been delighted to discover in 2013 that both the Duchess' grandmother and great aunt had worked at Bletchley Park during WWII, and they had set about getting her involved. It was a real coup getting the Duchess to open the visitor centre, and it had the desired effect: Bletchley Park was on the front page of most of the national press the next day.

I was invited to Bletchley Park on the day and took Steve Colgan as my plus one. Steve is a great friend and has kindly been working with me to

Me and Steve Colgan at Bletchley Park

add the historical elements to this book. We had a great day. It was absolutely wonderful to see the huts in their newly restored state – they have been renovated to look almost exactly as they would have looked during WWII. Inside each hut, images of people have been projected onto the walls, and as you walk into the room, audio of a conversation that might have been held there plays. I remembered the fantasy I'd had when I'd visited Bletchley Park with Jamillah Knowles, Mike Sizemore, and Christian Payne at the beginning of the campaign – that Bletchley Park could be a sort of living museum where history came alive. I think that vision has been realised. Being there now feels as close as it possibly can to stepping back in time and really experiencing the WWII code breaking environment. It is breathtakingly evocative of another time.

The campaign that I started in 2008 took three years to achieve its goal: to make sure that Bletchley Park will be here to tell its story, not just for our generation, but for our children and our grandchildren. The campaign was a sustained effort by hundreds, possibly thousands of people, all wanting to make a change in the world that they believed needed to happen. At the beginning, we had no idea whether it would work. The campaign had many ups and downs, joys and sorrows, successes and setbacks, quite a few of which you have read about. We didn't know if our efforts would work, but we kept going regardless because we wanted the change to happen.

At the beginning of the campaign, I thought it would take about six months before everyone saw our point of view, came on board with what we were trying to achieve, and made sure that Bletchley Park was financially stable. At the time of writing, that was six years ago. The campaign took much longer than I expected, but we made that change happen. We did it, and it was all absolutely worth all of the effort.

Even now though, the management at Bletchley Park, the Bletchley Park Trust and The National Museum of Computing still have to work hard to get funding and support for what they are doing. More and more people are realising the fundamental importance of Bletchley Park in our history and that we owe so much to the people that worked there – this is wonderful. What's still needed, though, is financial support.

Your purchase of this book will help, as we are giving ten per cent of profits to the Bletchley Park Trust and The National Museum of Computing. What I would really love, however, is for any of you that are in a position to, to set up a small regular payment to either, or both, trusts. The trusts are working hard to preserve our extremely important heritage. It doesn't need to be much – perhaps £5 per month – but if a critical mass of people do that, I know it will make a real, sustained difference.

And now at this final point it's over to you. Is there any change that you would like to see happen in the world? If you believe in something strongly I strongly urge you to follow your instincts and make that change happen. If you don't try, you will never know what you might have been able to achieve.

Me and Steve at the Unbound office

Acknowledgements

There are so many people that were a part of the campaign that it would take a whole book to name everyone. If you ever tweeted, Facebooked or cajoled innocent people inton helping to save Bletchley Park, thank you SO MUCH. Look what we did! Together, we made great change happen ☺

Thank you so much to everyone who worked tirelessly to get Bletchley Park the museum going including: Roger Bristow, Brian White, Chris and Lindsey Smith, Peter and Rowena Westcombe, Peter and Sue Jarvis, Tony and Margaret Sale and many others.

Thanks to everyone that spoke to me to help with background research, some already mentioned, also: Jean Valentine, David White from MKARS, Simon Greenish, Sam Crooks, Fred Piper, Tim Reynolds and Captain Jerry Roberts.

Thank you to all the BCSWomen who were part of the Women of Station X project: Jo Komisarczuk, Jill Dann, Lucy Hunt, Sarah Winmill, Rachel Burnett, Conrad Taylor and Genevieve Hibbs, and to Ann Day for interviewing all the veterans.

John Harper and the Bombe rebuild team first got me interested in Bletchley Park in 2003, if we hadn't spoken John I might never have known about the major role that Bletchley Park played in WWII. I would have left after my first visit none the wiser. Thank you.

Thanks to John Turner for early support for the campaign and writing the letter we sent into The Times in 2008.

Thanks to Chris Maigler and Maria Margeti for suggesting I start a blog and then setting it up for me.

Thanks to everyone from CPHC who signed the petition, the letter to The Times and supported and encouraged me throughout the campaign.

To @Sizemore, @Documentally, @Jemimah_Knight and @StephenFry who really catalyzed the social media campaign, thank you so much you really made a massive difference.

Thanks Twitter for being such a great platform, you enabled us to reach thousands of people across the world and encourage them to join the campaign.

Thanks to all the Amplified crew who took the time and effort to come up to Bletchley Park and interview veterans on Enigma reunion day 2009 and 2010: Toby Moores, Steve Lawson, Hannah Nicklin, Kate Arkless Gray, Benjamin Ellis, Julia and Nat Higginbottom, Maggie Philbin, Matt Rawlinson, Britt Warg, Gordon Tant, Graham Johnson, Drew Buddie and A L Ranson.

Many thanks are due to two of my heros Professor Brian Randell and Brian Oakley. Brian Randell has been a great role model for me during the campaign, he fought and was successful in getting recognition for Tommy Flowers the inventor and builder of Colossus. Brian Oakley dedicated years of his life to chronicling what went on at Bletchley Park and who did what.

To Pat Galea who has kept me laughing all the way through the campaign and been a major supporter of both the campaign and of Bletchley

Park itself. Cheer Dude!

Pink Punters, thank you so much fore letting me drive your double decker bus around Bletchley Park, and thanks Kelsey Griffin for organising it. Massive thanks also to everyone that came along that day to see me realise a life-time's ambition. What a fun day ☺

Massive thanks to the @goodfornothing crew for their fabulous energy and ideas.

Thanks Lisa Crispin and Anna Blake for providing one of the most unexpectedly fun days of the campaign in Colorado when we got stuck there due to a certain Icelandic volcano eruption. I still can't believe that I ended up blowing into a llamas nostrils and having an impromtu dressage lesson. Maybe it was a dream?

To Simon Meacham and Megan Smith who helped Bletchley Park to buy the Turing papers and so much more, to Peter Barron and team at Google London: Lynette Webb, Claudia Baker and Amy Brown, thanks for all your support and a fabulous garden party.

Thanks Robert Lllewelyn for a wonderful Carpool trip up to Bletchley.

To my lovely friends Heather Taylor and Benjamin Ellis thanks for giving me lots of encouragement and ideas at South By South West in Austin, Texas in 2012. I did it...finally.

Thanks Heidi Stephens for taking the time to help me with my pitch and helping me to get started.

Thanks Paul Clarke and Daren Forsyth for lots of Twitter support and in particular persuading me that crowdfunding our trip to Museums and the Web was a viable idea. You were right.

Steve Colgan thank you so much for being such a wonderful person to work with, you made it such fun, cheers Dude .

To everyone at Unbound who has helped me to make this book happen especially Justin, Isobel, Dan, Miranda, DeAndra, Lauren and of course Jimmy.

To some great proofreaders: my fab daughter in law Emma Hanes, my wonderful partner Dr Paul Boca, JP Rangaswami, Grady Booch, Pat Galea, Kate Day and Alan Burkitt-Gray.

Last and most importantly thanks to my family. Here we are outside Station X after a fabulous tour of Bletchley Park in March 2009. It was my twin sons Sam and Ollys' 23rd birthday, what better present could I give them for their birthday than a tour of Bletchley Park?

My lovely family put up with and supported my obsession with saving Bletchley Park over many years. I can't thank you all enough, I love you all dearly xxx

Image credits

A special thanks to the following for the use of images:

Shaun Armstrong / Mubsta.com
Matt Ball
Paul Boca
Jonathan Bowen
Peter Bryant
Stevyn Colgan
@Documentally
Lynda Feely at BCS
Kate Arkless Gray
Jamillah Knowles
Ade Oshiney
Rev Dr David W Perry
Mei Roberts
SamFry Ltd
Rui Vieira/PA Archive/PA Images

Supporters

Unbound is a new kind of publishing house. Our books are funded directly by readers. This was a very popular idea during the late eighteenth and early nineteenth centuries. Now we have revived it for the internet age. It allows authors to write the books they really want to write and readers to support the writing they would most like to see published.

The names listed below are of readers who have pledged their support and made this book happen. If you'd like to join them, visit: www.unbound.co.uk.

For Dad, love from Tom
@unclewilco from readersheds.co.uk

Tony Abbey
Helena Abbey
Billy Abbott
Karen Adams
Martin Adams
Sarah-Coffey Adkins
David H. Adler
David Albone
Bruce Alcorn
John Allum
Jon Alsbury
Nadia Alshahwan
Rachel Ambury
Mags Amond
Mark Amos
David Anderson
Eve Andersson
Caroline Andrews
Dr Peter Annison

Steven Appleby
Am Appleton
Rita Arafa
Geoff Archer
Jasmine Ardeleanu
Paul Ardeleanu
Helen Arney
Mark Arnold
Christine Arrowsmith BA(OU), MBCS, CITP, Dip. Mgmt.(OPEN)
Robert Arthur
Christine Asbury
Richard Atkin
Kate Atkins
Sam Atkins
Steve & Julie Atkinson
Damien Austin-Walker
Gabriela Avram
James Aylett

Louise Ayling
Ant Babajee
Andrew Back
Liz Bacon
Charnjit Bains
Daniel Baker
Martin Baker
Mark Baldwin
Matt Ball
Dave Ballantyne
Jason Ballinger
Victoria Banfield
Chris Bannister
Karen Barber
Julian Barker
Martyn Barmby
Ben Barnett
Gordon Barr (@gordonbarr)
Perdita Barran
Duncan Barratt
Roger Barraud
Peter Barrington
Nick Barron
Mark Barry
Paul Basham
Sarah Baskerville
William Bates
Kevin Baughan
Mary Baxter
Gisele Baxter
Ian Baxter
Osledy Bazó
Claire Beale
Sally Bean
Mike Beardshall
Pilgrim Beart
Peter Bebbington
Pete Beck
Yael Beeri
Sue Beesley

Adrian Belcher
Alex Bellars
Linda Bellos and Caroline Jones
Steve Bennington
Andy Bentley
Richard Benwell
Paul Bernal
Owain Betts
Dr Bex Lewis
Napoleon Biggs
Dave Binkley
Hannah Bird
Dorothy Birtalan
Jon Bishop
Carolyn Black
Emma Black
J. Flora Black
Owen and Jenny Blacker
William Blair
Mark Blewett
Nathan Bloomfield
Jonathon Blues
Paul Boca
Jean Boca
Nicola Boella
Cornelia Boldyreff
David Bond
William Bonwitt
Tracey Booth & Olivier Van Acker
Sarah Borne
Claire Borton
David Bover
Steve Bowbrick
Jonathan Bowen
Corrina Bower
Dione Bowie
David Bowie
Darren Bowles
Ryan Boyd
Chris Brace

Mike Bradley
Matt Brain
Hannah and Lena Breen
Professor Stephen Brewster
Mark Bridge
Steve Bridger
Martin Brookes
Alan Brookland
Oliver Brookshaw
Michael Brough
Linda Broughton
Laura Brown
Sara Brown
PJ Bryant
Alan Bucher
Carl Bulger
Paul Bullock
Jamie Bullock
Steve Bunce
Nicola & Sebastian Buntin
Sebastian Buntin
Adrian Burgess
Adam Burke
Edmund Burke
Alan Burkitt-Gray
Ajay Burlingham-Böhr
Pauline Burney
Rob Lloyd Burney
Christine Burns MBE
Bonnie Burton
Martin Bush
Gillian Butcher
Tony Butcher
Claire Butterfield
Melanie Byng
Astrid Byro
Jane Caccavale
Ian Calcutt
Gary Callard
David Callier

Sarah Louise Cameron
Kathryn Camfield
Niki Campbell
Rosie Campbell
Karen Campey
Andy & Joy Candler
Phillipa Candy
Andrea Capiluppi
Eamonn Carey
Chrissie Carlton (@techiefairy)
Gavin S Carpenter
John Carroll
Kevin Carson
Colin Carter
Lois Carter
Sarah Carter
Lucinda Casey
Lucinda Casey
Karen Catlin
Britta Cats
Roger Cavanagh
Karan Chadda
Mason Challinor
David Lars Chamberlain
Thomas Chambers
Darren Chandler
Linda Chandler
John Chandler
Kim Chandler McDonald
Alison Chapman
Chris Chapman
John Chapman
Paul Charlton-Thomson
Jacob Cheyette
Lauren Child
Brian Choo-Kang
Karen Claber
Pat Clack
Andy Clapham
Michelle Clark

Anne Clarke

Emma Clarke

Paul Clarke

Robert Clements

Leon Clowes

Garrett Coakley (@garrettc)

Eddie Coates-Madden

Matthew Cocking

Bernie Cohen

Stephen Colegrave

Mark Coleman

Peter Coleman

Stevyn Colgan (@stevyncolgan)

Judith Collard

Richard Collins

Stuart Colville

Brian Condon

Liz Conlan

Bernadette Cook

Pete Cook

Simon Cook

John Cooke

Susan Cooklin

Adrienne Cooper

Barry Cooper

Charles and Deborah Cooper

Katie Cooper

Robert Cooper

Max Cooter

Matt Cope (@PhotonQyv)

Richard Coppen

Sue Corbett

Jim Cordy

Tom Cossons

Steve Counsell

Nicola Cousen

Lesley Cowley

Bonnie Cox

Lee & Debbie Cox

Ian Crawford

John Crawford

Malcolm Crawford

David Cripps

Lisa Crispin

Bibiana Cristòfol

Emma Critchley

Marj Crockett

Catherine Cronin

James Cronin

Dave Cross

Deby Cruddas (@FizzyPetal)

Alice Cruickshank

Daniel Crussell

Kevin Culbert

Sue Cullen

Patrick Culligan

Fintan Culwin

Jim Cunningham

Collette Curry

Alan Curry

Ruth Curtis

Mike Czerski

Michael Dailly

Sharon Dale

Richard Dallaway

Lona Dallessandro

Peter Dalling

Robert Dallison

Tim Dalton

Lhosa Daly

Martin Daly

Dana Damian

Sebastian Danicic

Mick Dann

Geoffrey Darnton

Stephen Darvill

Dave (hedgecutter.com)

Tom Davenport

Ali Davidson

Christine Davidson

Gruff Davies

Roz Davies

Trefor Davies

Roger Davis

Tony Davis

Jonathan Davison

Edd Dawson

Gary Day-Ellison

Thomas Dean

Chris Dearden

Sven Decabooter

Hannah Dee

Martin Dehnel

Andy Delaney

Reid Derby

Jasdev Dhaliwal

Kalwinder Singh Dhindsa

David Dibben

Rhona Dick

Angela Dobb

Ian Dogherty

Louise Doherty

Craig Dolan

Jacky Dols

David Donaghy

Andy Donaldson

Claire Donlan

Ian Douglas

Lawrence T Doyle

Sandy Driskell

Vikki Drummond

Tim Duckett

Chris Dudley

Janet Dudley

Christopher Dudman

Vivienne Dunstan

Stewart and Maja Dunn

Sophie Duport

Mark Durbin

Jamie 'wibble' Duxbury

Benjamin Dyer

Nick Earl

John Earland

Ruth Eastham

Terence & Elizabeth Eden

Lee Edwards

Stuart Edwards

Tom Eeles

Stephen Eldridge

Richard Elen

John Elliott

Benjamin Ellis

Joshua Ellis

Steve Ellis

Rob Englebright

Chris Evans

David Evans

Jack Evans

PJ Evans

Mikael Falkvidd

Kerrie Farrar

Leslie David Farrell

Louise Farrow

Sarah Fenwick-Stubbs & Peter Stubbs

Michael Fernandez

Georgina Ferry

Andrew Field

Louise Findlay-Wilson

James Firth

Guy Fitzgerald

Bård Fjukstad

Simon Flaxman

Jane Fleming

Molly Fletcher

Chris Floyd

Julie Fogg

Sarah Forbes

Neil C Ford

Rebekah Ford

Gary Forster

Aaron Fothergill
Mike Frankland
Professor Mike Fraser
Lee Friend
Rennie Fritchie
Uta Frith
Michael Fuller
Jane Fullman
David Funnell
Pat Galea
James Gallie
Mark Gamble
Kimmi Gan
Claire Garside
Martin Garthwaite
Dagna Gaythorpe
Rebecca George
Richard George
Jemima Gibbons
Suna Gibbs
Matt Gibbs
Amanda Gibbs
David Gilbert
John Gilbert
Cyrus Gilbert-Rolfe
Tim and Helen Gilchrist
Victoria Gill
Richard Gillin
David Gilray (@davidgilray)
Bruno Girin
Karl Gjertsen
Mr David Glover
Bernard Golden
Pablo Gomez
Yvonne Goodwin
Denise Gorse
Richard Gough
Clive Gould
Paul Gould
Jill Goulder

Neil Graham
Voula Grand
Mr Grasshead
Iain Gray
Kenneth Gray
Richard Gray
Carl Green
Paul Greenfield
Brian D. Gregory
Jenny Gregory
Mike Griffiths
Neil Griffiths
Steven Griffiths
Andy Grigg
Luke Groves
Ian Guest
Trevor Guy
Kevin Hadfield
Miriam Halahmy
Dom Hale
Simon Hallpike
Gabrielle Halverson
Margaret Hames
John Hammersley
Jonathan Hammond
Pete Hammond
Mike Hardcastle
John Harding
John Hardy
Sean Harkin
Mark Harman
James Harold Davenport
Mark Harper
Mel Harper
Carl Harris
Michael Harris
Carrie Hartnell
Dave Harvey
Joanna Haseltine
Richard Hearle

George Heinrichs
Ilja Heitlager
John Helliwell
Alan Henderson
Martin Henson
Richard Herbert
Jennifer Hewitt
Tony Hey
Jez Higgins
Graham High
Natasha Higman
Robert Hill
Mark Hillary
Steve Hills
Mike Hinchey
Chris Hinde
Ruth Hinsley
Jill Hodges
Ian Hodgetts
Amelia Hodsdon
Keith Holland
Jessamy Hollinghurst
Abi Holloway
Niki Holmes-Bridges
Karen Holtorp
Leigh Honeywell
Clare Hooper
Emily Hopkins
Siegfried Hornecker
Punita Hossain
Emma C Howe (née Birch)
Adam Hoyle
Lucian Hudson
Philip Hughes
Linda Humphries
Lucy Hunt
Renee Hunt
Gil Huntley
Cate Huston
Steve Hutchings

Carl Hutchinson
Susanne Huttner
Paul Hutton
Roland Ibbett
Caroline Ingram
Andrew Ireland
Lois Ireson
Alastair Irons
Huma Islam
Johari Ismail
Glen Ivey
Stephane Ivic
Mike Jackson
Joanne Jacobs
Kathy Jacobs
Norman Jaffe
Steve Jalim
Bonnie James
Chris James
Mivy James
Chris Jamson
Leonie Jennings
Liz Jesty
Kay Johannes
Daniel John and The John Family
Alex Johnson
Filce Johnson
Hannah Johnson
Ian Johnson
Paul Johnson
Steve Johnson
Yvonne Johnston
Gordon Joly
Alan Jones
Dr Alastair S Jones
Carolyn Jones
Cliff Jones
Mortimus Roy Jones
Nicholas Jones
Roger O. Jones

Simon & Kate Jones (@simonrjones)

Steve Jones

Terry Jones

Charlotte Joyce

Kevin Julier

Jem Kale

Carolyn Kammen

Kavita Kapoor

Sid Kargupta

David Kaskel

Rubi Kaur (@RubiRedBlue)

Len Keighley

Andrea Keightley

Andrew Kelly

James Kelly

Nick Kelly

Graham Kendall

Paul Kennedy

Jonathan Kent

John V. Keogh

Peter Kettle

Katz Kiely

Clare Killen

Alex Kinch

Rebecca King

Dr Steve King

Michael Kirk

Jemima Kiss

Matthew Knight

Ian Knock

Brendon Knoetze

Hugh Knowles

Tobias Kreisel

Christian Krog Madsen

Steve Kunzer

Aydin Kurt-Elli

Marta Kwiatkowska

Pierre L'Allier

Luis Lamb

Andrew Lambert

Thomas Lancaster

Michael Lane

Ann Latham

Catharine Latif

Hannah Leach

Jimmy Leach

Alison Leary

Rob Lee

Shani Lee

Dave Leedham

Leo Leibovici

Guy Levin

Craig Lewis

Iain Lewis

Joyce Lewis

Judith Lewis

Kate Lewis

Mike Lewis

Peter Lewis

William Lewis

Scott Liddell

Paula Lilburn

Karlin Lillington

Lian Tze Lim

Richard Linley

Robert Lister

Jonathan Littlewood

Sue Llewellyn

Bruce Lloyd

Kim Locke

Sarah Lockwood

Carol Long

David Loonam

Paul Lorton Jr

Michael N. Louka

Keith Loven

Dr. Gus K. Lott

Wendy Lowes

Chris Loxley-Ford

Hollie Lubbock

Mark Lubienski

James Lucas

Ross Luker

Elizabeth Lutgendorff

Allen Lutz

James Lyne

Kelly Lyons

Matthew MacAulay

Jamie Macdonald

Neil Macehiter

Jordan MacLeod

Shona MacNeilage

Cait MacPhee (@sciorama)

Tes Macpherson

Rob Macredie

Peter Madelaine

Chris Maigler

Catherine Makin

Audrey Mandela

Keith Mander

Dave Mansfield

Keith Mantell

Graeme Manuel-Jones

Tiziana Margaria

Bev Marks FTISA, M Inst SCE

Fabien Marry

Angela Marshall

Rachael Marshall

Charlotte Martin

Ursula Martin

Paul Maskens

Beth Massey

Katherine Mathieson

Nicole Mathison

Anthony Matthews

Letitia Matthews

William Matthews

Ingvar Mattsson

Lee Mauger (Hi Tom and Freya)

Geoffrey Maugham

James Mayhew

Natasha Mayo and David Mayo

Tony Mayston

Gerry McAllister

John McAllister

Greg McDougall

Barbara McGinlay

Adam McGreggor

Darren McGuicken

Rachael McKelvey

Gavin McKeown

Bill McMillan

Geoffrey McMullen

Stephen McQuillan

Stuart McRae

Fiona McRobie

Rod Medew

Sally Meecham

Phillip Meents

Tom Mellor

Lesley Merry

Victoria Merry

Kayleigh Messer

Bethany Metheringham

Greg Michaelson

Jonathan Michie

Frieda Midgley

Roger Miles

Helen Miller

Kat Miller

Ewan Milne

Margo Milne

Sara Milner

Alex Milway

Dipak Mistry

David Mitchell

Molly and Charlotte Mitchell

Trayton Mitchell

Michael Mokrysz

Thomas Moloney

James Monahan

Arthur Monk

Simon Monk

Andrew Montgomery-Hurrell

Dave and Jim Mooney

Jim Mooney

Graham Moonie-Dalton

C M Moore

Mike Moore

Richard Moore

Sharon Moore

Chris Morgan

Jan Morgan

Mat Morrison

Jim Mortleman

Caron Morton

Shirley Moth

Kevin Mothers

Rhiannydd Mounter

Leslie Muetzelfeldt

David Muir

Fiona Mullen

Malcolm Munro

Lorna Murphy

Paul Murphy

Alison Murray

Dianne Murray

Sarah Murray

Deidre Myatt

Kate Myers

Paul Nash

Carlo Navato

James Naylor

David Neill

Andrew Nesbitt

Christopher J Newman

Alice Newton

Eleonora Nicchiarelli

Pat Nice, Reconnix Limited

Sue Nieland

Nigel (@nmeth)

Nine Nine

Dennis North

Douglas & Vida Norton

Jim Norton

Iciar Novo Fernandez

The Noyce Family

Ben Nunney

Freda O'Byrne

Stephen O'Callaghan

Lauren O'Connell

Sharon O'Dea

Denis O'Hora

Barry O'Mahony

Mark O'Neill

L-J O'Neill

Nigel Ogden

Martin Ogunbiyi

Helen Oliver

Gail Ollis

Par Olsson

ONS Limited

Erwin Oosterhoorn

Matthew Oswald

Thomas Otter

Ruth Oulton

Chris Owen

Huw Owen

Vincent J. Owens

Kiran Oza

Louise Paddock

Sydney Padua

Stefan Paetow

Alison Pain

George Parapadakis

Nick Parfitt

Andy Parkes

Lee Parkes

Janet Parkinson

Adriano Parracciani

Ed Parsons
Lopa Patel
Mike Paterson
Mark Patten
Harry Payne
David Peacock
George Pearson
Mark Pearson
Sarah Pearson
Sarah Peers
Clemency Penn
Clifford Penton
Raquel Pereira da Cunha
    (@raquelsolman)
Gemma Perry
Jan Peters
Allan Hagen Petersen
Helen Petrie
Mark Philpott
Dr Stephen Pike
Andy Piper
Chris Pirillo
Frank Pitt
Alan Pollard
Finnegan Pope-Carter
Caroline Porter
Matthew Porter
Alexandra Poulovassilis
Anthony Pounder
Adrian Pratt
Sylwia Presley
J N Pritchard
Brumley Daniel Pritchett
Jules Procter
Munish Pruthi
Dave Puddephatt
Chris Pugh-Jones
Mike Pyott
Lauren Raddon
Nigel Rainer & Trudy How

Leslie Ramage
Steven Ramage
Brian Randell
Andy Randle
Coby Randquist
JP Rangaswami
Andrew Ratcliffe
Andrew Rawlins
Steve Rawson
Uday Reddy
Steve Reeves
Jason Reich
Mary Reid
Jian Ren
Tim Rhodes
Clarke Rice
Bernard Richards
Kathryn Richards
Chris Ridd
Steve Riddle
Tony Riding
Sandy Riegler
Linda Rising
Ian Ritchie
Richard, Sue, Ella and Rose Rixham
Paul Roach
Jim & Jacqui Robbins
Anthony Roberts
Graham Roberts
Hedd Roberts
Jean Roberts
Jenny Roberts
Mei and Jerry Roberts
Victoria Roberts
Hazel Robertson
Colin Robinson
Lynn Robson
Shaun Rock
Petre Rodan
Mart Hugh Rogers

Paul Roff
Susannah Rogers
Wojciech Rogozinski
Jacqueline de Rojas
Marc Roper
Marco Rosenthal
Emma Ross
Fiona Faith Ross
Catherine Rossi
Cristina Rotaru
Nick Rothwell
Jeff Rowell
Francesco de Rubertis
Steve Rudland
Dave Russell
Theresa Russell
Laurel Rutledge
Marie Ryal
Damien Ryan
Liz Ryan
Huong Sabherwal
Scott Sage
David Sainsbury
Bryn Salisbury
Richard Salmon
Mair Salts
Patrick Sammon
Miia 'Myrtti' Sample
Jayne Samuel-Walker
Giles Sandeman-Allen
Amanda Sander
Sally Jasmin Sarma
Mauricette Scheurer
Seb Schmoller
Steve Schneider
John Schoenbaum
Lynn Schreiber
Peter Schwindt
Anne-Marie Scott
Georgina Scott

Rose Seabury
Dr. David A. Seager
Owen Searle
Valerie Selby
Sue Sentance
Lori Shaffer
Mandy & Tim Sharland
Jo Sharples
Dr Nick Sharples
Andrew Shepherd
David Shepherd
Lynsay Shepherd
Keith Shering
Aliza Sherman
Keith Sherratt
Caroline Sherrington
Lucy Shimidzu
Stephanie Shirley
Jeremy Sibley
Rebecca Sickinger
Susan Sim
Carl Simmons
Catherine Simmons
Linda Simmons
Rachael Simmons
Luiz Simpson
Kevin Sinclair-Noble
Wendy Skinner
Jason Slater
Annika Small
Mark Smedley
Daisy Smith
Douglas Smith
Gavin Smith
Gillian Smith
Jools Smith
Matthew Smith
Paul Smith
Paul Martin Smith
Sam Smith

Simon Smith
Steve Smith, Wimborne
Susan Smith
Genevieve Smith-Nunes
Nicola Smyth
Lili Soh
Giuseppe Sollazzo (@puntofisso)
Andra Sommer-Steinort
Julie Sorrell
Carole Souter
Jenny Sparks
Martin Spenceley
Ellen Spertus
Lucinda Spokes
Edouard Spooner
Janice Staines
Ash Stanbrook
Andy Stanford-Clark
J. Lynn Stapleton
Nikki Steeden
Murray Steele
Edward Stenson
Chris Stephenson
Alan Stevens
Lisa Stevens
Peter Stevens
Lucy Stewart
Martin Stewart
Martin Stillman-Jones
Adam Stone
Sandra Stones
Michael Strawson
Eleni Stroulia
Mark Sunner
Gerry Sweeney
Andrea Swinburn
Stephen Swindley
Rebecca Sword
Matthew Sylvester
Andrzej Szkuta

Garrick T.
Tall Man with Glasses (@stuartwitts)
Tanya Tarr
Ezra Tassone
Alan D. Taylor
Andy Taylor
Clare Taylor
Heather Taylor
Jacqui Taylor
Paul Taylor
Christopher Teano
Melissa Terras
Paul Theobald
David Thomas
Kim Thomas
Rick Thomas
Sue Thomas
Bill Thompson / @billt
Margaret Thompson
Simon Thompson
Ian Thompson-Corr
Jon Thrower
Daniel Tighe
James Titcomb
Tom <3 » ∞ Karen
Gavin and Daniela Toms
Christine Topliss
Edgar M. Toro
Gene Eric Toye
Vianne Tourle
Travis & Emery Music Bookshop
Samantha Treverton
Iain Triffitt
Ma. Angela Tripon
Roger Troughton
Richard Truscott
John Tucker
Dermot Turing
Erik Turk
Melissa Turner

Richard Turner

Steve Turner

Ben Tuson

TwoTone and all our other llamas
sadly lost.

Simon Tyldesley

Emma Vallintine

Mike Vallis

Tony Vallis

Steve Van Domelen

Louis van Dompselaar

Katrien Van Look

Joek van Montfort

Keith van Rijsbergen

Sietske van Vugt

Hugh Varilly

Dai Vaughan

Craig Vaughton

Mark Vent

Ana Victoria Chiu

Soraya Viloria Montes de Oca

Ian Vincent

Dirk vom Lehn

Peter Wade

Julian Wagstaff

Joanne Wainwright

Norman Wainwright

Catherine Walker

Clare Wallace

Rob & Liz Walsh

Ian Walters

Denise Walters née Bagley

Hui-chang Wang

Martin Ward

Britt Warg

Kate Waring

Fiddian Warman

Lorraine Warren

Angela & Sam Watling

Deirdre Watson

Isabel Weatherly

Lynette Webb

Matthew Webster

Casper de Weerd

Hubert Weikert

Andreas Weinberger

James Weiner

Dean Welbourn

Julius Welby

Brad Welch

Chris Westcott

James Whatley

Rebecca Wheeler

Paul Whelan

Richard Whitaker

Steve Whitaker

Ben Whitehouse

Roger Whiteley

J E L Whitmore

Matthew Whittaker

Anna Wickenden

Geraint Wiggins

John Wiggins

Steve Wilde

Ian Wiles

Dino Wilkinson

Beckie Williams

Courtney Williams

Daniel Williams

David Williams

Gavin Williams

Jonathan Williams

Meri Williams

Sean Williams

Shirley Williams

Steve Williams

Susan Williams

Beth Williamson

Ian Williamson

Matt Wilmshurst

Adam Wilson

Amanda Wilson

Clyde Eugene Wilson, III, Chief
Warrant Officer (CWO4), U.S.
Navy, Retired

Johanna Wilson

Julian Wilson

Mark Wilson

Robin Wilton

Sara Wingate Gray in memoriam
Diana Rosemary Woodruffe
Cleaver, FO Civilian, TA: Hut 8 and
Block D(8), German Navy Enigma
Processing Section, Bletchley Park

Sarah Witherby

Hamish Wood

Pete Wood

Jim Woodcock

Thaddeus Woodman

Kate Woodroffe

Gerard Woods

Jane Woods

Jenny Woods

David Wooldridge

Anne Workman

Liz Worsley

Colin Wright

Colin & Rachel Wright

James Wright

John Wright

Rachel Wright

Debbie Wythe

Chris Yapp

Sophie Yauner

Catherine Yorke

John Yorke

Linda Youdelis

Derek & Margaret Young

John Young

Jon Young

Soh Kam Yung

Zak Zebrowski

Andrea Zisman

Endnotes

1. All names used are the names people had while working at BP and its outstations.
2. Members of the Women's Royal Naval Service (WRNS) have traditionally been nicknamed "Wrens". The Women's Auxiliary Air Force staff were known as WAAFs.
3. From a 2009 article she wrote for Ayton School's Old Scholars' Association. http://aytonoldscholars.org/magazines/magazine_09/mag2009_bletchley_park.html
4. At the peak of activity, 33,003 miles were being covered by 130 drivers/riders every day.
5. Once the code breaking work began the radio aerials were moved to nearby Whaddon Hall to avoid drawing attention to the BP site.
6. Quoted in Richmond, J. (2002) "Classics and Intelligence". *Classics Ireland*, Volume 9. Classical Association of Ireland.
7. The GC&CS was created in 1919. It eventually became what we know today as GCHQ (Government Communications Headquarters) in 1946 and is now based in Cheltenham.
8. Named after the eponymous hero of the 1899 comedy *The Gay Lord Quex* by Sir Arthur Wing Pinero. Quex is described in the play as "the wickedest man in London" and, like the fictional character, Sinclair lived extraordinarily well, eating the finest foods, keeping an enviable cellar and smoking expensive cigars which he kept in a crocodile skin case.
9. Although he did manage to decipher the text of the seemingly unfathomable Herodus papyrus as the result.
10. The wartime blackouts were a serious problem for anyone that needed to get around at night as vehicles were not allowed to show lights. One solution to this was to paint white lines on kerbs and around roadside objects such as lamp posts and trees. They could be seen in dim light from ground level but not by the Luftwaffe bombers high overhead. Some paint is still visible on trees today. However, the system wasn't ideal and accidents still happened. Several Bletchley Park dispatch riders were killed by collisions during the war.

11. Later on, a fourth rotor would also be added.
12. http://www.independent.co.uk/news/obituaries/obituary-sir-howard-smith-1346505.html
13. They are also sometimes known as Jeffries Sheets as codebreaker John Jeffries became BP's expert in their use.
14. Kozaczuk, W. (1984) *Enigma: How the German Machine Cipher was Broken, and how it was Read by the Allies in World War Two.* Edited and translated by Christopher Kasparek. Revised and augmented translation with appendices by Marian Rejewski. Frederick, Maryland: University Publications of America.
15. Quoted from the 1999 PBS documentary *World War II: Mind of a Code Breaker.*
16. *Abwehr* was the name used for German military intelligence.
17. From a 1993 Security Group Seminar presentation by Hinsley called "The influence of Ultra in the Second World War".
18. BTM would also make copies of the Polish Enigma Double machines that were christened "Letchworth Enigmas".
19. This Indicator is where Dilly Knox had found his "Cillis".
20. Figures from May 1945, when BP was at its largest, taken from *Figuring It Out at Bletchley Park 1939 – 1945* by Kerry Howard and John Gallehawk.
21. Navy, Army and Air Force Institutes – essentially a bar and canteen for people to relax in.
22. The Lorenz cipher machine was used in coded teleprinter transmissions. The British codename for all such messages was "fish" and the machine itself was nicknamed a "tunny" (another name for the blue-finned tuna).
23. Coffin makers were among the teams of local woodworking professionals brought in to do the construction work.
24. Pocket-sized encoding machines invented by Swedish cryptographer Boris Hagelin in the 1930s.
25. There is a persistent story that, in order to keep secret the fact that BP had cracked Enigma, Winston Churchill "sacrificed" the city of Coventry to German bombers. I've even had people try to tell me that this is the origin of the phrase "being sent to Coventry". The truth is that the story stems from a 1974 war memoir by one Group Captain F W Winterbotham and the story has been challenged by historians and Station X veterans ever since. Peter Calvocoressi, who was head of the Air Section at Bletchley Park, which translated and analysed all deciphered Luftwaffe messages, has said that Churchill was under the impression that the raid was to be on London. Others have stated that a message was received with details of massive bombing raids destined for UK cities but that the coded location "KORN" used by the Germans for Coventry wasn't yet known to UK military intelligence. The "Historic Coventry" website says that the RAF did detect the wave of bombers approaching the city which did give some time for preparations. However, despite 6,700 rounds being fired off by ground defences, the massive 515 bomber attack on 14th November 1940 killed over 500 people, destroyed 4,300

homes and damaged a third of all buildings in the city. One third of the city's munitions factories – the German's main target – were destroyed. As for the "sent to Coventry" story, it is significantly older than WWII, probably dating to the 1730s.

26. The use of a cover story involving a spotter plane or ship became common practice to keep secret the fact that Enigma had been cracked. And it did produce secondary propaganda benefits. Harry Hinsley says, "As a consequence of [this procedure] the Germans and the Italians assumed that we had 400 submarines whereas we had 25. And they assumed that we had a huge reconnaissance Air Force on Malta, whereas we had three aeroplanes!"

27. http://www.theguardian.com/theguardian/1999/jan/18/features11.g2

28. The Karno family were a big name in entertainment, particularly music hall. Fred Karno (1866-1941) is credited with inventing the "custard pie in the face" gag and, at one time, had both Charlie Chaplin and Stan Laurel working for him as comic actors. Many of the routines they developed with Karno ended up in their earliest silent films.

29. http://www.bbc.co.uk/history/ww2peopleswar/stories/60/a2377460.shtml

30. After the end of the World War I, Knox co-wrote (with Frank Birch) an entire Carroll-inspired play called *Alice in ID25*. He also named many of the component parts of cribs and ciphers after animals like beetles, starfish and lobsters because Carroll used so many animals in his stories. http://www.chch.ox.ac.uk/development/old-member-publications/2007/alice-i-d-25&print=true

31. http://www.theguardian.com/theguardian/2012/nov/22/ann-cunningham-obituary

32. It's easy to see why the quality and amount of food might have been an issue. Rationing was in place and yet BP had to conjure up over 22,000 meals every day when staffing was at its highest. It was a far cry from Captain Ridley's Shooting Party and its Savoy Grill chef.

33. http://www.hertsad.co.uk/news/bletchley_park_remembered_by_harpenden_woman_1_827524

34. It should be noted that Tandy's son Miles, who has researched his father's life in detail, remains sceptical about this story. While the serendipitous seaweed/logbook story is true, the method of his recruiting may just be a witty yarn. Tandy was an accomplished linguist and researcher and may well have been recruited to BP for those skills.

35. Seaweeds are a form of algae.

36. These poems, of course, were later to be turned into the award-winning stage show *Cats* by Andrew Lloyd-Webber.

37. Like the aforementioned Coventry story, there is absolutely no truth to the urban myth that British Intelligence held back information about the attack on Pearl Harbour in order to force the Americans to get involved in the war effort.

38. Bigrams and trigrams are commonly found pairs or trios of letters e.g. (in

English) ou, th, st, ing, ert etc. They stand out from random groups like pk, hd, yts, mnb etc.

39. Not Enigma, as some websites suggest – that was the domain of the Turing/ Welchman Bombes.

40. We'll learn more about this machine and others in a later chapter.

41. http://mosaicscience.com/story/how-zebra-got-its-stripes-alan-turing

42. There is a persistent urban myth that the logo on all Apple products – an apple with a bite out of it – is a tribute to Turing. Sadly, it isn't true. The logo's designer, Rob Janoff, has said that he didn't know anything about Turing and that the bite was added for scale. The logo needed to look like an apple – no matter how small it was reproduced – rather than something like a cherry. Maybe that's because a number of early competitors also had fruit-based names and logos like Apricot, Tangerine and Acorn. Even today, there are Raspberry Pis as well as Blackberry and Orange mobile phones.

43. One aspect he particularly hated was that the female hormones caused him to develop breast tissue. Remember, this was a man who prided himself on his physique and who nearly represented the UK in the Olympics.

44. Bletchley station used to be on a branch line that connected Oxford to Cambridge, which was one of the reasons why BP was chosen as an ideal location. That line no longer exists and trains now run through Bletchley connecting London to Liverpool and the Midlands (and I'm told by commuter friends that it is still quite commonplace for there to be "line problems at Bletchley"). Incidentally, there is a story that Christie came up with the name of Miss Marple after being stuck at Marple station, near Stockport.

45. Auxiliary Territorial Service – the women's branch of the army during WWII. In 1949 it became the Women's Royal Army Corps.

46. W Heath Robinson (1872-1944) was a British illustrator famed for his gadgets that invariably used hugely complicated systems to perform simple tasks like breaking an egg or heating a bath. In the USA, illustrator Rube Goldberg (1883-1970) did much the same kind of thing.

47. The original couple of MKIs were upgraded to become MKIIs.

48. Report number *NR 857 CBCB28 1153A BRITISH BOMBE*, written by staff of the United States Army 6812th Division Signal Security Detachment (Prov), seconded to Eastcote in North London between February 1944 and May 1945.

49. http://www.washingtonpost.com/wp-dyn/content/article/2007/09/04/ AR2007090402069.html

50. There was an element of luck involved too; the Japanese ciphers were due to be replaced at the beginning of April 1942. However, slow distribution meant that they didn't change until the end of May. Midway was fought on the 4th of June.

51. The "D" in D-Day doesn't stand for any particular word. D-Day is a military codename for "the day on which an operation commences or is due to commence". There are codes for days and hours using most letters of the alphabet. E-Day is code for "the day on which a military exercise commences".

F-Day means "the day that reserve forces are mobilised". H-Hour is "the specific time at which an operation or exercise commences, or is due to commence". There have been many D-Days although most people only associate the term with Operation Overlord.

52. The film was appallingly retitled *Hell, Heaven or Hoboken* for the US market. It's quite a delicious fact that, in the film, M E Clifton James played himself… playing himself and Monty. Clifton James was originally contacted by the Army's film unit after he'd been spotted playing Montgomery in a patriotic revue. The officer who recruited him was another actor, the then Lieutenant-Colonel David Niven.

53. From *Top Secret Ultra*.

54. From *The Secret Life of Bletchley Park* by Sinclair McKay.

55. Saying that, the sick rate never got higher than 5 per cent of staff.

56. From Marion Hill's *Bletchley Park People*.